Famous European Artists

Sarah Knowles Bolton

Famous European Artists

The present edition is a reproduction of previous publication of this classic work. Minor typographical errors may have been corrected without note, however, for an authentic reading experience the spelling, punctuation, and capitalization have been retained from the original text.

ISBN: 978-1-64799-218-7

PREFACE

Hermann Grimm says, "Reverence for what is great is a universal feeling.... When we look at great men, it is as if we saw a victorious army, the flower of a people, marching along.... They all speak one common language, know nothing of castes, of noble or pariah; and he who now or in times to come thinks or acts like them rises up to them, and is admitted into their circle."

Possibly, by reading of these great men some may be led to "think and act like them," and thus "be admitted into their circle." All of these possessed untiring industry and a resolute purpose to succeed. Most were poor in early life.

S. K. B.

CONTENTS

MICHAEL ANGELO

Who has ever stood in Florence, and been warmed by her sunlight, refreshed by her fragrant flowers, and ennobled by her divine art, without saying with the poet Rogers,—

> "Of all the fairest cities of the earth,
> None is so fair as Florence. 'Tis a gem
> Of purest ray; and what a light broke forth
> When it emerged from darkness! Search within,
> Without, all is enchantment! 'Tis the Past
> Contending with the Present; and in turn
> Each has the mastery."

Pitiful in her struggles for freedom, the very centre of art and learning in the fifteenth century, she has to-day a charm peculiarly her own.

"Other though not many cities have histories as noble, treasures as vast; but no other city has them living, and ever present in her midst, familiar as household words, and touched by every baby's hand and peasant's step, as Florence has.

"Every line, every road, every gable, every tower, has some story of the past present in it. Every tocsin that sounds is a chronicle; every bridge that unites the two banks of the river, unites also the crowds of the living with the heroism of the dead.

"The beauty of the past goes with you at every step in Florence. Buy eggs in the market, and you buy them where Donatello bought those which fell down in a broken heap before the wonder of the crucifix. Pause in a narrow by-street in a crowd, and it shall be that Borgo Allegri, which the people so baptized for love of the old painter and the new-born art. Stray into a great dark church at evening time, where peasants tell their beads in the vast marble silence, and you are where the whole city flocked, weeping, at midnight, to look their last upon the dead face of their Michael Angelo. Buy a knot of March anemones or April arum lilies, and you may bear them with you through the same city ward in which the child Ghirlandaio once played amidst the gold and silver garlands that his father fashioned for the young heads of the Renaissance. Ask for a shoemaker, and you shall find the cobbler sitting with his board in the same old twisting, shadowy street-way where the old man Toscanelli drew his charts that served a fair-haired sailor of Genoa, called Columbus."

Florence, Shelley's "Smokeless City," was the ardently loved home of Michael Angelo. He was born March 6, 1475, or, according to

1

some authorities, 1474, the Florentines reckoning time from the incarnation of Christ, instead of his birth.

Lodovico Buonarotti, the father of Michael Angelo, had been appointed governor of Caprese and Chiusi, and had moved from Florence to the Castle of Caprese, where this boy, his second child, was born. The mother, Francesca, was, like her husband, of noble family, and but little more than half his age, being nineteen and he thirty-one.

After two years they returned to Florence, leaving the child at Settignano, three miles from the city, on an estate of the Buonarottis'. He was intrusted to the care of a stone-mason's wife, as nurse. Living among the quarrymen and sculptors of this picturesque region, he began to draw as soon as he could use his hands. He took delight in the work of the masons, and they in turn loved the bright, active child. On the walls of the stone-mason's house he made charcoal sketches, which were doubtless praised by the foster-parents.

Lodovico, who was quite too proud for manual labor, designed that his son should become a dealer in silks and woollens, as probably he would thus amass wealth. With such a project in mind, he was certainly unwise to place the child in the exhilarating air of the mountains, where nature would be almost sure to win him away from the counting-room.

When the boy was old enough he was sent by his father to a grammar school in Florence, kept by Francesco of Urbino, a noted grammarian. He made little progress in his studies, for nearly all of his time was spent in drawing and in visiting the ateliers of the different artists of the city. Vasari says he was beaten by his father and other elders; but the beatings did no good,—indeed, they probably made the quiet, self-poised lad more indifferent to trade and more devoted to art.

Fortunately, in these early years, as has so often happened to men of genius, Michael Angelo found a congenial friend, Francesco Granacci, a talented youth of good family, lovable in nature, and a student in art. He was a pupil of one of the best painters in Italy, Domenico Ghirlandaio. He loaned drawings to Michael Angelo, and made the boy of fourteen more anxious than ever to be an artist.

Lodovico at last saw that a lad so absorbed in art would probably be a failure in silk and wool, and placed him in the studio of Ghirlandaio, with the promise of his receiving six gold florins the first year, eight the second, and ten the third.

Granacci, who was nineteen, and Michael Angelo now worked happily together. The master had undertaken to paint the choir of the Church of Santa Maria Novella, and thus the boys were brought into important work.

One day, when the painters were absent, Michael Angelo drew the scaffolding, with all who worked on it, so perfectly that Ghirlandaio exclaimed, when he saw it: "This youth understands more than I do myself." He also corrected one of the master's drawings, the draped

2

form of a woman. Sixty years afterwards, when this sketch was shown to Michael Angelo, he said, "I almost think that I knew more art in my youth than I do in my old age."

The young artist now painted his first picture, a plate of Martin Schöngauer's of Germany, representing St. Anthony tormented by devils. One pulls his hair, one his garments, one seizes the book hanging from his girdle, one snatches a stick from his hand, while others pinch, and tease, and roll over him. Claws, scales, horns, and the like, all help to make up these monsters. Michael Angelo went to the fish-market, and carefully studied the eyes and scales of the fish, with their colors, and painted such a picture that it was mistaken for the original.

After a year spent with Ghirlandaio, the master seems to have become envious, and the three-years' contract was mutually broken, through a fortunate opening for Michael Angelo. Cosmo de' Medici, "Pater Patriæ," had collected ancient and modern sculptures and paintings, and these art treasures were enriched by his grandson, Lorenzo the Magnificent, who opened them to students, with prizes for the best work. He founded an academy and placed it under the charge of Bertoldo, the favorite disciple of Donatello.

Lorenzo made himself the idol of the people by his generosity, consideration, and unquestioned ability to lead. He arranged public festivities, and wrote verses to be sung by girls as they danced in the public square, in the month of May. All the young people knew and loved him.

On one of these festive occasions, when the triumphal procession of Paulus Æmilius was being represented, Granacci found an opportunity of winning Lorenzo's favor, and thereby gained access to the art treasures. At once he thought of his friend, and Michael Angelo was soon studying the marbles and pictures of the great Medici.

The boy of fifteen quickly made friends with the stone-masons, and, getting from them a piece of marble, began to copy the antique masque of a faun. However, his work was not like the original, but the mouth was open so that the teeth were visible. When Lorenzo came among the pupils he observed the masque and praised it, but said to the boy, "You have made your faun so old, and yet you have left him all his teeth; you should have known that at such an advanced age there are generally some wanting."

At once Michael Angelo broke out a tooth, filling the gum as though it had dropped out. When Lorenzo came again he was delighted, and told the boy to send for his father. Lodovico came reluctantly, for he was not yet reconciled to the choice of "art and poverty" which his son had made.

Lorenzo received him cordially and asked his occupation. "I have never followed any business," was the reply; "but I live upon the small income of the possessions left me by my ancestors. These I endeavor to keep in order, and, so far as I can, to improve them."

"Well," said Lorenzo, "look around you; and, if I can do anything for you, only apply to me. Whatever is in my power shall be done."

Lodovico received a vacant post in the customhouse, and Michael Angelo was taken into the Medici palace and treated as a son. For three years he lived in this regal home, meeting all the great and learned men of Italy: Politian, the poet and philosopher; Ficino, the head of the Platonic Academy; Pico della Mirandola, the prince and scholar, and many others.

Who can estimate such influence over a youth? Who can measure the good that Lorenzo de' Medici was doing for the world unwittingly? To develop a grand man from a boy, is more than to carve a statue from the marble.

Michael Angelo was now of middle height, with dark hair, small gray eyes, and of delicate appearance, but he became robust as he grew older.

Politian was the tutor of the two Medici youths, Giovanni and Giulio, who afterwards became Leo X and Clement VII. He encouraged Michael Angelo, when eighteen, to make a marble bas-relief of the battle of Hercules with the Centaurs. This is still preserved in the Buonarotti family, as the sculptor would never part with it. The head of the faun is in the Uffizi gallery.

Michael Angelo now executed a Madonna in bronze, and copied the wonderful frescos of Masaccio in the Brancacci Chapel of Santa Maria del Carmine (usually called the Carmine Chapel), the same which inspired Fra Angelico, Raphael, and Andrea del Sarto. "The importance of these frescos arises from the fact that they hold the same place in the history of art during the fifteenth century as the works of Giotto, in the Arena Chapel at Padua, hold during the fourteenth. Each series forms an epoch in painting, from which may be dated one of those great and sudden onward steps which have in various ages and countries marked the development of art. The history of Italian painting is divided into three distinct and well-defined periods, by the Arena and Brancacci Chapels, and the frescos of Michael Angelo and Raphael in the Vatican."

While Michael Angelo was copying these paintings of Masaccio, he took no holidays, and gave the hours of night to his labors. Ambition made work a delight. He studied anatomy like a devotee. Dead bodies were conveyed from the hospital to a cell in the convent of Santo Spirito, the artist rewarding the prior by a crucifix almost as large as life, which he carved from wood.

The youth could but know his superiority to others, and was not always wise enough to conceal his contempt for mediocrity, or for the young men who played at life. One of his fellow-students, Torrigiani, grew so angry at him, probably from some slighting remark, that he

4

struck him with his fist, disfiguring his face for life. Michael Angelo is said to have merely replied to this brutal assault, "You will be remembered only as the man who broke my nose." Torrigiani was at once banished, and died miserably in the Spanish Inquisition.

In April, 1492, Lorenzo the Magnificent died, in the very prime of his life. Michael Angelo was so overcome that for a long time he was unable to collect his thoughts for work. The self-reliant young man, cold outwardly, had a warm and generous heart.

He went home to the Buonarotti mansion, opened a studio, purchased a piece of marble and made a Hercules four feet in height. It stood for many years in the Strozzi Palace in Florence, was sold to France, and is now lost.

Piero de' Medici succeeded to his father Lorenzo, who is said to have remarked that "he had three sons: the first good, the second clever, the third a fool. The good one was Giuliano, thirteen years old at the death of his father; the clever one was Giovanni, seventeen years old, but a cardinal already by favor of the pope, whose son had married a daughter of Lorenzo's; and the fool was Piero."

In January, 1494, an unusual storm occurred in Florence, and the snow lay from four to six feet deep. Piero, with childish enthusiasm, sent for Michael Angelo and bade him form a statue of snow in the courtyard of the palace. The Medici was so pleased with the result that he brought the artist to sit at his own table, and to live in the same rooms assigned to him by Lorenzo his father.

Piero is said, however, to have valued equally with the sculptor a Spaniard who served in his stables, because he could outrun a horse at full gallop.

Piero was proud, without the virtues of his father, and soon alienated the affections of the Florentines. Savonarola, the Dominican monk of San Marco, was preaching against the luxuries and vices of the age. So popular was he, says Burlamacchi, that "the people got up in the middle of the night to get places for the sermon, and came to the door of the cathedral, waiting outside till it should be opened, making no account of any inconvenience, neither of the cold, nor the mud, nor of standing in winter with their feet on the marble; and among them were young and old, women and children, of every sort, who came with such jubilee and rejoicing that it was bewildering to hear them, going to the sermon as to a wedding.

"Then the silence was great in the church, each one going to his place; and he who could read, with a taper in his hand, read the service and other prayers. And though many thousand people were thus collected together, no sound was to be heard, not even a 'hush,' until the arrival of the children who sang hymns with so much sweetness that heaven seemed to have opened. Thus they waited three or four hours till the padre entered the pulpit, and the attention of so great a mass of people, all with eyes and ears intent upon the preacher, was wonderful; they listened so that when the sermon reached its end it seemed to them that it had scarcely begun."

Piero's weakness and Savonarola's power soon bore fruit. Michael Angelo foresaw the fall of the Medici, and, unwilling to fight for a ruler whom he could not respect, fled to Venice. But his scanty supply of money was soon exhausted, and he returned to Bologna, on his way back to Florence.

At Bologna, the law required that every foreigner entering the gates should have a seal of red wax on his thumb, showing permission. This Michael Angelo and his friends neglected to obtain, and were at once arrested and fined. They would have been imprisoned save that Aldovrandi, a member of the council, and of a distinguished family, set them free, and invited the sculptor to his own house, where he remained for a year. Together they read Dante and Petrarch, and the magistrate soon became ardently attached to the bright youth of nineteen.

In the Church of San Petronio are the bones of St. Domenico in a marble coffin; on the sarcophagus two kneeling figures were to be placed by Nicolo Pisano, a contemporary of Cimabue. One was unfinished in its drapery, and the other, a kneeling angel holding a candelabrum, was not even begun. At Aldovrandi's request Michael Angelo completed this work. So exasperated were the artists of Bologna at his skill that he felt obliged to leave their city, and return to Florence. What a pitiful exhibition of human weakness!

Meantime Piero had fled from Florence. Charles VIII. of France had made a triumphal entrance into the city, and Savonarola had become lawgiver. "Jesus Christ is the King of Florence," was written over the gates of the Palazzo Vecchio, hymns were sung in the streets instead of ballads, the sacrament was received daily, and worldly books, even Petrarch and Virgil, and sensuous works of art, were burned on a huge pile. "Even Fra Bartolomeo was so carried away by the enthusiasm of the moment as to bring his life-academy studies to be consumed on this pyre, forgetful that, in the absence of such studies, he could never have risen above low mediocrity. Lorenzo di Credi, another and devoted follower of Savonarola, did the same."

Michael Angelo, though an ardent admirer of Savonarola, and an attendant upon his preaching, seems not to have lost his good judgment, or to have considered the making of a sleeping Cupid a sin. When the beautiful work was completed, at the suggestion of a friend, it was buried in the ground for a season, to give it the appearance of an antique, and then sold to Cardinal San Giorgio for two hundred ducats, though Michael Angelo received but thirty as his share. Soon after, the cardinal ascertained how he had been imposed upon, and invited the artist to Rome, with the hope that the hundred and seventy ducats could be obtained from the dishonest agent who effected the sale. Vasari states that many persons believed that the agent, and not

6

Michael Angelo, buried the statue for gain, which seems probable from all we know of the artist's upright character.

Michael Angelo went to the Eternal City in June, 1496. He was still young, only twenty-one. "The idea," says Hermann Grimm, in his scholarly life of the artist, "that the young Michael Angelo, full of the bustle of the fanatically excited Florence, was led by his fate to Rome, and trod for the first time that soil where the most corrupt doings were, nevertheless, lost sight of in the calm grandeur of the past, has something in it that awakens thought. It was the first step in his actual life. He had before been led hither and thither by men and by his own indistinct views; now, thrown upon his own resources, he takes a new start for his future, and what he now produces begins the series of his masterly works."

Michael Angelo's first efforts in Rome were for a noble and cultivated man, Jacopo Galli: a Cupid, now lost, and a Bacchus, nearly as large as life, which Shelley declared "a revolting misunderstanding of the spirit and the idea of Bacchus." Perhaps the artist did not put much heart into the statue of the intoxicated youth. His next work, however, the Pietà, executed for Cardinal St. Denis, the French ambassador at Rome, who desired to leave some monument of himself in the great city, made Michael Angelo famous. Sonnets were written to the Pietà, the Virgin Mary holding the dead Christ.

Of this work Grimm says: "The position of the body, resting on the knees of the woman; the folds of her dress, which is gathered together by a band across the bosom; the inclination of the head, as she bends over her son in a manner inconsolable and yet sublime, or his, as it rests in her arms dead, exhausted, and with mild features,—we feel every touch was for the first time created by Michael Angelo, and that that in which he imitated others in this group, was only common property, which he used because its use was customary....

"Our deepest sympathy is awakened by the sight of Christ,—the two legs, with weary feet, hanging down sideways from the mother's knee; the falling arm; the failing, sunken body; the head drooping backwards,—the attitude of the whole human form lying there, as if by death he had again become a child whom the mother had taken in her arms; at the same time, in the countenance there is a wonderful blending of the old customary Byzantine type,—the longish features and parted beard, and the noblest elements of the national Jewish expression. None before Michael Angelo would have thought of this; the oftener the work is contemplated, the more touching does its beauty become,—everywhere the purest nature, in harmony both in spirit and exterior.

"Whatever previously to this work had been produced by sculptors in Italy passes into shadow, and assumes the appearance of attempts in which there is something lacking, whether in idea or in execution; here, both are provided for. The artist, the work, and the circumstances of the time, combine together; and the result is something that deserves to be called perfect. Michael Angelo numbered four and twenty years when he had finished his Pietà. He was the first master in Italy, the first in the world from henceforth, says Condivi; indeed, they go so far as to maintain, he says further, that Michael Angelo surpassed the ancient masters."

How could Michael Angelo have carved this work at twenty-four? His knowledge of anatomy was surprising. He had become imbued with great and noble thoughts from Savonarola's preaching, and from his ardent reading of Dante and Petrarch; he was eager for fame, and he believed in his own power. And, besides all this, he was in love with art. When a friend said to him, years afterwards, "'Tis a pity that you have not married, that you might have left children to inherit the fruit of these honorable toils," he replied, "I have only too much of a wife in my art, and she has given me trouble enough. As to my children, they are the works that I shall leave; and if they are not worth much, they will at least live for some time. Woe to Lorenzo Ghiberti if he had not made the gates of San Giovanni; for his children and grandchildren have sold or squandered all that he left; but the gates are still in their place. These are so beautiful that they are worthy of being the gates of Paradise."

The Pietà is now in St. Peter's. When some person criticised the youthful appearance of the Virgin, and captiously asked where a mother could be found, like this one, younger than her son, the painter answered, "In Paradise."

"The love and care," says Vasari, "which Michael Angelo had given to this group were such that he there left his name—a thing he never did again for any work—on the cincture which girdles the robe of Our Lady; for it happened one day that Michael Angelo, entering the place where it was erected, found a large assemblage of strangers from Lombardy there, who were praising it highly; one of them, asking who had done it, was told, 'Our Hunchback of Milan;' hearing which, Michael Angelo remained silent, although surprised that his work should be attributed to another. But one night he repaired to St. Peter's with a light and his chisels, to engrave his name on the figure, which seems to breathe a spirit as perfect as her form and countenance."

Michael Angelo was now urged by his father and brother to return to Florence. Lodovico, his father, writes him: "Buonarotto tells me that you live with great economy, or rather penury. Economy is good, but penury is bad, because it is a vice displeasing to God and to the people of this world, and, besides, will do harm both to soul and body."

However, when his son returned, after four years in Rome, carrying the money he had saved to establish his brothers in business, the proud father was not displeased with the "penury." This self-denial the great artist practised through life for his not always grateful or appreciative family. He said in his old age, "Rich as I am, I have always lived like a poor man."

Matters had greatly changed in Florence. Savonarola and his two principal followers, excommunicated by Pope Alexander VI., because they had preached against the corruptions of Rome, calling his court the Romish Babylon, had been burned at the stake.

While the mob had assisted at the death of the great and good friar, the people of Florence were sad at heart. Michael Angelo, who loved him and deeply loved republican Florence, was sad also, and perhaps thereby wrought all the more earnestly, never being frivolous either in thought or work.

Upon his return to Florence, Cardinal Piccolomini, afterwards Pius III, made a contract with him for fifteen statues of Carrara marble to embellish the family chapel in the cathedral of Siena. Three years were allowed for this work. The artist finished but four statues, Peter, Paul, Gregory, and Pius, because of other labors which were pressed upon him.

The marble Madonna in the Church of Notre Dame at Bruges was carved about this time. "This," says Grimm, "is one of Michael Angelo's finest works. It is life-size. She sits there enveloped in the softest drapery; the child stands between her knees, leaning on the left one, the foot of which rests on a block of stone, so that it is raised a little higher than the right. On this stone the child also stands, and seems about to step down. His mother holds him back with her left hand, while the right rests on her lap with a book. She is looking straight forward; a handkerchief is placed across her hair, and falls softly, on both sides, on her neck and shoulders. In her countenance, in her look, there is a wonderful majesty, a queenly gravity, as if she felt the thousand pious glances of the people who look up to her on the altar."

An opportunity now presented itself for the already famous sculptor to distinguish himself in his own city. Years before a marble block, eighteen feet high, had been brought from Carrara to Florence, from which the wool-weavers' guild intended to have a prophet made for Santa Maria del Fiore. One sculptor had attempted and failed. Others to whom it was offered said nothing could be done with the one block, but more pieces of marble should be added.

Michael Angelo was willing to undertake the making of a statue. He was allowed two years in which to complete it, with a monthly salary of six gold florins. His only preparation for the work was a little wax model which he moulded, now in the Uffizi. He worked untiringly, so that he often slept with his clothes on, to be ready for his beloved statue as soon as the morning dawned. He had shut himself away from the public gaze by planks and masonry, and worked alone, not intrusting a stroke to other hands. He felt what Emerson preached years later, that "society is fatal." The great essayist urged that while we may keep our hands in society "we must keep our head in solitude." Great thoughts are not born usually in the whirl of social life.

Finally, when the statue was finished in January, 1504, and the colossal David stood unveiled before the people, they said: "It is as great a miracle as if a dead body had been raised to life." Vasari says Michael Angelo intended, by this work, to teach the Florentines that as David "had defended his people and governed justly, so they who were then ruling that city should defend it with courage and govern it uprightly."

The statue weighed eighteen thousand pounds, and required forty men four days to drag it by ropes a quarter of a mile to the place where it was to stand in the Piazza della Signoria. Notwithstanding that the praise of the sculptor was on every lip, still there was so much jealousy among the artists that some of their followers threw stones at the statue during the nights when it was being carried to the Piazza, and eight persons were arrested and put in prison.

Vasari tells a story which, whether true or false, illustrates the character of those who profess much because they know little. "When the statue was set up, it chanced that Soderini, whom it greatly pleased, came to look at it while Michael Angelo was retouching it at certain points, and told the artist that he thought the nose too short. Michael Angelo perceived that Soderini was in such a position beneath the figure that he could not see it conveniently; yet, to satisfy him, he mounted the scaffold with his chisel and a little powder gathered from the floor in his hand, when striking lightly with the chisel, but without altering the nose, he suffered a little of the powder to fall, and then said to the gonfaloniere, who stood below, 'Look at it now.'

"'I like it better now,' was the reply; 'you have given it life.' Michael Angelo then descended, not without compassion for those who desire to appear good judges of matters whereof they know nothing." But the artist very wisely made no remarks, and thus retained the friendship of Soderini. In 1873, after nearly four centuries, this famous statue was removed to the Academy of Fine Arts in the old Monastery of St. Mark, lest in the distant future it should be injured by exposure.

Work now poured in upon Michael Angelo. In three years he received commissions to carve thirty-seven statues. For the cathedral of Florence he promised colossal statues of the twelve apostles, but was able to attempt only one, St. Matthew, now in the Florentine Academy. For Agnolo Doni he painted a Madonna, now in the Tribune at Florence. The price was sixty ducats, but the parsimonious Agnolo said he would give but forty, though he knew it was worth more. Michael Angelo at once sent a messenger demanding a hundred ducats or the picture, but, not inclined to lose so valuable a work by a famous artist, Agnolo gladly offered the sixty which he at first refused to pay. Offended by such penuriousness, Michael Angelo demanded and received one hundred and forty ducats!

In 1504, Gonfaloniere Soderini desired to adorn the great Municipal Hall with the paintings of two masters, Leonardo da Vinci and Michael Angelo. The latter was only twenty-nine, while Da Vinci was over fifty. He had recently come from Milan, where he had been painting the "Last Supper," which, Grimm says, "in moments of admiration, forces from us the assertion that it is the finest and sublimest composition ever produced by an Italian master."

And now with this "first painter in Italy" the first sculptor, Michael Angelo, was asked to compete, and he dared to accept the offer.

He chose for his subject an incident of the Pisan war. As the weather was very warm, the Florentines had laid aside their armor and were bathing in the Arno. Sir John Hawkwood, the commander of the opposing forces, seized this moment to make the attack. The bathers rushed to the shore, and Michael Angelo has depicted them climbing the bank, buckling on their armor, and with all haste returning the assault.

"It is not possible," says Grimm, "to describe all the separate figures, the fore-shortenings, the boldness with which the most difficult attitude is ever chosen, or the art with which it is depicted. This cartoon was the school for a whole generation of artists, who made their first studies from it."

Da Vinci's painting represented a scene at the battle of Anghiari, where the Florentines had defeated the Milanese in 1440. "While these cartoons thus hung opposite to each other," says Benvenuto Cellini, "they formed the school of the world." Raphael, Andrea del Sarto, and others made studies from them. Da Vinci's faded, and Michael Angelo's was cut in pieces by some enemy.

Before the artist had finished his painting he was summoned to Rome by Pope Julius II., the great patron of art and literature, who desired a monument for himself in St. Peter's. The mausoleum was to be three stories high; with sixteen statues of the captive liberal arts, and ten statues of Victory treading upon conquered provinces, for the first story; the sarcophagus of the pope, with his statue and attendant angels, for the second; and, above all, more cherubs and apostles.

"It will cost a hundred thousand crowns," said the artist.

"Let it cost twice that sum," said the pope.

At once Michael Angelo hastened to the marble quarries of Carrara, in the most northern part of Tuscany, where he remained for eight months. His task was a difficult one. He wrote to his father after he had gone back to Rome, "I should be quite contented here if only my marble would come. I am unhappy about it; for not for two days only, but as long as I have been here, we have had good weather. A few days ago, a bark, which has just arrived, was within a hair's-breadth of perishing. When from bad weather the blocks were conveyed by land, the river overflowed, and placed them under water; so that up to this day I have been able to do nothing. I must endeavor to keep the pope in good humor by empty words, so that his good temper may not fail. I hope all may soon be in order, and that I may begin my work. God grant it!"

When the marble reached Rome, the people were astonished, for there seemed enough to build a temple, instead of a tomb. The sculptor resided in a house near the Vatican, a covered way being constructed by the pope between the atelier and the palace, that he might visit the artist familiarly and see him at his work.

Meantime an envious artist was whispering in the ears of Julius that it was an evil omen to build one's monument in one's lifetime, and that he would be apt to die early. This was not agreeable news, and when Michael Angelo returned from a second journey to Carrara the pope refused to advance any money, and even gave orders that he should not be admitted to the palace.

With commendable pride the artist left Rome at once, and hastened to Florence, leaving a letter in which he said, "Most Holy Father,—If you require me in the future, you can seek me elsewhere than in Rome."

The proud Julius at once perceived his mistake, and sent a messenger to bid him return, on pain of his displeasure. But Michael Angelo paid no attention to the mandate. Then Julius II applied to Soderini the Gonfaloniere, who said to the sculptor, "You have treated the pope in a manner such as the King of France would not have done! There must be an end of trifling with him now. We will not for your sake begin a war with the pope, and risk the safety of the state."

The Sultan Bajazet II., who had heard of Michael Angelo's fame, now urged him to come to Turkey and build a bridge between Constantinople and Pera, across the Golden Horn. Soderini tried to persuade him that he had better "die siding with the pope, than live passing over to the Turk," and meantime wrote Julius that he could do nothing with him. The pope saw that kindness alone would win back the self-reliant and independent artist, and finally prevailed upon him to return to Rome.

When he arrived, Julius, half angry, said, "You have waited thus long, it seems, till we should ourselves come to seek you."

An ecclesiastic standing near officiously begged his Holiness not to be too severe with Michael Angelo, as he was a man of no education, and as artists did not know how to behave except where their own art was concerned.

The pope was now fully angry, and exclaimed, "Do you venture to say things to this man which I would not have said to him myself? You are yourself a man of no education, a miserable fellow, and this he is not. Leave our presence." The man was borne out of the hall, nearly fainting.

Michael Angelo was at once commissioned to make a bronze

statue of Julius, fourteen feet high, to be placed before the Church of St. Petronio, in Bologna. When the pope wished to know the cost, the artist told him he thought it would be about three thousand ducats, but was not sure whether the cast would succeed.

"You will mould it until it succeeds," said the pope, "and you shall be paid as much as you require."

When the clay model was ready for the pope to look at, he was asked if he would like to be represented holding a book in his left hand.

"Give me a sword!" he exclaimed; "I am no scholar. And what does the raised right hand denote? Am I dispensing a curse, or a blessing?"

"You are advising the people of Bologna to be wise," replied Michael Angelo.

The bronze statue was a difficult work. The first cast was unsuccessful. The sculptor wrote home, "If I had a second time to undertake this intense work, which gives me no rest night or day, I scarcely think I should be able to accomplish it. I am convinced that no one else upon whom this immense task might have been imposed would have persevered. My belief is that your prayers have kept me sustained and well. For no one in Bologna, not even after the successful issue of the cast, thought that I should finish the statue satisfactorily; before that no one thought that the cast would succeed."

After the statue was completed, Michael Angelo, at the earnest request of the helpless Buonarotti family, went back to Florence, and carried there what he had earned. Grimm naïvely remarks, "I could almost suppose that it had been designed by Fate, as may be often observed in similar cases, to compensate for Michael Angelo's extraordinary gifts by a corresponding lack of them in the family." The case of Galileo, struggling through life for helpless relatives, is similar to that of Michael Angelo.

He was soon summoned again to Rome, not to complete the monument, as he had hoped, but to paint the ceiling of the Sistine Chapel. He hesitated to undertake so important a work in painting, and begged that Raphael be chosen; but the pope would not consent.

He therefore began to make designs, and sent for some of his boyhood friends to aid him, Granacci and others. His method was to make the first draught in red or black chalk on a very small scale. From this he marked out the full-sized cartoons or working drawings, nailing these to the wall, and cutting away the paper around the figures. He soon found that his assistants were a hinderance rather than a help, and, unable to wound their feelings by telling them, he shut up the chapel and went away. They understood it, and, if some were hurt or offended, Granacci was not, but always remained an earnest friend.

Michael Angelo now worked alone, seeing nobody except his color-grinder and the pope. His eyes became so injured by holding his head back for his work that for a long period afterwards he could read only by keeping the page above his head. After he had painted for some time the walls began to mould, and, discouraged, he hastened to the pope, saying, "I told your Holiness, from the first, that painting was not my profession; all that I have painted is destroyed. If you do not believe it, send and let some one else see." It was soon found that he had made the plaster too wet, but that no harm would result.

He worked now so constantly that he scarcely took time to eat or sleep, and became ill from overexertion. In the midst of his labors and illness, he writes his father, "Do not lose courage, and let not a trace of inward sadness gain ground in you; for, if you have lost your property, life is not lost, and I will do more for you than all you have lost. Still, do not rely upon it; it is always a doubtful matter. Use, rather, all possible precaution; and thank God that, as this chastisement of heaven was to come, it came at a time when you could better extricate yourself from it than you would perhaps have been earlier able to do. Take care of your health, and rather part with all your possessions than impose privations on yourself. For it is of greater consequence to me that you should remain alive, although a poor man, than that you should perish for the sake of all the money in the world.
Your Michael Angelo."

He writes also to his younger brother, Giovanni Simone, who appears to have spent much and earned little: "If you will take care to do well, and to honor and revere your father, I will aid you like the others and will soon establish you in a good shop.... I have gone about through all Italy for twelve years, leading a dog's life; bearing all manner of insults, enduring all sorts of drudgery, lacerating my body with many toils, placing my life itself under a thousand perils, solely to aid my family; and now that I have commenced to raise it up a little, thou alone wishest to do that which shall confound and ruin in an hour everything that I have done in so many years and with so many fatigues."

Meantime the pope, as eager as a child to see the painting which he knew would help to immortalize himself, urged the artist to work faster, and continually asked when it would be finished and the scaffolding taken down. "When I can, holy father," replied the artist. "When I can—when I can! I'll make thee finish it, and quickly, as thou shalt see!" And he struck Michael Angelo with the staff which he held in his hand.

The sculptor at once left the painting and started for Florence. But Julius sent after him, and gave him five hundred crowns to pacify him. It certainly would have been a pecuniary saving to the pontiff not to have given way to his temper and used his staff!

When half the ceiling was completed, at Julius's request the scaffolding was removed, and all Rome crowded to see the wonderful work on All Saints' Day, 1509.

Kugler says, "The ceiling of the Sistine Chapel contains the most

14

perfect works done by Michael Angelo in his long and active life. Here his great spirit appears in its noblest dignity, in its highest purity; here the attention is not disturbed by that arbitrary display to which his great power not unfrequently seduced him in other works."

The paintings represent God the Father separating the light from the darkness; he creates the sun and moon; surrounded by angels, he commands the waters to bring forth all kinds of animals which can live in the sea; he breathes into man the breath of life; he forms Eve; both are driven from the garden; Abel is sacrificed; the flood comes; Noah and his family are saved in the ark.

Grimm thus describes a portion of this marvellous painting: "Adam lies on a dark mountain summit. His formation is finished; nothing more remains than that he should rise, and feel for the first time what life and waking are. It is as if the first emotion of his new condition thrilled through him; as if, still lying almost in a dream, he divined what was passing around him. God hovers slowly down over him from above, softly descending like an evening cloud. Angel forms surround him on all sides, closely thronging round him as if they were bearing him; and his mantle, as if swelled out by a full gust of wind, forms a flowing tent around them all. These angels are children in appearance, with lovely countenances: some support him from below, others look over his shoulder. More wonderful still than the mantle which embraces them all is the garment which covers the form of God himself, violet-gray drapery, transparent as if woven out of clouds, closely surrounding the mighty and beautiful form with its small folds, covering him entirely down to the knees, and yet allowing every muscle to appear through it. I have never seen the portrait of a human body which equalled the beauty of this. Cornelius justly said that since Phidias its like has not been formed....

"God commands and Adam obeys. He signs him to rise, and Adam seizes his hand to raise himself up. Like an electric touch, God sends a spark of his own spirit, with life-giving power, into Adam's body. Adam lay there powerless; the spirit moves within him; he raises his head to his Creator as a flower turns to the sun, impelled by that wonderful power which is neither will nor obedience....

"The next picture is the creation of Eve. Adam lies on his right side sunk in sleep, and completely turned to the spectator. One arm falls languidly on his breast, and the back of the fingers rest upon the ground.... Eve stands behind Adam; we see her completely in profile.... We feel tempted to say she is the most beautiful picture of a woman which art has produced.... She is looking straight forward; and we feel that she breathes for the first time: but it seems as if life had not yet flowed through her veins, as if the adoring, God-turned position was not only the first dream-like movement, but as if the Creator himself had formed her, and called her from her slumber, in this position."

The pope was anxious to have the scaffolding again erected, and

15

the figures touched with gold. "It is unnecessary," said Michael Angelo. "But it looks poor," said Julius, who should have thought of this before he insisted on its being shown to the public. "They are poor people whom I have painted there," said the artist; "they did not wear gold on their garments," and Julius was pacified.

Raphael was now working near Michael Angelo in the Vatican palace, but it is probable that they did not become friends, though each admired the genius of the other, and Raphael "thanked God that he had been born in the same century as Michael Angelo." But there was rivalry always between the followers of the two masters.

Raphael was gentle, affectionate, sympathetic, intense, lovable; Michael Angelo was tender at heart but austere in manner, doing only great works, and thinking great thoughts. "Raphael," says Grimm, "had one excellence, which, perhaps, as long as the world stands, no other artist has possessed to such an extent,—his works suit more closely the average human mind. There is no line drawn above or below. Michael Angelo's ideals belong to a nobler, stronger generation, as if he had had demigods in his mind, just as Schiller's poetical forms, in another manner, often outstep the measure of the ordinary mortal.... Leonardo sought for the fantastic, Michael Angelo for the difficult and the great; both labored with intense accuracy, both went their own ways, and impressed the stamp of nature on their works. Raphael proceeded quietly, often advancing in the completion only to a certain point, at which he rested, apparently not jealous at being confounded with others. He paints at first in the fashion of Perugino, and his portraits are in the delicate manner of Leonardo: a certain grace is almost the only characteristic of his works. At length he finds himself in Rome, opposed alone to Michael Angelo; then only does the true source of power burst out within him; and he produces works which stand so high above all his former ones that the air of Rome which he breathed seemed to have worked wonders in him.... Raphael served the court with agreeable obsequiousness; but under the outward veil of this subservient friendliness there dwelt a keen and royal mind, which bent before no power, and went its own way solitarily, like the soul of Michael Angelo."

The Sistine Chapel was finished, probably, in 1512, and Michael Angelo returned with ardor to the Julius monument, which, however, had been reduced in plan from the original. He worked on the central figure, Moses, with great joy, believing it would be his masterpiece. "This statue," says Charles Christopher Black of Trinity College, Cambridge, "takes rank with the Prometheus of Æschylus, with the highest and noblest conceptions of Dante and Shakespeare."

"He sits there," says Grimm, "as if on the point of starting up, his head proudly raised; his hand, under the arm of which rest the tables of the law, is thrust in his beard, which falls in heavy, waving locks on his breast; his nostrils are wide and expanding, and his mouth looks as if

16

the words were trembling on his lips. Such a man could well subdue a rebellious people, drawing them after him, like a moving magnet, through the wilderness and through the sea itself.

"What need we information, letters, supposititious records, respecting Michael Angelo, when we possess such a work, every line of which is a transcript of his mind?"

Emerson truly said, "Nothing great was ever achieved without enthusiasm." No work either in literature or art can ever be great, or live beyond a decade or two, unless the author or artist puts himself into it,—his own glowing heart and earnest purpose. Mr. Black well says, "The highest aim of art is not to produce a counterpart of nature, but to convey by a judicious employment of natural forms, and a wise deviation where required, the sentiment which it is the artist's object to inculcate."

The statues of the two chained youths, or "Fettered Slaves," which were too large after the monument had been reduced in size, were sent to France. The "Dying Slave" will be recalled by all who have visited the Renaissance sculptures of the Louvre. Grimm says, "Perhaps the tender beauty of this dying youth is more penetrating than the power of Moses.... When I say that to me it is the most elevated piece of statuary that I know, I do so remembering the masterpieces of ancient art. Man is always limited. It is impossible, in the most comprehensive life, to have had everything before our eyes, and to have contemplated that which we have seen, in the best and worthiest state of feeling.... I ask myself what work of sculpture first comes to mind if I am to name the best, and at once the answer is ready,—the dying youth of Michael Angelo.... What work of any ancient master do we, however, know or possess which touches us so nearly as this,—which takes hold of our soul so completely as this exemplification of the highest and last human conflict does, in a being just developing? The last moment, between life and immortality,—the terror at once of departing and arriving,—the enfeebling of the powerful youthful limbs, which, like an empty and magnificent coat of mail, are cast off by the soul as she rises, and which, still losing what they contained, seem nevertheless completely to veil it!

"He is chained to the pillar by a band running across the breast, below the shoulders; his powers are just ebbing; the band sustains him; he almost hangs in it; one shoulder is forced up, and towards this the head inclines as it falls backwards. The hand of this arm is placed on his breast; the other is raised in a bent position behind the head, in such an attitude as in sleep we make a pillow of an arm, and it is fettered at the wrist. The knees, drawn closely together, have no more firmness; no muscle is stretched; all has returned to that repose which indicates death."

A year after the Sistine Chapel was finished, Pope Julius died, and was succeeded by Leo X., at whose side the artist had sat when a boy, in the palace of Lorenzo the Magnificent. He was a man of taste and culture, and desired to build a monument to himself in his native Florence. He therefore commissioned Michael Angelo to build a beautiful, sculptured façade for the Church of San Lorenzo, erected by Cosmo de' Medici from designs of Brunelleschi.

For nearly four years the sculptor remained among the mountains of Carrara, and the adjacent ones of Serravezza, taking out heavy blocks of marble, making roads over the steep rocks for their transportation, and studying architecture with great assiduity.

Meantime, Michael Angelo writes to his "Dearest father: Take care of your health, and see whether you are not still able to get your daily bread; and, with God's help, get through, poor but honest. I do not do otherwise; I live shabbily, and care not for outward honor; a thousand cares and works burden me; and thus I have now gone on for fifteen years without having a happy, quiet hour. And I have done all for the sake of supporting you, which you have never acknowledged or believed. God forgive us all! I am ready to go on working as long as I can, and as long as my powers hold out."

Later he hears that his father is ill, and writes anxiously to his brother, "Take care, also, that nothing is lacking in his nursing; for I have exerted myself for him alone, in order that to the last he might have a life free of care. Your wife, too, must take care of him, and attend to his necessities; and all of you, if necessary, must spare no expenses, even if it should cost us everything."

Finally the façade of San Lorenzo was abandoned by Leo X., who decided to erect a new chapel north of the church, for the reception of monuments to his brother and nephew, Giuliano and Lorenzo. The artist built the new sacristy, bringing thither three hundred cart-loads of marble from Carrara.

Leo died in 1521, and was succeeded by Adrian, who lived only a year, and then by Clement VII., the cousin of Leo X He was a warm friend of Michael Angelo, and so desirous was he of keeping the artist in his service that he endeavored to have him take holy orders, but the offer was refused.

Like the other popes he wished to immortalize his name, and therefore gave the artist the building of the Laurentian library, adjoining San Lorenzo.

Meantime the relatives of Pope Julius were justly angry because his tomb was not completed, and threatened to imprison the sculptor for not fulfilling his contract. All art work was soon discontinued through the sacking of Rome by Charles V. of Germany, in 1527. Upon the inlaid marble floor of the Vatican the German soldiers lighted their fires, and with valuable documents made beds for their horses which stood in the Sistine Chapel. Rome had ninety thousand inhabitants under Leo X A year after the conquest, she had scarcely a third of that number.

The Florentines now expelled the Medici, revived the republic, and appointed Michael Angelo to superintend the fortifications and defences of Florence. He had always loved liberty. Now he loaned his funds freely to the republic, fortified the hill of San Miniato, was sent to Ferrara by the government to study its fortifications, and also on an embassy to Venice. He showed himself as skilful in engineering as in architecture or painting.

With quick intuition he soon perceived that Malatesta Baglioni, the captain-general of the republic, was a traitor, and, warned that he himself was to be assassinated, he fled to Venice.

Here, in exile, he probably wrote his beautiful sonnets to Dante, whose works he so ardently admired.

> "How shall we speak of him? for our blind eyes
> Are all unequal to his dazzling rays.
> Easier it is to blame his enemies,
> Than for the tongue to tell his highest praise.
> For us he did explore the realms of woe;
> And, at his coming, did high heaven expand
> Her lofty gates, to whom his native land
> Refused to open hers. Yet shall thou know,
> Ungrateful city, in thine own despite,
> That thou hast fostered best thy Dante's fame;
> For virtue, when oppressed, appears more bright.
> And brighter, therefore, shall his glory be,
> Suffering of all mankind most wrongfully,
> Since in the world there lives no greater name."
>
> *Southey.*

Venice offered Michael Angelo all possible inducements to remain, and Francis I of France eagerly besought the artist to live at his court; but his heart was in Florence, and thither he returned, and bravely helped to defend her to the last. When the Medici were again triumphant, and freedom was dead, the artist being too great a man to imprison or kill, he was publicly pardoned by the pope, and went sadly to his work on the monuments in the Medici Chapel of San Lorenzo.

Here he labored day and night, eating little and sleeping less, ill in body and suffering deeply in heart for his beloved Florence; working into the speaking stone his sorrow and his hopes. In 1534 the Medici Chapel was completed,—a massive piece of architecture, executed at an almost fabulous expense. On one side is the tomb of Giuliano de' Medici, the son of Lorenzo the Magnificent, with his statue in a sitting posture, holding in his hand the bâton of a general. Beneath him, over the tomb, are the statues Day and Night. Opposite is the tomb of Lorenzo de' Medici, the grandson of Lorenzo the Magnificent, and the father of Catherine de' Medici. It is clad in armor, with a helmet overshadowing the grave features. The Italians call it Il Pensiero ("Thought," or "Meditation").

Hawthorne said of this statue, "No such grandeur and majesty have elsewhere been put into human shape. It is all a miracle—the deep repose, and the deep life within it. It is as much a miracle to have achieved this as to make a statue that would rise up and walk.... This statue is one of the things which I look at with highest enjoyment, but also with grief and impatience, because I feel that I do not come at all to that which it involves, and that by and by I must go away and leave it forever. How wonderful! To take a block of marble, and convert it wholly into thought, and to do it through all the obstructions and impediments of drapery."

Some authorities believe that the statue usually called Lorenzo was intended for Giuliano. Michael Angelo himself, when remonstrated with because the portraits were not correct likenesses, replied that he "did not suppose people a hundred years later would care much how the dukes looked!"

Under this statue are Dawn and Twilight. Ruskin calls these, with Night and Day, "Four ineffable types, not of darkness nor of day—not of morning nor evening, but of the departure and the resurrection, the twilight and the dawn, of the souls of men."

Day is a gigantic figure of a man; Night, of a woman in a profound sleep, with her foot resting on a thick bundle of poppy-heads. When this statue was exhibited for the first time, Giovanni Batista Strozzi wrote a verse, and attached it to the marble:—

"Carved by an Angel, in this marble white
Sweetly reposing, lo, the Goddess Night!
Calmly she sleeps, and so must living be:
Awake her gently; she will speak to thee."

To which Michael Angelo wrote the following reply:—

"Grateful is sleep, whilst wrong and shame survive
More grateful still in senseless stone to live;
Gladly both sight and hearing I forego;
Oh, then, awake me not. Hush—whisper low."

Of Day, Mrs. Oliphant says, in her "Makers of Florence," "Bursting herculean from his strong prison, half heroic, nothing known of him but the great brow and resolute eyes, and those vast limbs, which were not yet free from the cohesion of the marble, though alive with such strain of action."

Twilight is the strong figure of a man. Dawn, or Morning, Grimm considers "the most beautiful of all. She is lying outstretched on the gently sloping side of the lid of the sarcophagus. Not, however, resting,

20

but as if, still in sleep, she had moved towards us; so that, while the upper part of the back is still reclining, the lower part is turned to us. She is lying on her right side; the leg next us, only feebly bent at the knee is stretching itself out; the other is half drawn up, and with the knee bent out, as if it was stepping forward and seeking for sure footing. An entire symphony of Beethoven lies in this statue."

In 1534, the same year in which the Medici statues were finished, Michael Angelo's father died, at the age of ninety. The artist gave him a costly burial, and wrote a pathetic poem in his memory. The beloved brother, Buonarotto, had died in Michael Angelo's arms. His young mother had died years before when he went to Rome, scarcely more than a boy.

"Already had I wept and sighed so much,
I thought all grief forever at an end,
Exhaled in sighs, shed forth in bitter tears.

******

For thee, my brother, and for him who was
Of thee and me the parent, love inspires
A grief unspeakable to vex and sting.

******

Full ninety times the sun had bathed his face
In the wet ocean, ending his annual round
Ere thou attainedst to the Peace Divine.

******

There, where (to Him be thanks!) I think thee now,
And hope to see again if my cold heart
Be raised from earthly mire to where thou art.

******

And if 'twixt sire and son the noblest love
Still grows in Heaven, where every virtue grows,
While giving glory to my heavenly Lord,
I shall rejoice with thee in Heaven's bliss."

Clement was now dead, and Paul III was in the papal chair. He, like the others, desired that Michael Angelo should do some great work to immortalize his reign. Clement had wished the artist to paint the "Last Judgment" in the Sistine Chapel, and when Paul urged the

21

carrying-out of this plan, Michael Angelo excused himself on account of the contract with the heirs of Julius II.

"It is now thirty years," cried Paul III, "that I have had this desire; and, now that I am pope, shall I not be able to effect it? Where is the contract, that I may tear it?"

One day he appeared in the studio of the painter, bringing with him eight cardinals, all of whom wished to see the designs for the "Last Judgment."

The artist was still at work on Moses. "This one statue is sufficient to be a worthy monument to Pope Julius," said the cardinal of Mantua. Paul III refused to release Michael Angelo, and he began work on the Sistine Chapel.

The painting was not completed until nearly eight years had passed. There are three hundred figures and heads in this vast fresco. Says M. F. Sweetser, in his concise and excellent life of Michael Angelo, "About Christ are many renowned saints,—the Madonna, gazing mildly at the blessed and redeemed souls; Adam and Eve, curiously regarding the Judge; and a group of pleading apostles, bearing their emblems. These are surrounded by a vast throng of saints and martyrs, safe in Heaven, all of whom exemplify the saying that 'Michael Angelo nowhere admits, either into heaven or hell, any but the physically powerful.' Below the Judge are four angels blowing trumpets towards the four quarters of the universe, and four others holding the books by which the dead are to be judged. Under these the land and sea are giving up their dead.... As a work of art, the Last Judgment was one of the grandest productions of the famous art-century."

Biagio da Cesena, the pope's master of ceremonies, complained that so many naked figures made the painting more appropriate for bath-rooms and stables than for a chapel. What was the surprise of Biagio, when the painting was thrown open to the public, to find that the infernal judge Minos, with ass's ears, was his own portrait! He begged the pope to punish the artist; but Paul replied, "If the painter had placed thee in purgatory, I should have used every effort to help thee; but since he has put thee in hell, it is useless to have recourse to me, because ex infernis nulla est redemptio."

Paul IV. later complained that the figures were shamefully nude, and desired to have them covered. "Tell his Holiness," said Michael Angelo, "that this is a mere trifle, and can be easily done; let him mend the world, paintings are easily mended." Paul finally had the nude figures draped by Daniele da Volterra, who thereupon bore the nickname of "the breeches-maker."

While painting this picture, the artist fell from the scaffold and injured his leg seriously. He refused to allow anything to be done for him, but his friend, the surgeon Rontini, forced his way into the house, and cared for him until he recovered.

These eight years had been the happiest of Michael Angelo's life.

22

Before this time he had been cold in manner, often melancholy, and sometimes overbearing; now he was gentle, cheerful, and affectionate. He had written home in early life, "I have no friends; I need none, and wish to have none." Now he had found, what every human being needs, a friend whose tastes and aspirations were like his own. At sixty, he met and loved Vittoria Colonna, a woman whose mind was henceforward to be his inspiration, and whose sweet nature was to be his rest and satisfaction forever. For such a mind as Michael Angelo's there are few kindred spirits. Fortunate was he that the blessed gift came, even though late in life.

Vittoria was the daughter of Fabrizio Colonna, and the widow of Marchese di Pescara, the two highest nobles and generals of her time. Tenderly reared and highly educated, she had married at nineteen, her husband soon after engaging in the wars of the time. He was wounded at Pavia, and died before his young wife could reach him. He was buried at Milan, but the body was afterwards removed to Naples with great magnificence.

Vittoria, childless, well-nigh heart-broken, turned to literature as her solace. She desired to enter a convent; but the bishop of Carpentros, afterwards a cardinal, and an intimate friend of Vittoria, hastened to Paul III, who forbade the abbess and nuns of San Silvestro, on pain of excommunication, to permit her to take the veil. Vittoria must not be lost to the world.

When her poems were published, says T. Adolphus Trollope, in his life of this charming woman, "copies were as eagerly sought for as the novel of the season at a nineteenth-century circulating library. Cardinals, bishops, poets, wits, diplomatists, passed them from one to another, made them the subject of their correspondence with each other and with the fair mourner."

Hallam says, "The rare virtues and consummate talents of this lady were the theme of all Italy in that brilliant age of her literature."

Vittoria Colonna is one of the best illustrations in history of what a noble and intellectual woman can do for the upbuilding of society. Many gifted men gave her a sincere affection, and she held that affection while life lasted. She was well read in history, religious matters, and classic literature. Her first visit to Rome was a continued ovation. Even the Emperor Charles V. called upon her. Unselfish, sympathetic, with a gentle and winsome manner that drew every one into confidence, she proved herself a companion for the most highly educated, and a helper for the lowly.

When she visited Ferrara, Duke Hercules II., who had married Renée of France, the daughter of Louis XII., received her, says Trollope, "with every possible distinction on the score of her poetical celebrity, and deemed his city honored by her presence. He invited, we are told, the most distinguished poets and men of letters of Venice and Lombardy to meet her at Ferrara. And so much was her visit prized that when Cardinal Giberto sent thither his secretary, Francesco della Torre, to persuade her to visit his episcopal city, Verona, that ambassador wrote to his friend Bembo, at Venice, that he had like to have been banished by the Duke, and stoned by the people, for coming there with the intention of robbing Ferrara of its most precious treasure, for the purpose of enriching Verona."... The learned and elegant Bembo writes of her that he considered her poetical judgment as sound and authoritative as that of the greatest masters of the art of song.... Bernardo Tasso made her the subject of several of his poems. Giovio dedicated to her his life of Pescara, and Cardinal Pompeo Colonna his book on "The Praises of Women;" and Contarini paid her the far more remarkable compliment of dedicating to her his work "On Free Will."

"Paul III was," as Muratori says, "by no means well disposed towards the Colonna family. Yet Vittoria must have had influence with the haughty and severe old Farnese. For both Bembo and Fregoso, the Bishop of Naples, have taken occasion to acknowledge that they owed their promotion to the purple in great measure to her."

It is probable that she first met Michael Angelo in the year 1536. He was then sixty-one, and she forty-six. "A woman," says Grimm, "needs not extreme youth to captivate the mind of a man who discovers in her the highest intelligence.... She belonged to that class of women who, apparently with no will of their own, never seek to extort anything by force, and yet obtain everything which is placed before them.... How tenderly she exercised her authority over Michael Angelo, who had never before been approached; whom she now for the first time inspired with the happiness of yielding to a woman, and for whom the years which she passed at that time in Rome she made a period of happiness, which he had never before known.... Whenever we contemplate the life of great men, the most beautiful part of their existence is that, when meeting with a power equal to their own, they find one worthy of measuring the depths of their mind.... There is no deeper desire than that of meeting such a mind; no greater happiness than having found it; no greater sorrow than to resign this happiness, whether it be that it has never been enjoyed, or that it has been lost."

Francesco d'Ollanda, a portrait-painter, has described one of the Sundays which he spent in the company of Michael Angelo and Vittoria, "the latter of whom he calls beautiful, pure in conduct, and acquainted with the Latin tongue; in short, she is adorned with every grace which can redound to a woman's praise."

When Michael Angelo arrived at her home on that Sunday, Vittoria, "who could never speak without elevating those with whom she conversed and even the place where she was, began to lead the conversation with the greatest art upon all possible things, without, however, touching even remotely upon painting. She wished to give Michael Angelo assurance." She said to him, "I cannot but admire the manner in which you withdraw yourself from the world, from useless conversation, and from all the offers of princes who desire paintings from your hand,—how you avoid it all, and how you have disposed the labor of your whole life as one single, great work."

"Gracious lady," replied Michael Angelo, "these are undeserved praises; but, as the conversation has taken this turn, I must here complain of the public. A thousand silly reproaches are brought against artists of importance. They say that they are strange people, that they are not to be approached, that there is no bearing with them. No one, on the contrary, can be so natural and human as great artists.... How should an artist, absorbed in his work, take from it time and thought to drive away other people's ennui?... An artist who, instead of satisfying the highest demands of his art, tries to suit himself to the great public, who has nothing strange or peculiar in his personal exterior, or rather what the world calls so,—will never become an extraordinary mind. It is true, as regards the ordinary race of artists, we need take no lantern to look for them; they stand at the corner of every street throughout the world, ready for all who seek them.... True art is made noble and religious by the mind producing it. For, for those who feel it, nothing makes the soul so religious and pure as the endeavor to create something perfect, for God is perfection, and whoever strives after it is striving after something divine. True painting is only an image of the perfection of God, a shadow of the pencil with which he paints,—a melody, a striving after harmony."

And then, says d'Ollanda, "Vittoria began a eulogium upon painting; she spoke of its ennobling influence upon a people,—how it led them to piety, to glory, to greatness, until the tears came into her eyes from the emotion within."

For ten or twelve years, in the midst of long separations and many sorrows, this affection of Vittoria and Michael Angelo shed its transcendent light over two great lives. It was impossible not to love a woman with such tenderness, sympathy, and sincerity. We may admire a beautiful or a brilliant woman, but if she lacks tenderness and sincerity the world soon loses its allegiance. When political changes made it necessary for her to leave Rome and go to the Convent of St. Catherine at Viterbo, Michael Angelo wrote her daily, while he painted in the Pauline Chapel, after the "Last Judgment" was finished, the "Crucifixion of Peter," and the "Conversion of Paul." In 1542 she wrote him tenderly, "I have not answered your letter before, thinking that if you and I continue to write according to my obligation and your courtesy, it will be necessary that I leave St. Catherine's Chapel, without finding myself with the sisters at the appointed hours, and that you must abandon the Pauline Chapel, and not keep yourself all the day long in sweet colloquy with your paintings ... so that I from the brides of Christ, and you from his vicar, shall fall away."

However she may chide him for writing too frequently, his words and works are most precious to her. When he paints for her a picture, she writes, "I had the greatest faith in God, that he would give you a supernatural grace to paint this Christ; then I saw it, so wonderful that it surpassed in every way my expectations. Being emboldened by your miracles, I desired that which I now see marvellously fulfilled, that is, that it should stand in every part in the highest perfection, and that one could not desire more nor reach forward to desire so much. And I tell you that it gave me joy that the angel on the right hand is so beautiful; for the Archangel Michael will place you, Michael Angelo, on the right hand of the Lord at the judgment day. And meanwhile I know not how to serve you otherwise than to pray to this sweet Christ, whom you have so well and perfectly painted, and to entreat you to command me as altogether yours in all and through all."

What delicate appreciation of the genius of the man she loved! How it must have stimulated and blessed him! But more than all else she loved Michael Angelo for the one thing women value most in men, the strength and constancy of a nature that gives a single and lasting devotion.

She gave to Michael Angelo a vellum book, containing one hundred and three of her sonnets, and sent him forty new ones which she composed at the convent of Viterbo. These he had bound up in the same book which he received from her; her for whom, he said, "I would have done more than for any one else whom I could name in the world." He wrote back his thanks with the sweet self-abnegation of love.

"And well I see how false it were to think
That any work, faded and frail, of mine,
Could emulate the perfect grace of thine.
Genius, and art, and daring, backward shrink.
A thousand works from mortals like to me
Can ne'er repay what Heaven has given thee."

She inspired him to write poetry. "The productions of our great artist's pen," says John Edward Taylor, "rank unquestionably in the number of the most perfect of his own or any subsequent age. Stamped by a flow of eloquence, a purity of style, an habitual nobleness of sentiment, they discover a depth of thought rarely equalled, and frequently approaching to the sublimity of Dante."

Several of his most beautiful sonnets were to Vittoria:—
"If it be true that any beauteous thing
Raises the pure and just desire of man
From earth to God, the eternal fount of all,
Such I believe my love: for, as in her
So fair, in whom I all besides forget,

I view the gentle work of her Creator;
I have no care for any other thing
Whilst thus I love. Nor is it marvellous,
Since the effect is not of my own power,
If the soul doth by nature, tempted forth,
Enamored through the eyes,
Repose upon the eyes which it resembleth,
And through them riseth to the primal love,
As to its end, and honors in admiring:
For who adores the Maker needs must love his work."

"If a chaste love, exalted piety,
If equal fortune between two who love,
Whose every joy and sorrow are the same,
One spirit only governing two hearts,—
If one soul in two bodies made eterne,
Raising them both to Heaven on equal wings,—
If the same flame, one undivided ray,
Shine forth to each, from inward unity,—
If mutual love, for neither's self reserved,
Desiring only the return of love,—
If that which one desires the other swift
Anticipates, impelled by an unconscious power,—
Are signs of an indissoluble faith,
Shall aught have power to loosen such a bond?"

John Edward Taylor.

In 1544 the Colonna estates were confiscated by the pope, after a contest between Paul III and the powerful Colonnas, in which the latter were defeated, and Vittoria retired to the Benedictine Convent of St. Anna. Here her health failed. The celebrated physician and poet Fracastoro said, "Would that a physician for her mind could be found! Otherwise, the fairest light in this world will, from causes by no means clear, be extinguished and taken from our eyes."

At the beginning of 1547 she became dangerously ill, and was conveyed to the palace of her relative Giuliano Cesarini, the only one of her kindred in Rome. She died towards the last of February, 1547, at the age of fifty-seven.

She requested to be buried like the sisters with whom she last resided, and so entirely were her wishes carried out that her place of sepulture is unknown.

Michael Angelo staid beside her to the very last. When she was gone he almost lost his senses. Says his pupil, Condivi, "He bore such a love to her that I remember to have heard him say that he grieved at nothing so much as that when he went to see her pass from this life he had not kissed her brow or her face, as he kissed her hand. After her death he frequently stood trembling and as if insensible."

He wrote several sonnets to her memory.

"When the prime mover of my many sighs
Heaven took through death from out her earthly place,
Nature, that never made so fair a face,
Remained ashamed, and tears were in all eyes.
O fate, unheeding my impassioned cries!
O hopes fallacious! O thou spirit of grace,
Where art thou now? Earth holds in its embrace
Thy lovely limbs, thy holy thoughts the skies.
Vainly did cruel Death attempt to stay
The rumor of thy virtuous renown,
That Lethe's waters could not wash away!
A thousand leaves, since he hath stricken thee down,
Speak of thee, nor to thee would heaven convey,
Except through death, a refuge and a crown."

Henry W. Longfellow.

The monument of Julius had at last been completed, and placed in the Church of San Pietro in Vincola. In 1546, Antonio di San Gallo, the director of the building of St. Peter's, died, and Michael Angelo was commissioned to carry forward the work. Fortunately Vittoria lived to see this honor conferred upon him.

He was now seventy-one years old. For the remaining eighteen years of his life, he devoted himself to this great labor, without compensation. When Paul III, with Cardinal Marcello, summoned Michael Angelo to talk over some alleged defects, the aged artist boldly replied to the cardinal, "I am not nor will I consent to be obliged to tell, to your eminence or any one else, what I ought or wish to do. Your office is to bring money and guard it from thieves, and the designing of the building is left to me." Then he said to the pope, "Holy Father, you see what I gain; if these fatigues which I endure do not benefit my soul, I lose both time and labor." The pope, who loved him, placed his hands on his shoulders, saying, "You benefit both soul and body: do not doubt."

When asked if the new dome would not surpass that of the Duomo of Florence, by Brunelleschi, he said, "It will be more grand, but not more beautiful."

Michael Angelo lived very simply in Rome, though he had amassed a large property, most of which he left to his nephew Leonardo, to whom and his family he was tenderly attached. When this nephew was married, the sculptor wrote him "not to care about a great dowry, but that you should look to a healthy mind, a healthy body, good blood, and good education, and what sort of family it is.... Above all, seek the counsel of God, for it is a great step."

Michael Angelo was devotedly attached to Urbino, who had been his servant for twenty-six years, and who loved him so much, says Vasari, "that he had nursed him in sickness, and slept at night in his clothes beside him, the better to watch for his comforts." One day the artist said to him, "When I die, what wilt thou do?"—"Serve some one else," was the reply. "Thou poor creature, I must save thee from that," said the sculptor, and immediately gave him two thousand crowns.

At Urbino's death, when his master was about eighty, Michael Angelo wrote Vasari, in deep grief, of his "infinite loss." "Nor have I now left any other hope than that of rejoining him in Paradise. But of this God has given me a foretaste, in the most blessed death that he has died; his own departure did not grieve him, as did the leaving me in this treacherous world, with so many troubles. Truly is the best part of my being gone with him, nor is anything now left me except an infinite sorrow."

The artist was again and again urged to return to Florence, by the reigning dukes, but he replied, "You must see by my handwriting that I touch the twenty-fourth hour, and no thought is now born in my mind in which death is not mixed."

He was implored on every side to carve statues and paint pictures. He promised Francis I of France a work in marble, in bronze, and in painting. "Should death interrupt this desire," said Michael Angelo, "then, if it be possible to sculpture or paint in the other world, I shall not fail to do so, where no one becomes old."

He furnished plans for several Roman gates which Pius IV., who succeeded Paul IV., wished to rebuild, and made designs for various other buildings and public squares. He erected the Church of St. Mary of the Angels, amid the ruins of the Baths of Diocletian. "Nothing exists in architecture," says Mr. Heath Wilson, "which exceeds the plan of this church in beauty and variety of form. The general proportions are so harmonious, the lines of the plan so gracefully disposed, the form of the whole so original, that, without looking at the elevations, the eye is delighted by the evidence on all sides of the imagination, taste, and skill shown by the venerable architect in this superb work."

The great sculptor never ceased to work or to study. When old he drew a picture representing himself as an aged man in a cart, with these words underneath: Ancora impara (still learning). He painted but two portraits, one of Vittoria Colonna, and one of young Tommaso dei Cavalieri, whom he tenderly loved. To this youth, whom Varchi, the Florentine professor and court scholar, declared to be the most attractive young man he had ever known, Michael Angelo wrote this beautiful sonnet:—

29

"Through thee I catch a gleam of tender glow,
Which with my own eyes I had failed to see;
And walking onward step by step with thee,
The once oppressing burdens lighter grow.
With thee, my grovelling thoughts I heavenward raise,
Borne upward by thy bold, aspiring wing;
I follow where thou wilt,—a helpless thing,
Cold in the sun, and warm in winter days.
My will, my friend, rests only upon thine;
Thy heart must every thought of mine supply;
My mind expression finds in thee alone.
Thus like the moonlight's silver ray I shine:
We only see her beams on the far sky,
When the sun's fiery rays are o'er her thrown."

His last work was a group of the Virgin and the dead Christ, which he intended should be placed on an altar over his own tomb; but it was left unfinished from a flaw in the marble, and is now in the cathedral in Florence. Vasari found the aged artist working at it late at night, when he had arisen from his bed because he could not sleep. A tallow candle was placed in his pasteboard cap, so as to leave his hands free for work. Once, as they were looking at the statue, Michael Angelo suffered the lantern which he held in his hand to fall, and they were left in darkness. He remarked, "I am so old that Death often pulls me by the cape, and bids me go with him; some day I shall fall myself, like this lamp, and the light of life will be extinguished."

To the last Michael Angelo was always learning. He used often to visit the Vatican to study the Torso Belvedere, which he declared had been of the greatest benefit to him.

In 1563-64 he was elected vice-president of the Florentine Academy of Fine Arts. That winter his strength failed rapidly, though all was done for him that love and honor could possibly do, for he had many devoted friends among all classes, and was constantly aiding artists and others. He did not fear death, for he said, "If life be a pleasure, since death also is sent by the hand of the same master, neither should that displease us."

Between three and four o'clock in the afternoon of the 18th of February, 1564, the same month in which Vittoria died, the great man passed away, in the ninetieth year of his age. Daniele da Volterra, Condivi, and Cavalieri stood by his bedside. His last words to them were, "I give my soul to God, my body to the earth, and my worldly possessions to my nearest of kin."

The pope and the Romans were determined to keep the dead Michael Angelo in Rome; but his wish had been to lie in Florence. The body, therefore, was conveyed to the latter city, disguised as a bale of merchandise, and buried in Santa Croce, on Sunday night, March 12th, the Tuscan artists following with their lighted torches, accompanied by thousands of citizens. In the month of July a grand memorial service was held, in the Church of San Lorenzo, for the illustrious dead, paintings and statuary surrounding a catafalque fifty-four feet high.

After thirty years of voluntary exile, the melancholy, solitary, great-souled man lay in his native Florence. He had loved liberty and uprightness. He had been ambitious, and devoted to his masterly work, with the will-power and intensity which belong to genius. He had allowed no obstacles to stand in his path,—neither lack of money nor jealousy of artists. He had faith in himself. He spoke sometimes too plainly, but almost always justly. Cold and unapproachable though he was, children loved him, and for them he would stop and make sketches on the street. He had the fearlessness of one who rightly counts manhood above all titles. He was too noble to be trifling, or petty, or self-indulgent. Great in sculpture, painting, poetry, architecture, engineering, character, he has left an imperishable name. Taine says, "There are four men in the world of art and of literature exalted above all others, and to such a degree as to seem to belong to another race; namely, Dante, Shakespeare, Beethoven, and Michael Angelo."

LEONARDO DA VINCI

"The world perhaps contains no example of a genius so universal, so creative, so incapable of self-contentment, so athirst for the infinite, so naturally refined, so far in advance of his own and of subsequent ages. His countenances express incredible sensibility and mental power; they overflow with unexpressed ideas and emotions. Michael Angelo's personages alongside of his are simply heroic athletes; Raphael's virgins are only placid children, whose sleeping souls have not yet lived." Thus writes Taine of Da Vinci, in his "Travels in Italy."

Mrs. Jameson calls Leonardo da Vinci, in her "Early Italian Painters," "The miracle of that age of miracles. Ardent and versatile as youth; patient and persevering as age; a most profound and original thinker; the greatest mathematician and most ingenious mechanic of his time; architect, chemist, engineer, musician, poet, painter!"

Hallam, in his "History of the Literature of Europe," says of the published extracts from the great volumes of manuscript left by Leonardo, "These are, according to our common estimate of the age in which he lived, more like revelations of physical truths vouchsafed to a single mind, than the superstructure of its reasoning upon any established basis. The discoveries which made Galileo, Kepler, Castelli, and other names illustrious—the system of Copernicus—the very theories of recent geologists, are anticipated by Da Vinci within the compass of a few pages, not perhaps in the most precise language, or on the most conclusive reasoning, but so as to strike us with something like the awe of preternatural knowledge. In an age of so much dogmatism, he first laid down the grand principle of Bacon, that experiment and observation must be the guides to just theory in the investigation of nature.

"If any doubt could be harbored, not as to the right of Leonardo da Vinci to stand as the first name of the fifteenth century, which is beyond all doubt, but as to his originality in so many discoveries, which probably no one man, especially in such circumstances, has ever made, it must be by an hypothesis, not very untenable, that some parts of physical science had already attained a height which mere books do not record."

This man, whom Vasari thinks "specially endowed by the hand of God himself," was born in 1452, at Castello da Vinci, a village in the Val d'Arno, near Florence. His father, Piero Antonio da Vinci, was a notary of the republic, a man of considerable property and influence. When he was twenty-five, he married the first of his four wives, Albiera di Giovanni Amadori, in 1452, and brought home his illegitimate son, Leonardo, born the same year, whom she tenderly cared for as her own.

Of Leonardo's mother, Caterina, little is known, save that five years later she married, presumably in her own circle. Among the twelve other children who came into the home of the advocate, Leonardo was the especial pet and pride, probably because he seemed to have been given all the talents originally intended for the Da Vinci family.

The handsome boy, whose "beauty of person," says Vasari, "was such that it has never been sufficiently extolled," and with "a grace beyond expression," cheerful, eager, enthusiastic, and warmhearted, when sent to school, learned everything with avidity. "In arithmetic he often confounded the master who taught him, by his reasonings and by the difficulty of the problems he proposed." He had that omnivorous appetite for books which Higginson calls the sure indication of genius.

He loved nature intensely. He studied every flower and tree about the country home; made companions of the river Arno, the changing clouds, and the snow-capped mountains. Passionately fond of music, he not only learned to play on the guitar and lute, but invented a lyre of his own, on which he improvised both the song and the air.

On the margins of his books he sketched such admirable drawings that his father took them to Andrea Verrochio, a famous Florentine artist, who was "amazed," and advised that the youth become a painter. Leonardo entered the studio of Verrochio when he was about eighteen, and at once became deeply absorbed in his work. He began to make models in clay, arranging on these soft drapery dipped in plaster, which he drew carefully in black and white on fine linen; also heads of smiling women and children out of terra cotta: already he had that divine gift of painting the "Da Vinci smile," which seems to have been born with him and to have died with him. He studied perspective, and with his fellow-students made chemical researches into the improvement of colors.

Verrochio was engaged in painting a picture of St. John baptizing Christ, for the monks of Vallombrosa, and requested Leonardo to paint an angel in the left-hand corner, holding some vestments. When the work was finished, and Verrochio looked upon Leonardo's angel, "a space of sunlight in the cold, labored old picture," as W. H. Pater says, in his "Studies in the History of the Renaissance," Verrochio became so discouraged "because a mere child could do more than himself," that he would never touch the brush again. This work is now in the Academy of Fine Arts in Florence.

About this time, according to Vasari, Leonardo made his famous shield Rotella del Fico. "Ser Piero da Vinci, being at his country house, was there visited by one of the peasants on his estate, who, having cut down a fig-tree on his farm, had made a shield from part of it with his own hands, and then brought it to Ser Piero, begging that he would be pleased to cause the same to be painted for him in Florence. This the latter very willingly promised to do, the countryman having great skill

33

in taking birds and in fishing, and being often very serviceable to Ser Piero in such matters. Having taken the shield with him to Florence, therefore, without saying anything to Leonardo as to whom it was for, he desired the latter to paint something upon it.

"Accordingly, he one day took it in hand, but, finding it crooked, coarse, and badly made, he straightened it at the fire, and, giving it to a turner, it was brought back to him smooth and delicately rounded, instead of the rude and shapeless form in which he had received it. He then covered it with gypsum, and, having prepared it to his liking, he began to consider what he could paint upon it that might best and most effectually terrify whomsoever might approach it, producing the same effect with that formerly attributed to the head of Medusa. For this purpose, therefore, Leonardo carried to one of his rooms, into which no one but himself ever entered, a number of lizards, hedgehogs, newts, serpents, dragon-flies, locusts, bats, glow-worms, and every sort of strange animal of similar kind on which he could lay his hands; from this assemblage, variously adapted and joined together, he formed a hideous and appalling monster, breathing poison and flames, and surrounded by an atmosphere of fire; this he caused to issuefrom a dark and rifted rock, with poison reeking from the cavernous throat, flames darting from the eyes, and vapors rising from the nostrils in such sort that the result was indeed a most fearful and monstrous creature; at this he labored until the odors arising from all those dead animals filled the room with a mortal fetor, to which the zeal of Leonardo and the love which he bore to art rendered him insensible or indifferent.

"When this work, which neither the countryman nor Ser Piero any longer inquired for, was completed, Leonardo went to his father and told him that he might send for the shield at his earliest convenience, since, so far as he was concerned, the work was finished; Ser Piero went accordingly one morning to the room for the shield, and, having knocked at the door, Leonardo opened it to him, telling him nevertheless to wait a little without, and, having returned into the room, he placed the shield on the easel, and, shading the window so that the light falling on the painting was somewhat dimmed, he made Ser Piero step within to look at it. But the latter, not expecting any such thing, drew back, startled at the first glance, not supposing that to be the shield, or believing the monster he beheld to be a painting; he therefore turned to rush out, but Leonardo withheld him, saying,—'The shield will serve the purpose for which it has been executed; take it, therefore, and carry it away, for this is the effect it was designed to produce.'

"The work seemed something more than wonderful to Ser Piero, and he highly commended the fanciful idea of Leonardo; but he afterwards silently bought from a merchant another shield, whereon there was painted a heart transfixed with an arrow, and this he gave to the countryman, who considered himself obliged to him for it to the end of his life. Some time after, Ser Piero secretly sold the shield painted by Leonardo to certain merchants for one hundred ducats, and it subsequently fell into the hands of the Duke of Milan, sold to him by the same merchants for three hundred ducats."

Leonardo painted also the "Head of Medusa," in the Uffizi Gallery, twined about with green, hissing serpents.

For the King of Portugal he painted a cartoon for a tapestry curtain,—"Adam and Eve in the Garden of Eden." Of the flowers and fruits in this picture, Vasari says, "For careful execution and fidelity to nature, they are such that there is no genius in the world, however godlike, which could produce similar results with equal truth." This cartoon is lost.

The "Madonna della Caraffa," celebrated for the exquisite beauty of the flowers with dew upon them, which stood in a vase by the Virgin, and was highly prized by Clement VII., has also disappeared. The "Adoration of the Magi" and a "Neptune in his Chariot drawn by Sea-horses" were among Da Vinci's works at this time.

He was also studying military engineering, completed a book of designs for mills and other apparatus working by water, invented machines for dredging seaports and channels, and urged the making of a canal from Pisa to Florence, by changing the course of the Arno, a thing accomplished two hundred years later.

Still he did not neglect his painting. He went about the streets of Florence looking for picturesque or beautiful faces, which he transferred to his sketch-book, always carried at his girdle. He attended the execution of criminals to catch the expression of faces or contortion of limbs in agony. Yet so tender-hearted was he, that, Vasari says, "When he passed places where birds were sold, he would frequently take them from their cages, and, having paid the price demanded for them by the sellers, would then let them fly into the air, thus restoring to them the liberty they had lost."

He loved art. He said, "In the silence of the night, recall the ideas of the things which you have studied. Design in your spirit the contours and outlines of the figures that you have seen during the day. When the spirit does not work with the hands, there is no artist.... Do not allege as an excuse your poverty, which does not permit you to study and become skilful; the study of art serves for nourishment to the body as well as the soul.... When all seems easy, it is an unerring sign that the workman has but scant ability and that the task is above his comprehension."

Enjoying all athletic exercises; so strong thathe could bend a horseshoe in his hands; exceedingly fond of horses, of which he owned several,—he still found time to be the life and joy of the brilliant society of Florence; always leading, always fascinating with his intelligent conversation and elegant address. And yet the ambitious Leonardo was not satisfied in Florence. The Medici did not encourage him as they did Michael Angelo. Possibly they felt that he lacked a steady and dominant purpose. He finally made up his mind to try his fortune elsewhere, and wrote the following letter to Lodovico Sforza, Regent of Milan:—

"My Most Illustrious Lord,—Having seen and duly considered the experiments of all those who repute themselves masters and constructors of warlike instruments, and that the inventions and operations of the said instruments are not different from those in common use, I will endeavor, without derogating from any one else, to make known to your Excellency certain secrets of my own, and, at an opportune time, I shall hope to put them into execution, if they seem valuable to you. I briefly note these things below:—

"1. I have a method of making very light bridges, fit to be carried most easily, with which to follow the flight of enemies; and others, strong and secure against fire and battle; easy and commodious to lift up and to place in position. I have methods also to burn and destroy those of the enemy.

"2. I know, in case of the siege of a place, how to take away the water from the ditches, and to make an infinite variety of scaling-ladders and other instruments pertinent to such an expedition.

******

"4. I have also kinds of cannon most commodious and easy to carry, with which to throw inflammable matters, whose smoke causes great fright to the enemy, with serious injury and confusion.

"5. I have means, by excavations and straight and winding subterranean ways, to come to any given point without noise, even though it be necessary to pass under moats and rivers.

******

"8. When the operations of artillery are impossible, I shall construct mangonels, balistæ, and other engines of marvellous efficacy, and out of the common use; and, in short, according to the variety of events, I shall build various and infinite means of offence.

"9. And when it shall happen to be upon the sea, I have means of preparing many instruments most efficient in attack or defence, and vessels that shall make resistance to the most powerful bombardment; and powders and smokes.

"10. In time of peace I believe I can satisfy very well and equal all others in architecture, in designing public edifices and private houses, and in conducting water from one place to another. I can carry on works of sculpture, in marble, bronze, or terra cotta, also in pictures. I can do what canbe done equal to any other, whoever he may be. Also, I shall undertake the execution of the bronze horse, which will be the immortal glory and eternal honor of the happy memory of my lord your father, and of the illustrious honor of Sforza."

36

The result of this letter was a summons to the court at Milan, where Lodovico, though dissolute, was proud to surround himself with the most brilliant men and women of the age. Leonardo took with him a silver lyre, made in the shape of a horse's head, designed by himself, on which he played so skilfully that the duke and his court were enchanted. "Whatever he did," says Vasari, "bore an impress of harmony, truthfulness, goodness, sweetness, and grace, wherein no other man could ever equal him." Such a union of gentleness and sincerity with genius! Who could withstand its influence!

At Milan Leonardo remained for nineteen years, and here some of his most remarkable works were done.

One of the first pictures painted for the Regent was a portrait of a favorite, the beautiful Cecilia Gallerani, a gifted woman, skilled in music and poetry. Leonardo painted for her a picture of the Virgin, for which she probably was the model. The infant Saviour is represented as blessing a new-blown Madonna rose, the emblem of St. Cecilia.

The next portrait—it is now in the Louvre—was that of another beauty, loved by the duke, Lucrezia Crivelli, formerly called La Belle Féronnière, who was a favorite of Francis I "The face," says Mr. Sweetser, "is at once proud and melancholy, with a warm and brilliant coloring and soft pure lines, the head full of light, and even the shadows transparent." In honor of both these portraits Latin poems were written by the poets of the time.

Leonardo also painted two fine portraits of the lawful duke, Gian Galeazzo Sforza, and his wife, Isabella of Aragon, the latter picture "beyond all description beautiful and charming," now preserved in the Ambrosian Library. When these persons were married, Leonardo invented for the entertainment of the guests at the wedding feast a mechanical device called "The Paradise," a representation of the heavens and the revolving planets, which opened as the bride and bridegroom approached, while a person in imitation of the Deity recited complimentary verses.

Leonardo now began on the great equestrian statue of the warrior Francesco Sforza. He studied ancient works of art, especially the equestrian statue of Marcus Aurelius in Rome, made almost countless drawings of horses in repose or on the battle-field, many of which are still preserved at Windsor Castle, studied every movement of live horses and every muscle of dead ones, and did not complete his clay model for ten long years. A genius like Da Vinci spends ten years on the model of an equestrian statue, and yet some artists of the present day, men and women, paint and mouldhorses or human beings after a few weeks or months of study, and expect to win fame!

When the clay model was exhibited in public at the royal wedding of the sister of Gian Galeazzo to the Emperor Maximilian, the enthusiasm was very great. All Italy talked of it, and poets and critics extolled it as beyond the works of Greece or Rome. Unfortunately the ensuing wars depleted the treasury of Milan, and prevented the work from being cast in bronze. When the French entered Milan in 1499, it became a target for the archers. Two years later the Duke of Ferrara asked the use of the model that a bronze horse with a statue of himself might be made; but the King of France refused, and the model finally disappeared.

During these years Leonardo founded the Milan Academy. Probably many of the manuscript volumes which he left were notes of lectures delivered to the students. He must have spoken to them on botany, optics, mechanics, astronomy, hydrostatics, anatomy, perspective, proportion, and other matters. He wrote a book on the anatomy of the horse. "He also," says Vasari, "filled a book with drawings in red crayons, outlined with the pen, all copies made with the utmost care from bodies dissected by his own hand. In this book he set forth the entire structure, arrangement and disposition of the bones, to which he afterwards added all the nerves, in their due order, and next supplied the muscles, of which the first are affixedto the bones, the second give the power of cohesion or holding firmly, and the third impart the motion."

Leonardo said in his notes, "The painter who has obtained a perfect knowledge of the nature of the tendons and muscles, and of those parts which contain the most of them, will know to a certainty, in giving a particular motion to any part of the body, which and how many of the muscles give rise and contribute to it; which of them, by swelling, occasion their shortening, and which of the cartilages they surround. He will not imitate those who, in all the different attitudes they adopt or invent, make use of the same muscles in the arms, back, or chest, or any other parts.... It is necessary that a painter should be a good anatomist, that in his attitudes and gestures he may be able to design the naked parts of the human frame, according to the just rules of the anatomy of the nerves, bones, and muscles; and that, in his different positions, he may know what particular nerve or muscle is the cause of such a particular movement, in order that he may make that only marked and apparent, and not all the rest, as many artists are in the habit of doing; who, that they may appear great designers, make the naked limbs stiff and without grace, so that they have more the appearance of a bag of nuts than the human superficies, or, rather, more like a bundle of radishes than naked muscles."

Leonardo irrigated the dry plains of Lombardy by utilizing the waters of the Ticino River, visiting many cities and towns throughout Lombardy for this purpose, and carefully studying the canals of Egypt under the Ptolemies. He studied ancient architecture also. In his epitaph, composed in his lifetime, he calls himself, "The admirer of the ancients, and their grateful disciple. One thing is lacking to me, their science of proportion. I have done what I could; may posterity pardon me."

He designed a palace for Count Giovanni Melzi, at Vaprio, which became a favorite home for him, especially in the time of war—the residence of his beloved pupil, Francesco Melzi.

In 1492, after Leonardo had been eleven years at the Court of Milan, Lodovico, unscrupulous and immoral, married the gentle and saintly Beatrice d'Este. Leonardo conducted the grand wedding festivities, and designed and decorated the bride's apartments in the Castello della Rocca, making a beautiful bath-room in the garden, adorned with colored marbles and a statue of Diana. While the regent in no wise discontinued his profligate habits, he yet desired to please his wife, by gratifying her taste for religious things. As she had shown an especial fondness for the Dominican church and convent of Santa Maria delle Grazie, Lodovico ordered them reconstructed and embellished for her. In the refectory, the artist painted kneeling portraits of Beatrice, her husband, and their two little children, Maximilian and Francesco; but they have long since faded.

About the year 1496, Leonardo began his immortal work in the refectory, The "Last Supper." Here, where daily the sweet and broken-hearted wife came to remain for hours in meditation and prayer before the tomb of the Duchess Bianca, from which she sometimes had to be removed by force, Leonardo came daily to his masterpiece. Sometimes he would go to his work at daybreak, and never think of descending from his scaffolding to eat or drink till night, so completely absorbed was he in his work. "At other times," says Bandello, "he would remain three or four days without touching it, only coming for an hour or two, and remaining with crossed arms contemplating his figures, as if criticising them himself. I have also seen him at midday, when the sun in the zenith causes all the streets of Milan to be deserted, set out in all haste from the citadel, where he was modelling his colossal horse, and, without seeking the shade, take the shortest road to the convent, where he would add a few strokes to one of his heads, and then return immediately."

Leonardo made a cartoon of the whole picture, and separate studies of each figure. Ten of these are now in the Hermitage in St. Petersburg.

He was long absorbed in his head of Christ. He used to say that his hand trembled whenever he attempted to paint it. At last, in despair, he asked counsel of a friend, Bernardo Zenale, who comforted him by saying, "Oh, Leonardo, the error into which thou hast fallen is one from which only the Divine Being himself can deliver thee; for it is not in thy power nor in that of any one else to give greater divinity and beauty to any figures than thou hast done to these of James the Greater and the Less; therefore, be of good cheer, and leave the Christ imperfect, for thou wilt never be able to accomplish the Christ after such apostles."

Leonardo finished the work in about three years. Beatrice, as might have been expected from such an ill-assorted union, died of sorrow in five years after her marriage. Lodovico, as has been often the case before and since in the world's history, realized too late the wrong he had done, and now strove to remedy it by causing a hundred masses a day to be said for her soul, shutting himself up in remorse for two weeks in a chamber hung with black, only coming forth to do penance at the sanctuaries where his lovely and neglected wife had worshipped. He now wished to make her last resting-place, Santa Maria delle Grazie, as beautiful as possible, and hastened Leonardo at his work on the "Last Supper" that he might see it completed, meantime raising a magnificent tomb to the memory of his neglected Beatrice.

The prior of the convent could not understand why Leonardo should meditate over his work, and, likewise in haste to have the picture finished, complained to Lodovico, who courteously entreated the artist to go on as rapidly as possible. Vasari says, "Leonardo, knowing the prince to be intelligent and judicious, determined to explain himself fully on the subject with him, although he had never chosen to do so with the prior. He therefore discoursed with him at some length respecting art, and made it perfectly manifest to his comprehension that men of genius are sometimes producing most when they seem to be laboring least, their minds being occupied in the elucidation of their ideas, and in the completion of those conceptions to which they afterwards give form and expression with the hand. He further informed the duke that there were still wanting to him two heads, one of which, that of the Saviour, he could not hope to find on earth....

"The second head still wanting was that of Judas, which also caused him some anxiety, since he did not think it possible to imagine a form of feature that should properly render the countenance of a man who, after so many benefits received from his Master, had possessed a heart so depraved as to be capable of betraying his Lord, and the Creator of the world; with regard to that second, however, he would make search, and after all—if he could find no better—he need never be at any great loss, for there would always be the head of that troublesome and impertinent prior. This made the duke laugh with all his heart; he declared Leonardo to be completely in the right: and the poor prior, utterly confounded, went away to drive on the digging in his garden, and left Leonardo in peace."

The "Last Supper" was painted in oils instead of fresco, and soon began to fade. In 1515, when Francis I was in Milan, he was so impressed with the picture that he determined to carry it back to France, and tried to find architects who could secure it from injury by defences of wood and iron so that it could be transported, but none could be found able to do it, and the project was abandoned. The painting was soon damaged by the refectory lying for some time under water. Later one of the monks made a doorway through it, cutting off the feet of Christ. In 1726 an artist named Belotti restored(?) it, leaving nothing untouched but the sky. His work proved unsatisfactory, and Mazza repainted everything except the heads of Matthew, Thaddeus, and Simon. The indignant people soon compelled him to cease, and the prior who had permitted it was banished from the convent.

In 1796, when Napoleon entered Italy, the troops used the refectory as a stable. Three or four years later, it again lay under water for two weeks. At present, one is able to perceive only the general design as the work of Leonardo. Excellent copies were made by Da Vinci's pupils, so that the great picture has found its way into thousands of homes.

The Saviour and his apostles are seated at a long table, in a stately hall. On the left is Bartholomew; next, James the Less; then Andrew, Peter, Judas holding the money-bag, John, with Christ in the centre, Thomas on his right hand, then James the Greater, Philip, Matthew, Thaddeus, and Simon. The moment chosen by the painter is that given by Matthew: "And as they did eat, he said, Verily I say unto you, that one of you shall betray me. And they were exceeding sorrowful, and began every one of them to say unto him, Lord, is it I?"

Mrs. C. W. Heaton says of this picture, in her valuable life of Da Vinci, "In his dramatic rendering of the disciples, Leonardo has shown the boldest and grandest naturalism. They are all of them real, living men with passions like unto us—passions called for the moment by the fearful words of the Master, 'One of you shall betray me,' into full and various play."

Most who visit Milan to see the lace-work in stone of its exquisite cathedral, go also to the famous painting which tells alike the story of a great artist struggling to put immortal thoughts into his faces, and the story of the remorse of a human being in breaking the heart of a lovely woman. Had it not been to atone to Beatrice, probably the "Last Supper" would never have been painted in Santa Maria delle Grazie. Thus strangely has the bitterness of one soul led to the joy and inspiration of thousands!

In 1498, Louis XII came to the throne of France, and laid claim to the duchy of Milan, enforcing his claim by arms. Lodovico fled, but was captured by the French, and kept a prisoner for ten years, until his death. Leonardo went back to his old home in Florence, taking with him two persons, his friend Luca Paciolo, who had lived with him three years at Milan, the author of De Divina Proportione, for which book the artist made sixty drawings; and his beautiful pupil Salaï, his son as he called him, "a youth of singular grace and beauty of person, with curling and wavy hair, a feature of personal beauty by which Leonardo was greatly pleased." From this dear disciple the artist painted many of his angels' heads.

Florence had changed since he went away, scarcely more than a boy. Now he was in middle life, forty-eight years old, the famous painter of the "Last Supper," the polished and renowned scholar. His first work on his return was an altar-piece for the Annunciata Church,—the Madonna, St. Anna, and the infant Christ. The cartoon, now in the Royal Academy at London, caused the greatest delight. "When finished, the chamber wherein it stood was crowded for two days by men and women, old and young, as if going to a solemn festival, all hastening to behold this marvel of Leonardo's, which amazed the whole population."

He now painted two noble Florentine ladies, Ginevra Benci, a famous beauty, and the Mona Lisa, the third wife of Francesco del Giocondo, the latter of whom it is conjectured that Leonardo loved.

Vasari says, "Whoever shall desire to see how far art can imitate nature, may do so to perfection in this head, wherein every peculiarity that could be depicted by the utmost subtlety of the pencil has been faithfully reproduced. The eyes have the lustrous brightness and moisture which is seen in life, and around them are those pale, red, and slightly livid circles, also proper to nature, with the lashes, which can only be copied as these are with the greatest difficulty; the eyebrows also are represented with the closest exactitude, where fuller and where more thinly set, with the separate hairs delineated as they issue from the skin, every turn being followed and all the pores exhibited in a manner that could not be more natural than it is; the nose, with its beautiful and delicately roseate nostrils, might be easily believed to be alive; the mouth, admirable in its outline, has the lips uniting the rose-tints of their color with that of the face in the utmost perfection, and the carnation of the cheek does not appear to be painted, but truly of flesh and blood; he who looks earnestly at the pit of the throat cannot but believe that he sees the beating of the pulses, and it may be truly said that this work is painted in a manner well calculated to make the boldest master tremble, and astonishes all who behold it, however well accustomed to the marvels of art.

"Mona Lisa was exceedingly beautiful; and while Leonardo was painting her portrait, he took the precaution of keeping some one constantly near her, to sing or play on instruments, or to jest and otherwise amuse her, to the end that she might continue cheerful, and so that her face might not exhibit the melancholy expression often imparted by painters to the likenesses they take. In this portrait of Leonardo's, on the contrary, there is so pleasing an expression, and a smile so sweet, that while looking at it one thinks it rather divine than human, and it has ever been esteemed a wonderful work, since life itself could exhibit no other appearance."

No wonder Grimm says, "He who has seen the Mona Lisa smile is followed forever by this smile, just as he is followed by Lear's fury, Macbeth's ambition, Hamlet's melancholy, and Iphigenia's touching purity."

Pater says of the Mona Lisa, "'La Gioconda' is, in the truest sense,

Leonardo's masterpiece, the revealing instance of his mode of thought and work. In suggestiveness, only the 'Melancholia' of Dürer is comparable to it; and no crude symbolism disturbs the effect of its subdued and graceful mystery. We all know the face and hands of the figure, set in its marble chair, in that cirque of fantastic webs, as in some faint light under sea. Perhaps of all ancient pictures time has chilled it least.

******

"The fancy of a perpetual life, sweeping together ten thousand experiences, is an old one; and modern thought has conceived the idea of humanity as wrought upon by, and summing up in itself, all modes of thought and life. Certainly Lady Lisa might stand as the embodiment of the old fancy, the symbol of the modern idea."

One feels with Michelet, when he says, "It fascinates and absorbs me. I go to it in spite of myself, as the bird is drawn to the serpent." I have found myself going day after day to the Louvre to linger before two masterpieces; to grow better through the womanhood of the Venus de Milo, and to rest in the peaceful, contented smile of the Mona Lisa. Nobody can forget the perfect hand. One seems to feel the delicacy of the loving touch which Leonardo gave as he painted through those long yet short four years, leaving the portrait, as he declared, unfinished, because of his high ideal of what a painting should be. The husband did not purchase the picture of the artist—did he not value the beauty? It was finally sold to Francis I., for four thousand gold crowns, an enormous sum at that day.

After Da Vinci had been two years in Florence, Cæsar Borgia, the son of Pope Alexander VI., appointed him architect and general engineer. He travelled through Central Italy, making ramparts and stairways for the citadel of Urbino, machinery at Pesaro, designing a house and better methods of transporting grapes at Cesena, and finer gates at Cesenatico. At one place he lingered to enjoy the regular cadence of the waves beating on the shore; at another, his soul filled with music, he was soothed by the murmur of the fountains. But Cæsar was soon obliged to flee into Spain, and Leonardo could no longer hold the position of engineer.

Pietro Soderini, who had been elected gonfaloniere for life, was the friend of both Leonardo and Michael Angelo. He wished to have these two greatest artists paint each a wall in the Hall of the Palazzo Vecchio. Michael Angelo chose for his subject a group of soldiers surprised by the enemy while bathing in the Arno; Leonardo, a troop of horsemen fighting round a standard, a scene from the battle of Anghiari, fought by the Florentines against the North Italians. Vasari says, "Not only are rage, disdain, and the desire for revenge apparent in the men, but in the horses also; two of those animals, with their fore-

43

legs intertwined, are attacking each other with their teeth, no less fiercely than do the cavaliers who are fighting for the standard."

Vasari thinks it "scarcely possible adequately to describe ... the wonderful mastery he exhibits in the forms and movements of the horses.... The muscular development, the animation of their movements, and their exquisite beauty, are rendered with the utmost fidelity."

When the rival cartoons of Michael Angelo and Da Vinci were publicly exhibited, the excitement was great between the followers of each artist. When Da Vinci began to paint upon the wall, in oils, as in the "Last Supper," the colors so sank into it that he abandoned the work. Soderini accused him of having received money and not rendering an equivalent, which so wounded the pride, of the artist that his friends raised the amount which had been advanced to him, and offered it to the gonfaloniere, who generously refused to accept it. Da Vinci had already become offended with Soderini's treasurer, who offered him a portion of his pay in copper money. Leonardo would not take it, saying, "I am no penny-painter."

In 1504, Da Vinci's father died, and the artist became involved in lawsuits with the other twelve children, who seem to have disputed his share in the property.

At this time Leonardo made drawings for the raising of the Church of San Giovanni (the Baptistery), and the placing of steps beneath it. "He supported his assertions with reasons so persuasive that while he spoke the undertaking seemed feasible, although every one of his hearers, when he had departed, could see for himself that such a thing was impossible." They could not understand that they had a genius in their midst some centuries in advance of his age. He made three bronze figures over the portal of the Baptistery, "without doubt the most beautiful castings that have been seen in these latter days."

Tired of lawsuits, and his ineffectual efforts toward the raising of the Baptistery, he gladly went back to Milan, having been invited thither by Maréchal de Chaumont, the French governor, after an absence in Florence of six years. He seems to have been straitened in circumstances, for he had but thirty crowns left, and of these he generously gave thirteen to make up the marriage portion of the sister of his beloved Salaï.

For seven years during this second sojourn in Milan, he was prosperous and happy. He built large docks and basins, planned many mills, enlarged and improved the great Martesan canal, two hundred miles long, "which brings the waters of the Adda through the Valtellina and across the Chiavenna district, contributing greatly to the fertility of the garden of Northern Italy," and painted several pictures. "La Monaca," now in the Pitti Palace, is the half-length figure of a young nun. Taine says, "The face is colorless excepting the powerful and strange red lips, and the whole physiognomy is calm, with a slight expression of disquietude. This is not an abstract being, emanating from the painter's brain, but an actual woman who has lived, a sister of Mona Lisa, as complex, as full of inward contrasts, and as inexplicable."

"Flora," a beautiful woman in blue drapery, holding a flower in her left hand, believed by many to be a portrait of Diana of Poitiers, is at the Hague, where the Hollanders call it "Frivolity" or "Vanity." Leda, the bride of Jupiter, with the twins, Castor and Pollux, "playing among the shell-chips of their broken egg," is also at the Hague.

Probably the celebrated La Vierge aux Rochers ("The Virgin among the Rocks") was painted at this time. Of this Théophile Gautier says, "The aspect of the Virgin is mysterious and charming. A grotto of basaltic rocks shelters the divine group, who are sitting on the margin of a clear spring, in the transparent depths of which we see the pebbles of its bed. Through the arcade of the grotto, we discover a rocky landscape, with a few scattered trees, and crossed by a stream, on the banks of which rises a village. All this is of a color as indefinable as those mysterious countries one traverses in a dream, and accords marvellously with the figures. What more adorable type than that of the Madonna! it is especially Leonardo's, and does not in any way recall the Virgins of Perugino or Raphael. Her head is spherical in form; the forehead well developed; the fine oval of her cheeks is gracefully rounded so as to enclose a chin most delicately curved; the eyes with lowered eyelids encircled with shadow, and the nose, not in a line with the forehead, like that of a Grecian statue, but still finely shaped; with nostrils tenderly cut, and trembling as though her breathing made them palpitate; the mouth a little large, it is true, but smiling with a deliciously enigmatic expression that Da Vinci gives to his female faces, a tiny shade of mischief mingling with the purity and goodness. The hair is long, loose, and silky, and falls in crisp meshes around the shadow-softened cheeks, according with the half-tints with incomparable grace."

This picture was originally on wood, but has been transferred to canvas. There are three pictures of this scene; the one in the collection of the Duke of Suffolk is believed to be the original, while that in the Louvre is best known.

Of the Virgin seated on the knees of St. Anne, now in the Louvre, Taine says, "In the little Jesus of the picture of St. Anne, a shoulder, a cheek, a temple, alone emerge from the shadowy depth. Leonardo da Vinci was a great musician. Perhaps he found in that gradation and change of color, in that vague yet charming magic of chiaroscuro, an effect resembling the crescendoes and decrescendoes of grand musical works."

"St. John the Baptist," in the Louvre, is one of the few pictures, among the many attributed to Leonardo, which critics regard as authentic. "St. Sebastian," now in the Hermitage in St. Petersburg, was purchased by the Tsar of Russia in 1860, for twelve thousand dollars.

When the French were driven out of Lombardy, Da Vinci left Milan, in 1514, and, taking his devoted pupils, Salaï, Francesco Melzi, and a few others with him, started for Rome, whither Michael Angelo and Raphael had already gone. Leo X was on the papal throne: he cordially welcomed him, and bade him "work for the glory of God, Italy, Leo X., and Leonardo da Vinci." However, the pope gave him very little to do. "The pontiff," says Vasari, "was much inclined to philosophical inquiry, and was more especially addicted to the study of alchemy. Leonardo, therefore, having composed a kind of paste from wax, made of this, while it was still in its half-liquid state, certain figures of animals, entirely hollow and exceedingly slight in texture, which he then filled with air. When he blew into these figures he could make them fly through the air, but when the air within had escaped from them they fell to the earth.

"One day the vine-dresser of the Belvedere found a very curious lizard, and for this creature Leonardo constructed wings made from the skins of other lizards, flayed for the purpose; into these wings he put quicksilver, so that when the animal walked the wings moved also, with a tremulous motion; he then made eyes, horns, and a beard for the creature, which he tamed and kept in a case; he would then show it to the friends who came to visit him, and all who saw it ran away terrified."

When the pope asked him to paint a picture, Leonardo immediately began to distil oils and herbs for the varnish, whereupon the pontiff exclaimed, "Alas! this man will assuredly do nothing at all, since he is thinking of the end before he has made a beginning to his work." It is supposed that Leonardo painted for Leo X the "Holy Family of St. Petersburg," with the bride of Giuliano de Medici as the St. Catherine.

Louis XII of France having died, the brilliant young Francis I succeeded him January 1, 1515, and soon after won back Lombardy to himself in battle. At once Leonardo, who had been painter to King Louis while in Milan, joined himself to Francis, not wishing to remain in Rome. He was received by that monarch with the greatest delight, and given the Château of Cloux with its woods, meadows, and fish-ponds, just outside the walls of the king's castle at Amboise. Here he abode with his dear pupils, who were content to live in any country so they were with Da Vinci; and was allowed a pension of seven hundred crowns of gold and the title of Painter to the King.

He was sixty-three. He had done many great things, but now, with ease and every comfort, perchance his genius would be more brilliant than ever. When about this age, Michael Angelo had completed his wonderful statues in the Medici chapel, and later even painted his "Last Judgment" and planned the great dome of St. Peter's.

But Leonardo, the versatile, luxury-loving, "divine Leonardo," no longer urged to duty by necessity, did nothing further for the world. He mingled in the gayeties of the court, walked arm in arm in his gardens with the beautiful Salaï, his long white hair falling to his shoulders, and made a unique automaton for the great festivities of the conquering young king at Pavia, a lion filled with hidden machinery by means of which it walked up to the throne, and, opening its breast, showed it filled with a great number of fleurs-de-lis. He soon fell into a kind of languor that presaged the sure coming of death.

In early life he had been so devoted to science that Vasari tells us "by this means he conceived such heretical ideas that he did not belong to any religion, but esteemed it better to be a philosopher than a Christian." Now he turned his thoughts toward the Catholic church, and made his will, which recommends his soul "to God, the glorious Virgin Mary, his lordship St. Michael, and all the beautiful angels and saints of Paradise." He wishes that at his obsequies "there shall be sixty torches carried by sixty poor persons, who shall be paid for carrying them according to the discretion of the said Melzi, which torches shall be shared among the four churches above named."

To his beloved pupils, ever with him, he gives his property. Nine days after this, says Vasari, May 2, 1519, at the age of sixty-seven, Leonardo died in the arms of his devoted King, Francis I.; but later historians have considered this doubtful. He was buried under the flag-stones in the Church of St. Florentin at Amboise.

In the religious wars which followed, the church was demolished, the gravestones sold, and the lead coffins melted for their metal. Many persons have tried to find the grave of the great master, and M. Arsène Houssaye made a last and perhaps successful attempt in 1863. He says, "More than one Italian had gone to Amboise for the purpose of finding the tomb of Leonardo da Vinci, and had gazed sadly on the spot where the church once stood, now covered by thick growing covert.

"The gardener's daughter had been often questioned, and it was she who first gave me the idea, some years ago, of seeking for the tomb of the painter of the 'Last Supper,' but I do not know whether the fact of her having the painter's name sometimes on her lips arose from the fact of her hearing him spoken of by her father or by visitors. She it was who pointed out to me the spot where the great painter of Francis I might be found; a white-cherry tree was growing there, whose fruit was so rich from the fact of its growing above the dead.

"On Tuesday, the 23d of June, 1863, the first spadeful of earth was turned up before the mayor and the archbishop of Amboise. I set the men to work on three different spots, some to reconnoitre the foundations of the church, others to look for the ossuary, and the rest to search the tombs. It was necessary to dig down deeply, the soil having risen over the site of the church to the height of two or three yards....

"The 20th of August we lighted on a very old tomb, which had been, at the demolition of St. Florentin, covered with unequal stones. No doubt the original tombstone had been broken, and, out of respect for the dead, replaced by slabs belonging to the church, and bearing still some rude traces of fresco painting.... It was in the choir of the church, close to the wall, and toward the top of the plantation, where grew the white-cherry tree.

"We uncovered the skeleton with great respect; nothing had occurred to disturb the repose of death, excepting that towards the head the roots of the tree had overturned the vase of charcoal. After displacing a few handfuls of earth, we saw great dignity in the attitude of the majestic dead.... The head rested on the hand as if in sleep. This is the only skeleton we discovered in this position, which is never given to the dead, and appears that of a deep thinker tired with study.... I had brought with me from Milan a portrait of Leonardo da Vinci ... and the skull we had taken from its tomb corresponded exactly with the drawing. Many doctors have seen it, and consider it to be the skull of a septuagenarian. Eight teeth still remain in the jaws, four above and four below.... The brow projects over the eyes, and is broad and high; the occipital arch was ample and purely defined. Intellect had reigned there, but no especial quality predominated.

"We collected near the head some fragments of hair or beard, and a few shreds of brown woollen material. On the feet were found some pieces of sandals, still keeping the shape of the feet....

"The skeleton, which measured five feet eight inches, accords with the height of Leonardo da Vinci. The skull might have served for the model of the portrait Leonardo drew of himself in red chalk a few years before his death. M. Robert Fleury, head master of the Fine Art School of Rome, has handled the skull with respect, and recognized in it the grand and simple outline of this human yet divine head, which once held a world within its limits."

In 1873 Italy raised a monument to her great genius, at Milan. His statue stands on a lofty pedestal, which has four bas-reliefs, representing scenes from his life. At the four corners are placed statues of his principal scholars,—Cesare da Sesto, Marco d' Oggione, Beltraffio, and Andrea Solario.

All Leonardo's precious manuscripts were bequeathed to Francesco Melzi, and unfortunately became scattered. About the end of the seventeenth century they were mostly in the Ambrosian Library at Milan; but the French under Napoleon took fourteen of the principal manuscripts, leaving only two, which now form the "Codex Atlantico" at Milan. The latter is a collection of four hundred of Leonardo's drawings and manuscripts. One volume on mathematics and physics is among the Arundel Manuscripts, at the British Museum. At Holkham is a manuscript of the Libro Originali di Natura.

In 1651 Raphael Trichet Dupresne, of Paris, published a selection from Da Vinci's works on painting, the Trattato della Pittura, which has been reprinted twenty-two times in six different languages, "one of the best guides and counsellors of the painter." A "Treatise on the Motion and Power of Water" was published later. In 1883 Jean Paul Richter, Knight of the Bavarian Order of St. Michael, after years of labor over the strange handwriting of Da Vinci, from right to left across the page, published much of the work of the great painter, reproducing his sketches by photogravure. He had access to the manuscripts in the Royal Library at Windsor, the Institute of France, the Ambrosian Library at Milan, the Louvre, the Academy of Venice, the Uffizi, the Royal Library of Turin, the British and South Kensington Museums, and Christ Church College, Oxford.

Richter says, "Da Vinci has been unjustly accused of having squandered his powers by beginning a variety of studies, and then, having hardly begun, thrown them aside. The truth is that the labors of three centuries have hardly sufficed for the elucidation of some of the problems which occupied his mighty mind."

Leonardo's astronomical speculations, his remarks on fossils, at that time believed to be mere freaks of nature, his close study of botany, his researches in chemistry, color, heat, light, mechanics, anatomy, music, acoustics, and magnetism, have been an astonishment to every reader.

Among his inventions were "a proportional compass, a lathe for turning ovals, an hygrometer; an ingenious surgical probe, a universal joint, dredging machines, wheelbarrows, diving-suits, a porphyry color-grinder, boats moved by paddle-wheels, a roasting-jack worked by hot air, a three-legged sketching-stool which folded up, a revolving cowl for chimneys, ribbon-looms, coining presses, saws for stone, silk spindles and throwers, wire-drawing and file-cutting, and plate-rolling machines." No wonder he was called the "all-knowing Leonardo."

All his work as a poet is lost, save one sonnet:—

> "Who cannot do as he desires, must do
> What lies within his power. Folly it is
> To wish what cannot be. The wise man holds
> That from such wishing he must free himself.
> Our joy and grief consist alike in this:
> In knowing what to will and what to do;
> But only he whose judgment never strays
> Beyond the threshold of the right learns this.
> Nor is it always good to have one's wish;
> What seemeth sweet full oft to bitter turns.
> My tears have flown at having my desire.
> Therefore, O reader of these lines, if thou
> Wouldest be good, and be to others dear,
> Will always to be able to do right."

In Richter's works of Leonardo are many fables: "A razor, having come out of the sheath in which it was usually concealed, and placed itself in the sunlight, saw how brightly the sun was reflected from its surface. Mightily pleased thereat, it began to reason with itself after this fashion: 'Shall I now go back to the shop which I have just quitted? Certainly it cannot be pleasing to the gods that such dazzling beauty should be linked to such baseness of spirit. What a madness it would be that should lead me to shave the soaped beards of country bumpkins! Is this a form fitted to such base mechanical uses? Assuredly not. I shall withdraw myself into some secluded spot, and, in calm repose, pass away my life.'

"Having therefore concealed itself for some months, on leaving its sheath one day and returning to the open air, it found itself looking just like a rusty saw, and totally unable to reflect the glorious sun from its tarnished surface. It lamented in vain this irreparable loss, and said to itself, 'How much better had I kept up the lost keenness of my edge, by practising with my friend the barber. What has become of my once brilliant surface? This abominable rust has eaten it all up.' If genius chooses to indulge in sloth, it must not expect to preserve the keen edge which the rust of ignorance will soon destroy."

Richter also gives many pages of terse moral sentiments, showing that Da Vinci, in his more than thirty years of writing,—he began to write when he was about thirty,—had thought deeply and probably conformed his life to his thoughts.

"It is easier to contend with evil at the first than at the last.

"You can have no dominion greater or less than that over yourself.

"If the thing loved is base, the lover becomes base.

"That is not riches which may be lost; virtue is our true good, and the true reward of its possessor. That cannot be lost, that never deserts us, but when life leaves us. As to property and external riches, hold them with trembling; they often leave their possessor in contempt, and mocked at for having lost them.

"Learning acquired in youth arrests the evil of old age; and if you understand that old age has wisdom for its food, you will so conduct yourself in youth that your old age will not lack for nourishment.

"The acquisition of any knowledge is always of use to the intellect; because it may thus drive out useless things, and retain the good.

"Avoid studies of which the result dies with the worker.

"Reprove your friend in secret, and praise him openly."

In the midst of the corruption of that age, we hear no word breathed against the character of this eager, brilliant, many-sided man. He won from his pupils the most complete devotion, and he seems to have given as fond an affection in return. This possibly satisfied the craving of the human heart for love. Perhaps, after all, life did not

50

appear as satisfactory as he could have wished, with all his worship of the beautiful, for he says, "When I thought I was learning to live, I was but learning to die." He seemed at the zenith of his powers when death came; but who shall estimate the value of a life by its length? He said, "As a day well spent gives a joyful sleep, so does life well employed give a joyful death.... A life well spent is long."

RAPHAEL OF URBINO

"In the history of Italian art Raphael stands alone, like Shakespeare in the history of our literature; and he takes the same kind of rank—a superiority not merely of degree, but of quality.... His works have been an inexhaustible storehouse of ideas to painters and to poets. Everywhere in art we find his traces. Everywhere we recognize his forms and lines, borrowed or stolen, reproduced, varied, imitated,—never improved.

"Some critic once said, 'Show me any sentiment or feeling in any poet, ancient or modern, and I will show you the same thing either as well or better expressed in Shakespeare.' In the same manner one might say, 'Show me in any painter, ancient or modern, any especial beauty of form, expression, or sentiment, and in some picture, drawing, or painting after Raphael I will show you the same thing as well or better done, and that accomplished which others have only sought or attempted.'

"To complete our idea of this rare union of greatness and versatility as an artist with all that could grace and dignify the man, we must add such personal qualities as very seldom meet in the same individual—a bright, generous, genial, gentle spirit; the most attractive manners, the most winning modesty."

Thus writes Mrs. Jameson of the man of whom Vasari said, "When this noble artist died, well might Painting have departed also, for when he closed his eyes, she too was left, as it were, blind.... To him of a truth it is that we owe the possession of invention, coloring, and execution, brought alike, and altogether, to that point of perfection for which few could have dared to hope; nor has any man ever aspired to pass before him."

Raphael of Urbino was born at Colbordolo, a small town in the Duchy of Urbino, April 6, 1483. His father, Giovanni Santi, was a painter of considerable merit, and was possessed also of poetic ability, as he wrote an epic of two hundred and twenty-four pages, in honor of Federigo of Montefeltro, then Duke of Urbino. This duke was a valiant soldier, and a patron of art and literature, who for years kept twenty or thirty persons copying Greek and Latin manuscripts for his library.

The mother of Raphael, Magia, the daughter of Battista Ciarla, a merchant at Urbino, was a woman of unusual sweetness of disposition and beauty of character. Unfortunately she died when Raphael was eight years old. Her three other children died young.

These years must have been happy ones to the gentle, loving child. Their home was in the midst of the snowy peaks of the Apennines, looking towards the blue Adriatic. It is not strange that he became a worshipper of the beautiful. Nature soon grows to be an inspiring companion to those who love her. She warms the heart with her exquisite pictures of varied earth and sky; she caresses us with the glow of sunlight and the fragrance of flowers; she sings us to rest with the melody of the sea and the murmur of the trees and the brooks.

Giovanni Santi married for his second wife Bernardina, the daughter of the goldsmith, Pietro di Parte, a woman of strong character, but lacking the gentleness of Magia. Two years after this marriage he died, leaving Raphael doubly orphaned at eleven years of age. What prospect was there that this boy, without father or mother, without riches or distinguished family, would work his way to renown?

The will of Giovanni left the Santi home to Bernardina as long as she remained a widow, and the child to her care and that of his brother, a priest, Don Bartolomeo. The latter does not appear to have been a very saintly minister, for he and Bernardina quarrelled constantly over the property, quite forgetting the development of the boy left in their charge. Finally Magia's brother, Simone di Battista Ciarla, came to an understanding with the disputants, and arranged that the lad, who had worked somewhat in his father's studio, should be placed under some eminent painter.

Pietro Perugino was chosen, an artist who had one of the largest schools in Italy, and who was noted especially for his coloring and profound feeling. It is said that when he examined the sketches of the boy, he exclaimed, "Let him be my pupil: he will soon become my master."

Perugino had been a follower of Savonarola, but after he had seen that good man put to death, he gave up his faith in God and man. When he was on his death-bed, he refused to see a confessor, saying, "I wish to see how a soul will fare in that Land, which has not been confessed."

For nine years Raphael worked under Perugino at Perugia, studying perspective and every department of art, and winning the love of both master and pupils. When he was seventeen, Passavant, in his life of Raphael, says, the young artist painted his first works, his master being in Florence: a banner for the church of the Trinita of Città di Castello, and the "Crucifixion." The banner has the "Trinity" on one sheet of canvas, and the "Creation of Man" on the other. The "Crucifixion" was bought by Cardinal Fesch at Rome, and at the sale of his paintings, in 1845, was purchased for about twelve thousand five hundred dollars. It is now in Earl Dudley's collection.

About this time the "Coronation of the Virgin" was painted for Madonna Maddalina degli Oddi, a lady of great influence, who obtained for Raphael several commissions, concerning which he expresses great joy in his letters. How many are willing to employ an artist after he is famous; how few before! A woman had the heart and the good sense to help him in these early years, and she helped the whole art world thereby.

This picture was kept in the Franciscan church at Perugia until 1792, when it was sent to Paris, but was restored to Italy by the treaty of 1815, and is now in the Vatican.

For a friend of Perugia he painted the beautiful Connestabile Madonna. "The mother of the Saviour," says Passavant, "a figure of virginal sweetness, is walking in the country, in early spring, when the trees are still bare, and the distant mountains are covered with snow. She is walking along pensively, reading in a little book, in which the child in her arms also looks attentively. Nothing could be found more exquisite. Everything in it shows that Raphael must have devoted himself to it with especial ardor."

This picture, only six and three-fourths inches square, was sold in 1871 to the Emperor of Russia for sixty-six thousand dollars.

Raphael left the studio of Perugino in the beginning of 1504, before he was twenty-one, and painted for the Franciscans, at Città di Castello, the "Marriage of the Virgin," now the chief ornament of the Brera gallery at Milan, and called the "Sposalizio." "The Virgin is attended by five women, and St. Joseph by five young men who were once Mary's suitors. The despair of the lovers is shadowed forth by the reeds they hold; they will never flower; and the handsomest youth is breaking his across his knees."

Grimm says of this picture, "Next to the Sistine Madonna, it may be considered Raphael's most popular work. In the figures of this composition we recognize types of all the different ages of man, which allow every one who stands before it, whether young or old, to feel as if the artist had been the confidant of all the thoughts and feelings appropriate to his period of life.... Raphael's elegance obtrudes itself nowhere, as with other artists is so often the case. Beside this, the harmony of his colors, which, although hitting against one another almost sharply, still have the effect of a bed of flowers whose varied hues combine agreeably. A youthful delight in the brilliancy of color is apparent, which later yielded to a different taste. Like Dürer, Raphael might have confessed, in his ripest years, that while young he loved a certain garishness of coloring, such as he had afterward renounced."

Raphael now returned to Urbino, where he painted for the reigning duke, "St. George slaying the Dragon" and "St. Michael attacking Satan." He made many friends among the noted people of the court, but, full of ambition, and having heard of the works of Da Vinci and Michael Angelo at Florence, he was extremely anxious to go to that city. A lady, as previously, took interest in the boyish artist, and wrote to Pietro Soderini, the Gonfaloniere of Florence, the following letter of introduction:—

"Most magnificent and powerful lord, whom I must ever honor as a father,—

"He who presents this letter to you is Raphael, a painter of Urbino, endowed with great talent in art. He has decided to pass some time in Florence, in order to improve himself in his studies. As the father, who was dear to me, was full of good qualities, so the son is a modest young man of distinguished manners; and thus I bear him an affection on every account, and wish that he should attain perfection. This is why I recommend him as earnestly as possible to your Highness, with an entreaty that it may please you, for love of me, to show him help and protection on every opportunity. I shall regard as rendered to myself, and as an agreeable proof of friendship to me, all the services and kindness that he may receive from your Lordship.

"From her who commends herself to you, and is willing to render any good offices in return.

"Joanna Feltra de Ruvere, [sic.]
"Duchess of Sora, and Prefectissa of Rome."

With this cordial letter from the sister of the Duke of Urbino, he entered the City of Flowers. He was now a youth of twenty-one, slight in figure, five feet eight inches tall, with dark brown eyes and hair, perfect teeth, and the kindest of hearts. He was received into the homes of the patricians, and was asked to paint pictures for them. Meantime he used every spare moment in study. Especially did the works of Masaccio and Leonardo da Vinci, says Passavant, "reveal to Raphael his own wonderful powers, until then almost concealed. Awakened suddenly, and excited with the inspiration that seemed all at once to flow in on him from every side, he pushed forward at once towards the perfection he was so soon to attain."

He copied the horsemen in Da Vinci's battle of Anghiari; made sketches from life of the children of the Florentines, in his book of drawings, now to be seen in the Academy of Venice; stood entranced before the gates of Ghiberti, and that marvel of beauty, the Campanile of Giotto.

Raphael now painted for his friend, Lorenzo Nasi, the "Madonna della Gran Duca," now in the Pitti Palace. Until the end of the last century this picture was in the possession of a poor widow, who sold it to a bookseller for twelve scudi. Finally the Grand Duke Ferdinand III. of Tuscany bought it, and carried it with him through all his journeys, praying before it night and morning. "The bold, commanding, and luminous style," says Passavant, "in which the painting stands out from the background, makes the figure and divine expression of the head still more impressive. Thanks to all these qualities united, this Madonna produces the effect of a supernatural apparition. In short, it is one of the masterpieces of Raphael."

Another Madonna on wood, thirty-five inches in diameter, owned by the Terranuova family until 1854, was purchased for the Berlin Museum, for thirty-four thousand dollars.

After some other works, Raphael went back to Urbino and Perugia, but, eager and restless for Florence, he soon returned to that city and was cordially welcomed. His enthusiasm inspired every artist, and his modest deference to the opinions of others won him countless friends; "the only very distinguished man," as Mrs. Jameson says, "of whom we read, who lived and died without an enemy or a detractor!" Between 1506 and 1508, besides the Temfi Madonna now of Munich, and the Colonna Madonna at Berlin, the Ansidei Madonna was painted for the Ansidei family of Perugia as an altar-piece in the church of S. Fiorenzo. It represents the Virgin on a throne, with Jesus on her right knee, and an open book on her left, from which mother and child are reading. The painting was purchased in 1884 by the National Gallery for the Duke of Marlborough for the enormous sum of three hundred and fifty thousand dollars.

On the marriage of his patrician friend, Lorenzo Nasi, he painted for him the "Madonna with the Goldfinch," called also the "Madonna del Cardellino," now in the Uffizi. The Virgin is seated holding a book, while St. John is offering to the infant Saviour a goldfinch, which the child is about to caress. Another picture, painted for his intimate friend Taddeo Taddei, a learned Florentine, "The Holy Family under the Palm Tree," round, and forty-two and three-fourths inches in diameter, was purchased by the Duke of Bridgewater, for sixty thousand dollars, and is now in the possession of Lord Ellesmere, in London.

Again Raphael returned to the court of Urbino, always winning to himself the most educated and the noblest among the distinguished men and women. Pietro Bembo, secretary to Leo X and a cardinal under Paul III, one of the most celebrated writers of the time, was very fond of Raphael; Count Baldassare Castiglione, a writer and diplomatist, was one of the artist's most loved companions; Bernardo Divizio da Bibiena, author of "La Calandra," the first prose comedy written in Italy, loved him as a brother; Francesco Francia and Fra Bartolomeo, the noted artists, were his ardent friends.

Something beside genius drew all these men and scores of others to Raphael. Vasari says, "Every vile and base thought departed from the mind before his influence. There was among his extraordinary gifts one of such value and importance that I can never sufficiently admire it, and always think thereof with astonishment. This was the power accorded to him by Heaven, of bringing all who approached his presence into harmony; an effect inconceivably surprising in our calling, and contrary to the nature of our artists, yet all, I do not say of the inferior grades only, but even those who lay claim to be great personages, became as of one mind once they began to labor in the society of Raphael, continuing in such unity and concord, that all harsh feelings and evil dispositions became subdued and disappeared at the sight of him.... Such harmony prevailed at no other time than his own. And this happened because all were surpassed by him in friendly courtesy as well as in art; all confessed the influence of his sweet and gracious nature, which was so replete with excellence, and so perfect in all the charities, that not only was he honored by men, but even by the very animals, who would constantly follow his steps and always loved him."

"We find it related that whenever any other painter, whether known to Raphael or not, requested any design or assistance of whatever kind at his hands, he would invariably leave his work to do him service; he continually kept a large number of artists employed, all of whom he assisted and instructed with an affection which was rather as that of a father to his children than merely as of an artist to artists. From these things it followed that he was never seen to go to court, but surrounded and accompanied, as he left his house, by some fifty painters, all men of ability and distinction, who attended him thus to give evidence of the honor in which they held him. He did not, in short, live the life of a painter, but that of a prince.

"Wherefore, O art of painting! well mightest thou for thy part, then, esteem thyself most happy, having, as thou hadst, one artist, among thy sons, by whose virtues and talents thou wert thyself exalted to heaven. Thrice blessed indeed mayest thou declare thyself, since thou hast seen thy disciples, by pursuing the footsteps of a man so exalted, acquire the knowledge of how life should be employed, and become impressed with the importance of uniting the practice of virtue to that of art."

Raphael allowed people to pursue their own course, without attempting to dominate. He said to Cesare da Sesto, one of Da Vinci's most distinguished pupils, "How does it happen, dear Cesare, that we live in such good friendship, but that in the art of painting we show no deference to each other." Finally, however, Cesare adopted Raphael's methods from choice.

Raphael was modest in manner, never monopolizing the time or conversation of others. He made the best of things, overlooking the petty matters which some persons allow to wear and imbitter their dispositions. He worked hard, performing an amount of labor which has been the astonishment of the world ever since his death; he was somewhat frail in body; he was not rich in this world's goods; sweet in nature and refined in spirit, it is to be presumed that he kept his troubles in his own heart, unspoken to others. He loved ardently, and was as ardently loved in return. He was appreciative, sympathetic, tender, and gracious.

Herrmann Grimm says, "Such men pass through life as a bird flies through the air. Nothing hinders them. It is all one to the stream whether it flows through the plain smoothly in one long line, or meanders round rocks in its winding course. It is no circuitous way for it, thus to be driven right and left in its broad course; it is sensible of no delay when its course is completely dammed. Swelling easily, it widens out into the lake, until at length it forces a path for its waves; and the power with which it now dashes on is just as natural as the repose with which it had before changed its course.

"Raphael, Goethe, and Shakespeare had scarcely outward destinies. They interfered with no apparent power in the struggles of their people. They enjoyed life; they worked; they went their way, and compelled no one to follow them. They obtruded themselves on none; and they asked not the world to consider them, or to do as they did. But the others all came of themselves, and drew from their refreshing streams. Can we mention a violent act of Raphael's, Goethe's, or Shakespeare's?

"Goethe, who seems so deeply involved in all that concerns us, who is the author of our mental culture, nowhere opposed events; he turned wherever he could advance most easily. He was diligent. He had in his mind the completion of his works. Schiller wished to produce and to gain influence; Michael Angelo wished to act, and could not bear that lesser men should stand in the front, over whom he felt himself master. The course of events moved Michael Angelo, and animated or checked his ideas. It is not possible to extricate the consideration of his life from the events going on in the world, while Raphael's life can be narrated separately like an idyl."

Raphael, while still under Perugino, had received from Donna Atalanta Baglioni the order for an "Entombment" for the Church of the Franciscans. This he painted in 1507. A century later the monks sold it to Pope Paul V., who had it removed to the Borghese Palace in Rome.

The body of Christ is being borne to the tomb by two men. The weeping Magdalen is holding his hand, and the Virgin is fainting in the arms of three women.

Grimm says, "The bearers of the body move along, conscious of carrying a noble burden. And Christ, himself, beauty, serenity, and mercy dwell in him in fullest measure, as if his spirit still both informed his body and glorified it. Only Raphael could undertake to paint this. No one before or after him could so simply and naturally picture the earthly form, irradiated with heavenly light."

"St. Catherine of Alexandria," painted at this time, now in the National Gallery of London, says Passavant, "is one of the works which nothing can describe; neither words nor a painted copy, nor engravings, for the fire in it appears living, and is perfectly beyond the reach of imitation."

"La Belle Jardinière," in the Louvre, considered one of the best and most beautiful of Raphael's works, represents the Virgin in the midst of rich landscape, the ground covered with grass and flowers, while the infant Christ looks up to her with great tenderness. It is said that the model was a lovely flower-girl to whom the painter was much attached.

While finishing this picture he was called to Rome by the famous Pope Julius II., and went to the Eternal City with great hope and delight.

He was now twenty-five, and the most important work of his life lay before him. Julius II had refused to take possession of the rooms in the Vatican which had been used by the depraved Alexander VI. He said, when it was suggested to remove the mural portraits of that pope, "Even if the portraits were destroyed, the walls themselves would remind me of that Simoniac, that Jew!"

Michael Angelo was already at work upon the great monument for Julius. Now the pope desired to enlarge and beautify the Vatican, and make that his monument as well. He received Raphael with the greatest cordiality. It is said that when Raphael knelt down before him, his chestnut locks falling upon his shoulders, the pope exclaimed, "He is an innocent angel. I will give him Cardinal Bembo for a teacher, and he shall fill my walls with historical pictures." Julius commissioned him to fresco the hall of the judicial assembly, called "La Segnatura." The first fresco, done between 1508 and 1509, is called "Theology" or the "Dispute on the Holy Sacrament" (La Disputa).

"In the upper part appear the three figures of the Holy Trinity, each surrounded by a glory. Above all is the Almighty Father, in the midst of the seraphim, cherubim, and a countless host of angels, who sing the 'Holy, holy, holy, Lord God of hosts.' Below the Father, amidst the saints of the celestial kingdom, the Saviour is enthroned; a little lower, the Holy Spirit is descending on men.

"At the right of the Saviour, the Virgin is seated, bending towards him in adoration; and at her left is St. John the Baptist, who is pointing towards him. On a large half-circle of clouds, which extends to the extreme limits of the picture, are seated patriarchs, prophets, and martyrs, representing the communion of saints. Commencing at the extreme point to the right of Christ, we see the apostle St. Peter, holding the Holy Scriptures and the two keys.... At his side, in the expectation of mercy and pardon, is Adam, the father of the human race. Near Adam is St. John, the apostle loved by Christ, writing down his divine visions; afterwards, David, the head of the terrestrial family of our Lord, the sweet psalmist who sang the praises of God; then St. Stephen, the first martyr; and lastly, a saint half concealed by the clouds.

"On the other side, at the right of the spectator, is St. Paul, holding a sword in remembrance of his martyrdom, and also as a symbol of the penetrating power of his doctrine. By his side is Abraham, with the knife to sacrifice Isaac, the first type of the sacrifice of Christ; then the apostle St. James, the third witness of the transfiguration of the Saviour, the religious type of hope, as St. Peter is of faith and St. John of love. Moses follows with the tables of the law. St. Lawrence corresponds to St. Stephen; and lastly we perceive a warlike figure, which is believed to be St. George, the patron saint of Liguria; in honor, no doubt, of Julius II., who was born in that country.

"The Holy Spirit, under the form of a dove, surrounded by four cherubim, who hold the four books of the Gospel open, is descending upon the assembly of believers.

"This sort of council, expressing theological life, is united in a half-circle around the altar, on which the Eucharist is exposed on a monstrance. Nearest to the altar, on both sides, come the four great fathers of the church, the columns of Roman Catholicism; to the left, St. Jerome, the type of contemplative life, absorbed in profound meditation on the Scriptures; near him are two books, one containing his 'Letters,' the other the Vulgate. Opposite is St. Ambrose, active especially in the militant church: he is raising his eyes and hands towards heaven, as if delighted with the angelic harmonies. St. Augustine, whom he converted to Christianity, is beside him, and is dictating his thoughts to a young man seated at his feet. His book on the 'City of God' is lying by him. St. Gregory the Great, clothed in the tiara and pontifical mantle, is opposite St. Augustine. His book on Job, with the superscription, 'Liber Moralium,' is also on the ground beside him."

Besides these, among the fifty or more figures, are other priests and philosophers, all discussing the great questions pertaining to the redemption of the world.

The pope was so overjoyed on the completion of this picture that he is said to have thrown himself upon the ground, exclaiming, with uplifted hands, "I thank thee, great God, that thou hast sent me so great a painter!"

With La Disputa the romance of Raphael's life begins. While he was painting this, tradition says that he fell in love with Margherita, the daughter of a soda-manufacturer, who lived near Santa Cecilia, on the other side of the Tiber. Passavant says, quoting from Missirini, "A small house, No. 20, in the street of Santa Dorotea, the windows of which are decorated with a pretty framework of earthenware, is pointed out as the house where she was born.

"The beautiful young girl was very frequently in a little garden adjoining the house, where, the wall not being very high, it was easy to see her from outside. So the young men, especially artists,—always passionate admirers of beauty,—did not fail to come and look at her, by climbing up above the wall.

"Raphael is said to have seen her for the first time as she was bathing her pretty feet in a little fountain in the garden. Struck by her perfect beauty, he fell deeply in love with her, and, after having made acquaintance with her, and discovered that her mind was as beautiful as her body, he became so much attached as to be unable to live without her." She has been called "Fornarina," because she was long supposed to be the daughter of a baker (fornajo).

On the rough studies made for the Disputa, now preserved in Vienna, London, and elsewhere, three love sonnets have been found in the artist's handwriting, showing that while he mused over heavenly subjects, with the faces of Peter and John before him, he had another face, more dear and beautiful than either, in his mind. Eugene Muntz, the librarian to the École Nationale des Beaux-Arts, who says of these sonnets, "So great is his delicacy of feeling, his reserve and discretion, that we can scarcely analyze his dominant idea," gives the following translation:—

"Love, thou hast bound me with the light of two eyes which torment me, with a face like snow and roses, with sweet words and tender manners. So great is my ardor that no river or sea could extinguish my fire. But I do not complain, for my ardor makes me happy.... How sweet was the chain, how light the yoke of her white arms around my neck. When those bonds were loosed, I felt a mortal grief. I will say no more; a great joy kills, and, though my thoughts turn to thee, I will keep silence."

"Just as Paul, descended from the skies, was unable to reveal the secrets of God," so Raphael is unable to reveal the thoughts of his beating heart. He thanks and praises love, and yet the pain of separation is intense. He feels like "mariners who have lost their star."

To this love he was probably constant through life, the short twelve years which remained. When he painted the Farnesina, the palace of the rich banker, Agostino Chigi, years afterward, Vasari says, "Raphael was so much occupied with the love which he bore to the lady of his choice, that he could not give sufficient attention to the work. Agostino, therefore, falling at length into despair of seeing it finished, made so many efforts by means of friends and by his own care that after much difficulty he at length prevailed on the lady to take up her abode in his house, where she was accordingly installed, in apartments near those which Raphael was painting; in this manner the work was ultimately brought to a conclusion."

He painted her portrait, now in the Barberini Palace, it is believed, in 1509. It represents a girl "only half-clothed, seated in a myrtle and laurel wood. A striped yellow stuff surrounds her head as a turban, and imparts something distinguished and charming to her features," says Passavant. " ... With her right hand she holds a light gauze against her breast. Her right arm, encircled with a golden bracelet, rests on her knees, which are covered by red drapery. On the bracelet Raphael has inscribed his name with the greatest care."

The face did not seem to me beautiful when I saw it in Rome a few years ago, but certainly does not lack expression, making one feel that the mind which Raphael discovered "to be as beautiful as the body" was equally potent with the warmhearted artist.

Grimm says, "The portrait of the young girl or woman in the Barberini Palace is a wonderful painting. I call it so because it bears about it in a high degree the character of mysterious unfathomableness. We like to contemplate it again and again.... Her hair is brilliantly black, parted over the brow, and smoothly drawn over the temples, behind the ear; the head is encircled with a gay handkerchief, like a turban, the knots of which lie on one side above the ear, pressing it a little with their weight.

"She is slightly bent forward. She sits there with her delicate shoulder a little turned to the left; she seems looking stealthily at her lover, to watch him as he paints, and yet not to stir from her position, because he has forbidden it. It seems to him, however, to be a source of the most intense pleasure to copy her accurately, and in no small matter to represent her otherwise than as he saw her before him. We fancy her to feel the jealousy, the vehemence, the joy, the unalterable good-humor, and the pride springing from the happiness of being loved by him. He, however, painted it all because he was capable of these feelings himself in their greatest depth. If his pictures do not betray this, his poems do."

Muntz says, "From a technical point of view, the work is a masterpiece. Never, perhaps, has Raphael given such delicacy and subtlety to his carnations; never did he create a fuller life; we can see the blood circulate; we can feel the beating pulse. Thus the picture is a continual source of envy and despair to modern realists."

Crowe and Cavalcaselle, in their life of Raphael, speak of the "warm tone of flesh burnished to a nicety and shaded with exceptional force," in this picture. "The coal-black eyes have a fascinating look of intentness, which is all the more effective as they are absolutely open, under brows of the purest curves.... The forehead has a grand arch, the cheeks are broad, the chin rounded and small. The contours are all circular. The flesh has a fulness which characterizes alike the neck, the drooping shoulders, and the arms and extremities."

Passavant thus speaks of a portrait in Florence, which belonged to the Grand Duke of Tuscany. "This portrait in the Pitti Palace bears a strong resemblance to the Madonna di San Sisto (Dresden Museum), with this difference, however, that the features of the Virgin are ennobled. The woman in the portrait is a handsome Roman, but of quite individual character. Her form is powerful, her costume sumptuous, her beautiful black eyes flash, her mouth is refined and full of grace.

"If this portrait, as may well be believed, represents the same person as that of the Barberini house, we are compelled to admit that the countenance, always intelligent, of this young girl, had become wonderfully animated in the time between the execution of the two portraits. However," he adds, "it would be indeed astonishing if constant intercourse with the author of so many masterpieces, and one of the most perfect human organizations that nature ever produced, should have failed to influence the facile character of a young girl. This second portrait, to judge by the manner in which it is painted, must belong to the last years of Raphael's life."

With this fervent and lasting love for Margherita in his heart,

Raphael painted the other three mural paintings in the Vatican hall: the "Parnassus," Apollo surrounded by the Nine Muses, Homer singing, Dante and Virgil conversing, with Pindar, Sappho, Horace, Petrarch, Ovid, and others; "Jurisprudence," with Emperor Justinian and Gregory IX., the one founding the laws of the State, the other the laws of the Church; the "School of Athens," with the masters of ancient philosophy and science assembled.

On the left we see the most ancient of the philosophic schools gathered around Pythagoras. Socrates, Plato, and Aristotle are surrounded by their pupils; Archimedes and Zoroaster are the central figures of the interested group. Diogenes sits on the central steps of the grand hall where more than fifty great men are assembled.

Passavant says, "In the 'School of Athens,' Raphael showed the full power of his genius, and that he was completely master both of his style and of his execution. In the part of this picture requiring great learning, it is possible, and indeed highly probable, that Raphael consulted the most erudite of his friends, and amongst others the Count Castiglione, who had just come to settle at Rome.

"However this may be, to Raphael alone belongs the great honor of having succeeded in representing, in a single living and distinct image, the development of Greek philosophy. It was Raphael who conceived the idea of grouping the personages according to the rank they occupy in history, and rendered the tendencies of these philosophers apparent, not merely by ingenious grouping, but also by their actions, their attitudes, and countenances.

"This fresco, in which he rose to such dignity and to such a grand style, is justly considered as the most magnificent work the master ever produced. It does, indeed, unite the technical experience of drawing, coloring, and touch—the conquests of the more modern schools—to the severity bequeathed to them by the more ancient ones....

"A great era in arts, as in literature, does not always follow the appearance of an extraordinary genius. It comes on gradually, and its progress may be noted. It has its infancy, and with it the simplicity belonging to that age; then its youth, with the grace and sentiments natural to youth; afterwards maturity, with its increased power.

"Raphael was the highest expression of the art of the sixteenth century; he attained its greatest perfection. He was a continuation of the chain of artists in his time, and was its last and brightest link."

Eugene Muntz calls this papal hall, the Stanza della Segnatura, "the most splendid sanctuary of modern art. The profundity of ideas, the nobility of the style, and the youthful vitality which prevails in every detail of the decoration, make up a monumental achievement which is without parallel in the annals of painting, without equal even among the other works of Raphael himself."

During the three years' work in this hall, Raphael painted several other pictures: the magnificent portrait of Pope Julius II, now in the

Pitti Palace; the "Madonna di Foligno," now in the Vatican, a large altar-piece for Sigismondo Conti di Foligno, private secretary to the pope; the Virgin seated on golden clouds surrounded by half-length angels against a blue sky. "A burning globe, with a rainbow above it, is falling from the sky. According to tradition this globe is a bomb, and bears reference to the danger incurred by Sigismondo at the siege of Foligno, his native town, and the rainbow may be considered symbolical of the reconciliation of the donor with God."

The Madonna della Casa d'Alba, round, on wood, only nine and one-half inches in diameter, was originally in a church at Nocera de Pagani, in the Neapolitan States, and later was owned by the Duke of Alba, at Madrid. The Duchess of Alba gave it to her doctor, in her will, for curing her of a dangerous disease. She died very soon, and the doctor was arrested on suspicion of poison, but was finally liberated. The painting came into the possession of the Emperor of Russia, for seventy thousand dollars, and is in the Hermitage.

The "Madonna del Pesce," the gem of the Italian Gallery of the Madrid Museum, which some persons rank equal to the Sistine Madonna, represents the Virgin holding the Child, who rests his hand on an open book. Tobias, holding a fish, and led by an angel, implores a cure for his father's blindness.

Raphael also executed for the wealthy Agostino Chigi, the protégé of Julius II and Leo X., the frescos in the Church Santa Maria della Pace. Cinelli tells this anecdote: "Raphael of Urbino had painted for Agostino Chigi, at Santa Maria della Pace, some prophets and sibyls, on which he had received an advance of five hundred scudi. One day he demanded of Agostino's cashier (Giulio Borghesi) the remainder of the sum at which he estimated his work. The cashier, being astonished at this demand, and thinking that the sum already paid was sufficient, did not reply. 'Cause the work to be estimated by a judge of painting,' replied Raphael, 'and you will see how moderate my demand is.'

"Giulio Borghesi thought of Michael Angelo for this valuation, and begged him to go to the church and estimate the figures of Raphael. Possibly he imagined that self-love, rivalry, and jealousy would lead the Florentine to lower the price of the pictures.

"Michael Angelo went, accompanied by the cashier, to Santa Maria della Pace, and, as he was contemplating the fresco without uttering a word, Borghesi questioned him. 'That head,' replied Michael Angelo, pointing to one of the Sibyls, 'that head is worth a hundred scudi.'... 'And the others?' asked the cashier. 'The others are not less.'

"Some who witnessed this scene related it to Chigi. He heard every particular, and, ordering, in addition to the five hundred scudi for five heads, a hundred scudi to be paid for each of the others, he said to his cashier, 'Go and give that to Raphael in payment for his heads, and behave very politely to him, so that he may be satisfied; for if he insists on my also paying for the drapery, we should probably be ruined.'"

From 1512 to 1514, Raphael frescoed the second Vatican hall, La Stanza d'Eliodoro. The first mural painting was "The Miraculous Expulsion of Heliodorus from the Temple at Jerusalem," the angels attacking him as he is taking the money destined for widows and orphans.

The second fresco is the "Miracle of Bolsena," where, in the reign of Urban IV, a priest, who doubted the reality of transubstantiation, saw the blood flow from the Host while he was celebrating mass. These are called the most richly colored frescos in the world, exceeding the celebrated ones of Titian in the Scuola di San Antonio, at Padua.

The third fresco represents the "Deliverance of St. Peter from Prison," and the fourth, Attila arrested in his march on Rome in 452, by the apparition of St. Peter and St. Paul. A frightful hurricane is raging at the time, and the Huns are filled with terror. Leo X., who had succeeded Julius II., desired to be immortalized instead of St. Leo, so, with a touch of human nature not entirely spiritual, caused himself and his court, driving the French under Louis XII out of Italy, to be painted in the picture. Passavant says, "A few very animated groups of soldiers had to be sacrificed; but on the whole the composition gained by the alteration, from the contrast of the calm gentleness of the pontiff with the ferocity of the barbarians. In execution this fresco may be considered as one of the most perfect by this master."

While this second room in the Vatican was being painted, Raphael, as usual, was engaged also in other work.

In the Chigi palace, or Farnesina, he painted the beautiful fresco, "Galatea." The subject is taken from the narrative of Philostratus about the Cyclops. "In the fresco," says Passavant, "Galatea is gently sailing on the waves. Love guides the shell, which is drawn by dolphins, and surrounded by tritons and marine centaurs, who bear the nymphs. Little cupids in the air are shooting arrows at them. All these figures form a contrast with the beautiful Galatea, whose languid eyes are raised to heaven, the centre of all noble aspirations.

"Galatea is an image of beauty of soul united to that of the body. It is, indeed, a sort of glorified nature; or, rather, a goddess clad in human form. Raphael's genius defies all comparison, and has attained in this masterpiece a height which approaches very nearly to perfection."

This fresco won the most enthusiastic praise. His friend, Count Castiglione, wrote him in hearty commendation, and Raphael replied,—

"As for 'the Galatea,' I should think myself a great master if it possessed one-half the merits of which you write, but I read in your words the love you bear to myself. To paint a figure truly beautiful, I should see many beautiful forms, with the further provision that you

65

should be present to choose the most beautiful. But, good judges and beautiful women being rare, I avail myself of certain ideas which come into my mind. If this idea has any excellence in art I know not, although I labor heartily to acquire it."

How modest the spirit of this letter, and how fully it shows that the young artist lived in an ideal world, filled with exquisite things of his own creating. Some natures always see roses instead of thorns, sunshine behind the clouds; believe in goodness and purity rather than in sin and sorrow; and such natures make the world lovelier by their uplifting words and hopes.

The famous artist, now thirty-one, had become wealthy, and had built for himself a tasteful and elegant home on the Via di Borgo Nuova, not far from the Vatican. "The ground floor of the façade was of rustic architecture, with five arched doors, four of which were for the offices, and the one in the centre for the entrance to the house. The upper story was of Doric order, with coupled columns, and five windows surmounted by triangular pediments. The entablature which surmounted the whole was of a severe style; imitated from the antique. This beautiful building no longer exists. The angle of the right of the basement, which now forms a part of the Accoramboni palace, is the only part that remains."

Raphael's friends, with that well-meant, but usually injudicious interference which is so common, were urging him to bring a wife into his home. His uncle, Simone di Battista di Ciarla, seems to have been anxious, for the artist writes him in 1514, "As to taking a wife, I will say, in regard to her whom you destined for me, that I am very glad and thank God for not having taken either her or another. And in this I have been wiser than you who wished to give her to me. I am convinced that you see yourself that I should not have got on as I have done."

Another person seemed equally anxious for his marriage. Cardinal Bibiena, who had been Raphael's intimate friend when he lived in Urbino, had long been desirous that he should marry Maria, the daughter of Antonio Divizio da Bibiena, his nephew. Evidently Raphael was engaged to her, for he writes to this uncle, Simone, "I cannot withdraw my word; we are nearer than ever to the conclusion." As the matter was deferred year by year—as many writers believe, because Raphael, loving Margherita, was unwilling to marry another— he was saved from the seeming necessity of keeping his promise, by Maria's death some time previous to his own. She is buried in Raphael's chapel in the Pantheon, not far from his grave. He had met and loved Margherita in 1508, six years earlier, and possibly after his engagement to Maria. Margherita was in his house when he died, and to her he left an adequate portion of his property.

This year, 1514, Bramante, the architect of St. Peter's, having died, Raphael was appointed his successor. Perceiving that the four columns which were to support the cupola had too weak a foundation, the first work was to strengthen these. He executed a plan of the church, which some think superior to that which Michael Angelo carried out after Raphael's death. He studied carefully the architectural works of Vitruvius, and planned several beautiful structures in Rome.

Raphael also had the oversight of all the excavations in and around Rome, so that pieces of antique statuary, which were often found, might be carefully preserved. "To this end," wrote Leo X., "I command every one, of whatever condition or rank he may be, noble or not, titled or of low estate, to make you, as superintendent of this matter, acquainted with every stone or marble which shall be discovered within the extent of country designated by me, who desire that every one failing to do so shall be judged by you, and fined from one hundred to three hundred gold crowns."

The third hall of the pope, called the Stanza del Incendio, was painted from 1514 to 1517. The first fresco is "The Oath of Leo III.," who, brought before the Emperor Charlemagne for trial, was acquitted through a supernatural voice proclaiming that no one had the right to judge the pope.

The second fresco is "The Coronation of Charlemagne by Leo III.," thus signifying that the spiritual power is above the temporal power. The two principal portraits are, however, Leo X and Francis I, who formed an alliance in 1515.

The third and finest picture is "The Conflagration of the Borgo Vecchio at Rome." The other pictures were executed in part by the pupils of Raphael. This was by his own hand. In 847 a fire broke out in Rome, which extended from the Vatican to the Mausoleum of Adrian. The danger from the high wind was very great, when Pope Leo IV implored divine aid, and at once the flames assumed the form of a cross, and the fire was quenched. "Several of the figures," says Passavant, "are considered as perfect and inimitable, amongst others the two beautiful and powerful women who are bringing water in vases, and whose forms are so admirably delineated under their garments agitated by the wind."

The last fresco shows the "Victory of Leo IV over the Saracens at Ostia." The pope, Leo IV, with the face of Leo X, is on the shore, engaged in prayer.

At this time Raphael made sepia sketches for the Loggie leading to the apartments of the pope; thirteen arcades, each arcade containing four principal pictures. Forty-eight of these scenes are taken from the Old Testament, and four from the life of Christ. Taken together, they are called "Raphael's Bible." Vasari said of the decorations in the Loggie, "It is impossible to execute or to conceive a more exquisite work." Catherine II of Russia had all these Loggie paintings copied on canvas, and placed in the Hermitage, in a gallery constructed for them, like that in the Vatican. This gallery cost a million and a half of dollars.

In these busy years, 1515 to 1516, the famous cartoons for the Sistine Chapel were made. Sixtus IV had built the chapel. Michael Angelo, under Julius II., had painted in it his "History of the Creation," and "Prophets and Sibyls." And now Raphael was asked to make cartoons for ten pieces of tapestry, to be hung before the wainscoting on high festivals. The cartoons are, "The Miraculous Draught of Fishes," "Christ's Charge to Peter," "The Martyrdom of St. Stephen," "The Healing of the Lame Man," "The Death of Ananias," "The Conversion of St. Paul," "Elymas struck with Blindness," "Paul and Barnabas at Lystra," "St. Paul Preaching at Athens," and "Saint Paul in Prison." The cartoons were sent to Arras, in Flanders, and wrought in wool, silk, and gold. Brought to Rome in 1519, they were hung in St. Peter's, on the feast of St. Stephen.

The enthusiasm of the Romans was unbounded. Vasari says this work "seems rather to have been performed by miracle than by the aid of man." These tapestries, after many changes, are now in the Vatican, much soiled and faded. Of the cartoons, twelve feet by from fourteen to eighteen feet, with figures above life-size, seven of them are to be seen in the South Kensington Museum. They were purchased at Arras by Charles I, on the recommendation of Rubens. They are yearly studied by thousands of visitors. Grimm calls the cartoons "Raphael's greatest productions." He considers the "Death of Ananias" "as the most purely dramatic of all his compositions."

"Compared with these," says Hazlitt, "all other pictures look like oil and varnish; we are stopped and attracted by the coloring, the pencilling, the finishing, the instrumentalities of art; but here the painter seems to have flung his mind upon the canvas. His thoughts, his great ideas alone, prevail; there is nothing between us and the subject; we look through a frame and see Scripture histories, and are made actual spectators in miraculous events.

"Not to speak it profanely, they are a sort of a revelation of the subjects of which they treat; there is an ease and freedom of manner about them which brings preternatural characters and situations home to us with the familiarity of every-day occurrences; and while the figures fill, raise, and satisfy the mind, they seem to have cost the painter nothing. Everywhere else we see the means; here we arrive at the end apparently without any means."

Raphael was now overwhelmed with orders for pictures. He had shown worldly wisdom—a thing not always possessed by genius—in having his works engraved by men under his own supervision, so that they were everywhere scattered among the people.

In 1516 he decorated the bath-room of his friend Cardinal Bibiena, who lived on the third floor of the Vatican. The first sketch represents the Birth of Venus; then Venus and Cupid, seated on dolphins, journey across the sea; she is wounded by Cupid's dart; she pulls out the thorn which has pierced her. The blood, falling on the white rose, gives us, according to tradition, the rich red rose. These paintings were certainly of a different nature from the others in the Vatican, and, while Passavant thinks it strange that a spiritually minded cardinal should have desired such pictures, they were nevertheless greatly admired and copied.

This same year, 1516, one of Raphael's most celebrated Madonnas was painted, the one oftener copied, probably, than any other picture in the world, "The Madonna della Sedia," now in the Pitti Palace. The Virgin, with an uncommonly sweet and beautiful face, is seated in a chair (sedia), with both arms encircling the infant Saviour, his baby head resting against her own. Grimm says, "Mary has been painted by Raphael in different degrees of earthly rank; the Madonna della Sedia approaches the aristocratic, but only in outward show, for the poorest mother might sit there as she does. Gold and variegated colors have been used without stint.... The dress of the mother is light blue; the mantle which she has drawn about her shoulders is green, with red and willow-green stripes and gold-embroidered border; her sleeves are red faced with gold at the wrists. A grayish brown veil with reddish brown stripes is wound about her hair; the little dress of the child is orange-colored, and the back of the chair red velvet. The golden lines radiating from the halo around the head of the child form a cross, and over the mother's and John's float light golden rings. All the tones are flower-like and clear.... A harmonious glow irradiates it, which, partaking of a spiritual as well as a material nature, constitutes the peculiarity of this work, and defies all attempts at reproduction. Pictorial art has produced few such works which actually in their beauty exceed nature herself, who does not seem to wish to unite so many advantages in one person or place....

"Raphael's Madonnas have the peculiarity that they are not distinctively national. They are not Italians whom he paints, but women raised above what is national. Leonardo's, Correggio's, Titian's, Murillo's, and Rubens's Madonnas are all in some respects affected by their masters' nationality; a faint suggestion of Italian or Spanish or Flemish nature pervades their forms. Raphael alone could give to his Madonnas that universal human loveliness, and that beauty which is a possession common to the European nations compared with other races.

"His Sistine Madonna soars above us as our ideal of womanly beauty; and yet, strange to say, despite this universality, she gives to each individual the impression that, owing to some special affinity, he has the privilege of wholly understanding her. Shakespeare's and Goethe's feminine creations inspire the same feeling....

"All Raphael's works are youthful works. After finishing the Sistine Madonna, he lived only three years. At thirty-five years of age (and he did not survive much beyond this), the largest portion of human life is often still in the future. The events of each day continue to surprise us, and to seem like adventures. Raphael was full of these fresh hopes and anticipations when a cruel fate snatched him away. His last works betray the same youthful exhilaration in labor as his first. His studies from nature made at this time have a freshness and grace which, regarded as personal manifestations of his genius, are as valuable as his paintings. He was still in process of development.... What in our later years we call illusions still enchanted him. The easy, untrammelled life at the court of the pope wore for him, to the last, a romantic glamour, and the admiration of those who only meant to flatter sounded sweet in his ears, even while he saw through it. Everything continued to serve him; with the gospel of defeat his soul was still unacquainted."

The Sistine Madonna, with the Virgin standing on the clouds in the midst of myriads of cherubs' heads, St. Sixtus kneeling on the left, and St. Barbara on the right, was painted in 1518 for the Benedictine Monastery of San Sisto, at Piacenza, from which it was purchased in 1754 by Augustus III, Elector of Saxony, for forty thousand dollars. It was received at Dresden with great joy, the throne of Saxony being displaced in order to give this divine product of genius a fitting home. It is said that the famous Correggio, standing before this picture, exclaimed with pride, "I too am an artist!"

Passavant says, "It was the last Virgin created by the genius of Raphael; and, as if he had foreseen that this Madonna would be his last, he made it an apotheosis."

It is interesting to sit in the Dresden gallery alone, before the Sistine Madonna, which has the face of the beloved Margherita, and note the hush that comes upon the people when they pass over the threshold. They seem to enter into the feelings of the artist. It is said that many a poor and lonely woman, bent with years, has wept before this painting.

The eyes of the Virgin look at you, but they do not see you. The eyes are thinking—looking back into her past with its mysteries; looking forward perchance into a veiled but significant future. These eyes, once seen, are never forgotten, and you go again and again to look at them.

Raphael's "Christ Bearing the Cross" (Lo Spasimo) is considered a masterpiece, from its drawing and expression. Some think it equal to "The Transfiguration." The ship which was carrying it to Palermo was lost with all on board. Nothing was recovered save this picture, which, uninjured, floated in a box into the harbor of Genoa. It is now in Madrid.

Another well-known work of Raphael is "St. Cecilia," listening to the singing of six angels, her eyes raised to heaven in ecstasy. A musical instrument is slipping from her hand while she listens, entranced, to playing so much more wonderful than her own. On her right are St. Paul and St. John; on her left Mary Magdalene, with St. Augustine.

70

Cecilia was a rich and noble Roman lady who lived in the reign of Alexander Severus. She was married at sixteen to Valerian, who, with his brother Tiburtius, was converted to Christianity by her prayers. Both these men were beheaded because they refused to sacrifice to idols, and Cecilia was shortly after condemned to death by Almachius, Prefect of Rome. She was shut up in her own bath-room, and blazing fires kindled that the hot vapor might destroy her; but she was kept alive, says the legend, "for God sent a cooling shower which tempered the heat of the fire."

The prefect then sent a man to her palace, to behead her, but he left her only half killed. The Christians found her bathed in her blood, and during three days she still preached and taught, like a doctor of the church, with such sweetness and eloquence that four hundred pagans were converted. On the third day she was visited by Pope Urban I., to whose care she tenderly committed the poor whom she nourished, and to him she bequeathed the palace in which she had lived, that it might be consecrated as a temple to the Saviour. She died in the third century.

This masterpiece of color was sent to Bologna, having been ordered by a noble Bolognese lady, Elena Duglioni, for a chapel which she built to St. Cecilia. Raphael sent the picture to his artist friend Francesco Francia, asking that he "make any correction he pleased, if he noticed any defect." It is stated that Francia was so overcome at the sight of this picture that he died from excessive grief because he felt that he could never equal it.

Shelley wrote concerning this work, "Standing before the picture of St. Cecilia, you forget that it is a picture as you look at it, and yet it is most unlike any of those things which we call reality. It is of the inspired and ideal kind, and seems to have been conceived and executed in a similar state of feeling to that which produced among the ancients those perfect specimens of poetry and sculpture which are the baffling models of succeeding generations. There is a unity and a perfection in it of an incommunicable kind. The central figure, St. Cecilia, seems wrapt in such inspiration as produced her image in the painter's mind; her deep, dark, eloquent eyes lifted up, her chestnut hair flung back from her forehead: she holds an organ in her hands; her countenance, as it were, calmed by the depth of her passion and rapture, and penetrated throughout with the warm and radiant light of life. She is listening to the music of heaven, and, as I imagine, has just ceased to sing, for the four figures that surround her evidently point, by their attitudes, towards her, particularly St. John, who, with a tender, yet impassioned gesture, bends his countenance towards her, languid with the depth of his emotion. At her feet lie various instruments of music, broken and unstrung. Of the coloring I do not speak; it eclipses Nature, yet it has all her truth and softness."

Raphael was now loaded with honors. Henry VIII urged him to

visit England and become attached to his court. Francis I was eager to make him court painter of France. Often the artist shut himself up in his palace, and applied himself so closely to his books and pictures that people said he was melancholy. He was so deeply interested in history that he thought of writing some historical works. He had planned and partially completed a book on ancient Rome, which should reproduce to the world the city in its former grandeur. He left a manuscript on art and artists, which Vasari found most valuable in his biographies. He sent artists into all the neighboring countries to collect studies from the antique. He loved poetry and philosophy.

Several artists lived in his home, for whom he provided as though they were his children. Among others in his house lived Fabius of Ravenna, concerning whom Calcagnini, the pope's secretary, wrote, "He is an old man of stoical probity, and of whom it would be difficult to say whether his learning or affability is the greater. Through him Hippocrates speaks Latin, and has laid aside his ancient defective expressions. This most holy man has this peculiar and very uncommon quality of despising money so much as to refuse it when offered to him, unless forced to accept it by the most urgent necessity. However, he receives from the pope an annual pension, which he divides amongst his friends and relations. He himself lives on herbs and lettuces, like the Pythagoreans, and dwells in a hole which might justly be named the tub of Diogenes. He would far rather die than not pursue his studies....

"He is cared for as a child by the very rich Raphael da Urbino, who is so much esteemed by the pope; he is a young man of the greatest kindness and of an admirable mind. He is distinguished by the highest qualities. Thus he is, perhaps, the first of all painters, as well in theory as in practice; moreover, he is an architect of such rare talent that he invents and executes things which men of the greatest genius deemed impossible. I make an exception only in Vitruvius, whose principles he does not teach, but whom he defends or attacks with the surest proofs, and with so much grace that not even the slightest envy mingles in his criticism.

"At present he is occupied with a wonderful work, which will be scarcely credited by posterity (I do not allude to the basilica of the Vatican, where he directs the works): it is the town of Rome, which he is restoring in almost its ancient grandeur; for, by removing the highest accumulations of earth, digging down to the lowest foundations, and restoring everything according to the descriptions of ancient authors, he has so carried Pope Leo and the Romans along with him as to induce every one to look on him as a god sent from heaven to restore to the ancient city her ancient majesty.

"With all this he is so far from being proud that he comes as a friend to every one, and does not shun the words and remarks of any one; he likes to hear his views discussed in order to obtain instruction and to instruct others, which he regards as the object of life. He respects and honors Fabius as a master and a father, speaking to him of everything and following his counsels."

A rare man, indeed, this Raphael; not proud, not envious, but confiding, learning from everybody, sincere and unselfish.

For the fourth hall in the Vatican, the Sala di Costantino, Raphael made the cartoon for "The Battle of Constantine." In the centre of the picture Constantine is dashing across the battle-field on a white horse, with his spear levelled at Maxentius, who, with his army, is driven back into the Tiber. The whole picture is remarkable for life and spirit.

Raphael now undertook the paintings in the Loggie of the Farnesina, for Agostino Chigi,—the fable of Cupid and Psyche, from Apuleius. "A certain king had three daughters, of whom Psyche, the youngest, excites the jealousy of Venus by her beauty. The goddess accordingly directs her son Cupid to punish the princess by inspiring her with love for an unworthy individual. Cupid himself becomes enamoured of her, shows her to the Graces, and carries her off. He visits her by night, warning her not to indulge in curiosity as to his appearance. Psyche, however, instigated by her envious sisters, disobeys the injunction. She lights a lamp, a drop of heated oil from which awakens her sleeping lover. Cupid upbraids her, and quits her in anger. Psyche wanders about, filled with despair. Meanwhile Venus has been informed of her son's attachment, imprisons him, and requests Juno and Ceres to aid her in seeking for Psyche, which both goddesses decline to do. She then drives in her dove-chariot to Jupiter, and begs him to grant her the assistance of Mercury. Her request is complied with, and Mercury flies forth to search for Psyche. Venus torments her in every conceivable manner, and imposes impossible tasks on her, which, however, with the aid of friends, she is enabled to perform. At length she is desired to bring a casket from the infernal regions, and even this, to the astonishment of Venus, she succeeds in accomplishing. Cupid, having at length escaped from his captivity, begs Jupiter to grant him Psyche; Jupiter kisses him, and commands Mercury to summon the gods to deliberate on the matter. The messenger of the gods then conducts Psyche to Olympus, she becomes immortal, and the gods celebrate the nuptial banquet. In this pleasing fable Psyche obviously represents the human soul purified by passions and misfortunes, and thus fitted for the enjoyment of celestial happiness."

Raphael had time only to make cartoons for the greater part of this work, while his pupils executed them. The paintings were criticised, and it was said that the talent of Raphael was declining.

Hurt by such an unwarrantable opinion, Raphael gladly accepted an order from Cardinal Giuliano de' Medici for a "Transfiguration" for the Cathedral of Narbonne. At the same time the cardinal ordered the "Raising of Lazarus" from Sebastiano del Piombo. Michael Angelo made the drawings for this picture, it is said, so that this work might

73

equal or surpass that of Raphael. When the latter was apprised of this, he replied cheerfully, "Michael Angelo pays me a great honor, since it is in reality himself that he offers as my rival and not Sebastiano."

The "Transfiguration," now in the Vatican, is in two sections. In the upper portion Christ has risen into the air above Mount Tabor, and has appeared to Peter, James, and John, on the mount. At this moment the voice is heard saying, "This is my beloved Son: hear him."

At the foot of the mount, an afflicted father, followed by a crowd of people, has brought his demoniac boy to the Apostles, to be healed. The disciples point to the Saviour as the only one who has the power to cast out evil spirits.

Vasari says, "In this work the master has of a truth produced figures and heads of such extraordinary beauty, so new, so varied, and at all points so admirable, that among the many works executed by his hand this, by the common consent of all artists, is declared to be the most worthily renowned, the most excellent, the most divine. Whoever shall desire to see in what manner Christ transformed into the Godhead should be represented, let him come and behold it in this picture.... But as if that sublime genius had gathered all the force of his powers into one effort, whereby the glory and the majesty of art should be made manifest in the countenance of Christ: having completed that, as one who had finished the great work which he had to accomplish, he touched the pencils no more, being shortly afterwards overtaken by death."

Before the "Transfiguration" was completed, Raphael was seized with a violent fever, probably contracted through his researches among the ruins of Rome. Weak from overwork, he seems to have realized at once that his labors were finished. He made his will, giving his works of art to his pupils; his beautiful home to Cardinal Bibiena, though the cardinal died soon after without ever living in it; a thousand crowns to purchase a house whose rental should defray the expense of twelve masses monthly at the altar of his chapel in the Pantheon, which he had long before made ready for his body; and the rest of his property to his relatives and Margherita.

He died on the night of Good Friday, April 6, 1520, at the age of thirty-seven. All Rome was bent with grief at the death of its idol. He lay in state in his beautiful home, on a catafalque surrounded by lighted tapers, the unfinished "Transfiguration" behind it.

An immense crowd followed the body to the Pantheon; his last beautiful picture, its colors yet damp, being carried in the procession.

His friend Cardinal Pietro Bembo wrote his epitaph in Latin: "Dedicated to Raphael Sanzio, the son of Giovanni of Urbino, the most eminent painter, who emulated the ancients. In whom the union of Nature and Art is easily perceived. He increased the glory of the pontiffs Julius II and Leo X by his works of painting and architecture.

He lived exactly thirty-seven years, and died on the anniversary of his birth, April 6, 1520.

"Living, great Nature feared he might outvie
Her works, and, dying, fears herself to die."

Count Castiglione wrote to his mother, "It seems as if I were not in Rome, since my poor Raphael is here no longer." The pope, Leo X, could not be comforted, and, it is said, burst into tears, exclaiming, "Ora pro nobis." The Mantuan Ambassador wrote home the day after Raphael's death, "Nothing is talked of here but the loss of the man who at the close of his three-and-thirtieth year thirty-seventh has now ended his first life; his second, that of his posthumous fame, independent of death and transitory things, through his works, and in what the learned will write in his praise, must continue forever."

Three hundred and thirteen years after his death his tomb was opened, in 1833, and the complete skeleton was found. After five weeks, the precious remains were enclosed in a leaden coffin, and that in a marble sarcophagus, and reburied at night, the Pantheon being illuminated, and the chief artists and cultivated people of the city bearing torches in the reverent procession.

Dead at thirty-seven, and yet how amazing the amount of work accomplished. He left two hundred and eighty-seven pictures and five hundred and seventy-six drawings and studies. Michael Angelo said Raphael owed more to his wonderful industry than to his genius. When asked once by his pupils how he accomplished so much, Raphael replied, "From my earliest childhood I have made it a principle never to neglect anything."

Passavant says, "He was the most ideal artist that God has ever created." His maxim was, "We must not represent things as they are, but as they should be."

Says Charles C. Perkins of Boston, "Throughout all his works there is not an expression of face, or a contour, whether of muscle or drapery, which is not exactly suited to its end; nor in the thousands of figures which he drew or painted can we recall an ungraceful or a mannered line or pose. This was because of all artists since the Greeks, he had the most perfect feeling for true beauty. The beautiful was his special field, and hence he is first among his kind. Leonardo had more depth, Michael Angelo more grandeur, Correggio more sweetness; but none of them approached Raphael as an exponent of beauty whether in young or old, in mortals or immortals, in earthly or divine beings.

"Raphael was in truth the greatest of artists, because the most comprehensive, blending as he did the opposing tendencies of the mystics and the naturalists into a perfect whole by reverent study of nature and of the antique. Bred in a devotional school of art, and transferred to an atmosphere charged with classical ideas, he retained enough of the first, while he absorbed enough of the second, to make him a painter of works Christian in spirit and Greek in elegance and purity of form and style."

Raphael will live, not only through his works but through the adoration we all pay to a lovable character. The perennial fountain of goodness and sweetness in Raphael's soul, which "won for him the favor of the great," as Giovio said, while living, has won for him the homage of the world, now that he is dead. He had by nature a sunny, kindly disposition: he had what every person living may have, and would do well to cultivate: a spirit that did not find fault, lips that spoke no censure of anybody, but praise where praise was possible, and such self-control that not an enemy was ever made by his temper or his lack of consideration for others. He was enthusiastic, but he had the self-poise of a great nature. True, his life was short. As Grimm says, "Four single statements exhaust the story of his life: he lived, he loved, he worked, he died young." He helped everybody, and what more is there in life than this?

TITIAN

"If I were required," says Mrs. Jameson, "to sum up in two great names whatever the art of painting had contemplated and achieved of highest and best, I would invoke Raphael and Titian. The former as the most perfect example of all that has been accomplished in the expression of thought through the medium of form; the latter, of all that has been accomplished in the expression of life through the medium of color. Hence it is that, while both have given us mind, and both have given us beauty, Mind is ever the characteristic of Raphael—Beauty, that of Titian.

"Considered under this point of view, these wonderful men remain to us as representatives of the two great departments of art. All who went before them, and all who follow after them, may be ranged under the banners of one or the other of these great kings and leaders. Under the banners of Raphael appear the majestic thinkers in art, the Florentine and Roman painters of the fifteenth and sixteenth centuries; and Albert Dürer, in Germany. Ranged on the side of Titian appear the Venetian, the Lombard, the Spanish, and Flemish masters. When a school of art arose which aimed at uniting the characteristics of both, what was the result? A something second-hand and neutral—the school of the Academicians and the mannerists, a crowd of painters who neither felt what they saw, nor saw what they felt; who trusted neither to the God within them, nor the nature around them; and who ended by giving us Form without Soul—Beauty without Life."

Ruskin says, "When Titian or Tintoret look at a human being, they see at a glance the whole of its nature, outside and in; all that it has of form, of color, of passion, or of thought; saintliness and loveliness; fleshly power and spiritual power; grace, or strength, or softness, or whatsoever other quality, those men will see to the full, and so paint that, when narrower people come to look at what they have done, every one may, if he chooses, find his own special pleasure in the work. The sensualist will find sensuality in Titian; the thinker will find thought; the saint, sanctity; the colorist, color; the anatomist, form; and yet the picture will never be a popular one in the full sense, for none of these narrower people will find their special taste so alone consulted as that the qualities which would insure their gratification shall be sifted or separated from others; they are checked by the presence of the other qualities, which insure the gratification of other men.... Only there is a strange undercurrent of everlasting murmur about the name of Titian, which means the deep consent of all great men that he is greater than they."

Strong praise indeed!—"the deep consent of all great men that he is greater than they;"—strong praise for the tireless worker, of whom

Ludovico Dolce wrote, who knew him personally, that "he was most modest; that he never spoke reproachfully of other painters; that, in his discourse, he was ever ready to give honor where honor was due; that he was, moreover, an eloquent speaker, having an excellent wit and a perfect judgment in all things; of a most sweet and gentle nature, affable and most courteous in manner; so that whoever once conversed with him could not choose but love him thenceforth forever." He was remarkably calm and self-poised through life, saying that a painter should never be agitated. And yet he was a man of strong feelings and tender affections.

Titian, the lover of the beautiful, was born at Arsenale, in the Valley of Cadore, in the heart of the Venetian Alps, in the year 1477. His father, Gregorio Vecelli, was a brave soldier, a member of the Council of Cadore, inspector of mines, superintendent of the castle, and, though probably limited in means, was universally esteemed for wisdom and uprightness. Of the mother, Lucia, little is known, save that she bore to Gregorio four children, Caterina, Francesco, Orsa, and Titian.

In this Alpine country, with its waterfalls and its rushing river, Piave, with its mountain wild-flowers, its jagged rocks and nestling cottages, the boy Titian grew to be passionately fond of nature; to idolize beauty of form and face, and to revel in color. The clouds, the sky, the cliffs, the greensward, were a constant delight. In after years he put all these changing scenes upon canvas, becoming the most famous idealist as well as the "greatest landscape-painter of the Venetian school."

The story is told, though it has been denied by some authorities, that before he was ten years of age he had painted, on the walls of his home at Cadore, with the juice of flowers, a Madonna, the Child standing on her knee, while an angel kneels at her feet. The father and relatives were greatly surprised and pleased, and the lad was taken to Venice, seventy miles from Cadore, and placed with an uncle, so that he might study under the best artists.

His first teacher seems to have been Sebastian Zuccato, the leader of the guild of mosaic-workers. He was soon, however, drawn to the studio of Gentile Bellini, an artist seventy years old, noted for his knowledge of perspective and skill in composition. He had travelled much, and had gathered into his home pictures and mosaics of great value: the head of Plato, a statue of Venus by Praxiteles, and other renowned works. What an influence has such a home on a susceptible boy of eleven or twelve years of age! Gentile was a man of tender heart as well as of refined taste. Asked to paint portraits of the sultan and sultana, the aged artist went to Constantinople in 1479 and presented the ruler with a picture of the decapitation of St. John. The sultan criticised the work, and, to show the painter the truth of the criticism, had the head of a slave struck off in his presence, whereupon the artist, sick at heart, returned at once to Venice.

The young Cadorine studied carefully the minute drawings of Gentile Bellini, but, with an originality peculiar to himself, sketched boldly and rapidly. The master was displeased, and the boy sought the studio of his brother, Giovanni Bellini, an artist with more brilliant style, and broader contrasts in light and shade.

Here he met Giorgione as a fellow-pupil, who soon became his warm friend. This man studied the works of Leonardo da Vinci, and became distinguished for boldness of design and richness of color. Titian was his assistant and devoted admirer.

Another person who greatly influenced the early life of Titian was Palma Vecchio of Bergamo, eminent for his portraits of women. Perhaps there was a special bond between these two men, for it is asserted that Titian loved Palma's beautiful daughter, Violante. Palma had three daughters, whom he frequently painted; one picture, now at Dresden, shows Violante in the centre between her two sisters; another, St. Barbara in the church of Santa Maria Formosa in Venice, Palma's masterpiece, and still another, Violante, at Vienna, with a violet in her bosom.

Titian's earliest works were a fresco of Hercules, on the front of the Morosini Palace; a Madonna, now in the Vienna Belvedere, which shows genuine feeling with careful finish; and portraits of his parents, now lost. His first important work was painted about the year 1500, when he was twenty-three, "Sacred and Profane Love," now in the Borghese Palace at Rome.

Eaton says of this, "Out of Venice there is nothing of Titian's to compare to his 'Sacred and Profane Love.'... Description can give no idea of the consummate beauty of this composition. It has all Titian's matchless warmth of coloring, with a correctness of design no other painter of the Venetian school ever attained. It is nature, but not individual nature; it is ideal beauty in all its perfection, and breathing life in all its truth, that we behold."

Crowe and Cavalcaselle, who have studied the more than one thousand pictures to which the name of Titian is attached, say in their life of the great painter, "The scene is laid in a pleasure ground surrounded by landscape, swathed in the balmy atmosphere of an autumnal evening. A warm glow is shed over hill, dale, and shore, and streaks of gray cloud alternate with bands of light in a sunset sky. To the right, in the distance, a church on an island, and a clump of cottages on a bend of land, bathed by the waters of the sea; and two horsemen on a road watch their hounds coursing a hare. To the left a block of buildings and a tower half illumined by a ray of sun crown the hillside, where a knight with his lance rides to meet a knot of villagers.

"Nearer to the foreground, and at measured intervals, saplings throw their branches lightly on the sky, which, nearer still, is intercepted in the centre of the space by a group of rich-leaved trees, rising fan-like behind the marble trough of an antique fountain.

Enchanting lines of hill and plain, here in shadow, there in light, lead us to the foreground, where the women sit on a lawn watered by the stream that issues from the fountain, and rich in weeds that shoot forked leaves and spikes out of the grass.

"Artless (Sacred) Love, on one side, leans, half-sitting, on the ledge of the trough, a crystal dish at her side, symbolizing her thoughts. Her naked figure, slightly veiled by a length of muslin, is relieved upon a silken cloth hanging across the arm, and helping to display a form of faultless shape and complexion. The left hand holds aloft the vase and emblematic incense of love; the right, resting on the ledge, supports the frame as the maiden turns, with happy earnestness, to gaze at her companion. She neither knows nor cares to heed that Cupid is leaning over the hinder ledge of the fountain and plashing in the water.... Not without coquetry, or taste for sparkling color, the chestnut hair of the naked maiden is twisted in a rose-colored veil; the cloth at her loins is of that golden white which sets off so well the still more golden whiteness of her skin. The red silk falling from her arm, and partly waving in the air, is of that crimson tone which takes such wonderful carminated changes in the modulations of its surface, and brings out by its breaks the more uniform pearl of the flesh."

To this figure of Sacred Love, into which the young painter evidently put his heart, he gave the beautiful and half-pensive face of Violante. Did he intend thus to immortalize her, while he immortalized himself? Very likely.

"Sated (Profane) Love sits to the left, her back resolutely turned towards Cupid, her face determined, haughty, but serene; her charms veiled in splendid dress, her very hands concealed in gloves.... A plucked rose fades unheeded by the sated one's side, and a lute lies silent under her elbow.... She seems so grand in her lawns and silks; her bosom is fringed with such delicate cambric; her waist and skirt, so finely draped in satin of gray reflexes; the red girdle, with its jewelled clasp, the rich armlets, the bunch of roses in her gloved hand, all harmonize so perfectly."

For the next six or seven years, while Venice was engaged in wars with the French and the Turks, little is known of the young Titian, save that he must have been growing in fame, as he painted the picture of the infamous Cæsar Borgia, the son of Pope Alexander VI., Jacopo da Pesaro, Bishop of Paphos, who had charge of the Papal squadron against the Turks, and other paintings, now lost. The picture of Pesaro was owned by Charles I. of England. In 1825 William I., King of the Netherlands, presented it to the city of Antwerp, where it is highly prized.

In 1507 the State of Venice engaged Giorgione to fresco the new Fondaco de' Tedeschi, a large public structure for the use of foreign merchants, which had two halls, eighty rooms, and twenty-six warehouses. A portion of this work was transferred to Titian. Above the portal in the southern face of the building, Titian painted a "Judith," the figure of a woman seated on the edge of a stone plinth, in front of a stately edifice. In her right hand she waves a sword, while with her left foot she tramples on a lifeless head. Two other grand frescos were painted by him, all now despoiled by the northern or "Tramontana" winds.

Says one writer, "Whilst Giorgione showed a fervid and original spirit, and opened up a new path, over which he shed a light that was to guide posterity, Titian exhibited in his creations a grander but more equable genius, leaning at first, indeed, on Giorgione's example, but expanding, soon after, with such force and rapidity as to place him in advance of his rival, on an eminence which no later craftsman was able to climb. Titian was characterized by this, that he painted flesh in which the blood appeared to mantle, whilst the art of the painter was merged in the power of a creator.

"He imagined forms of grander proportions, of more sunny impast, of more harmonious hues, than his competitors. With incomparable skill he gave tenderness to flesh, by transitions of half-tone and broken contrasted colors. He moderated the fire of Giorgione, whose strength lay in resolute action, fanciful movement, and a mysterious artifice in disposing shadows contrasting darkly with hot red lights, blended, strengthened, or blurred so as to produce the semblance of exuberant life."

It is said by some writers that Giorgione never forgave Titian for excelling him in the frescos of the Fondaco; but, however this may be, when the noted artist and poet died, soon after, at the age of thirty-four, Titian completed all his unfinished pictures. Giorgione loved tenderly a girl who deserted him through the influence of Morto da Feltri, an intimate friend, who lived under his roof. The latter was killed in the battle of Zara in 1519, after his friend Giorgione had died of a broken heart at the loss of his beloved.

Between 1508 and 1511 Titian painted several Madonnas, one in the Belvedere at Vienna, one in Florence, one in the Louvre, and the beautiful "Madonna and St. Bridget" now at Madrid.

"St. Bridget stands with a basin of flowers in her hand, in front of the infant Saviour, who bends out of the Virgin's arms to seize the offering, yet turns his face to his mother, as if inquiring shall he take it or not. Against the sky and white cloud of the distance, the form of St. Bridget alone is relieved. The Virgin and the saint in armor to the left stand out in front of hangings of that gorgeous green which seems peculiar in its brightness to the Venetians. With ease in action and movement, a charming expression is combined. The juicy tints and glossy handling are those of Titian's Palmesque period; and St. Bridget is the same lovely girl whose features Palma painted with equal fondness and skill in the panel called Violante, at the Belvedere of Vienna.... Titian shows much greater fertility of resource in the handling of flesh than Palma, being much more clever and subtle in harmonizing light with half-tint by tender and cool transitions of gray crossed with red, and much more effective in breaking up shadow with contrasting touches of livid tone, yet fusing and blending all into a polished surface, fresh as of yesterday, and of almost spotless purity, by the use of the clearest and finest glazings that it is possible to imagine."

Titian was now thirty-four, with probably the same love for Violante in his heart, but still poor, and struggling with untiring industry for the great renown which he saw before him.

At this time Titian painted one of his most noted works, thought by some to be his masterpiece, "The Tribute Money," now in the museum at Dresden. It was painted at the request of Alfonso d'Este, Duke of Ferrara. Scanelli, who wrote in 1655, tells this story concerning the picture.

"Titian was visited on a certain occasion by a company of German travellers, who were allowed to look at the pictures which his studio contained. On being asked what impression these works conveyed, these gentlemen declared that they only knew of one master capable of finishing as they thought paintings ought to be finished, and that was Dürer; their impression being that Venetian compositions invariably fell below the promise which they had given at their first commencement.

"To these observations Titian smilingly replied, that if he had thought extreme finish to be the end and aim of art, he too would have fallen into the excesses of Dürer. But, though long experience had taught him to prefer a broad and even track to a narrow and intricate path, yet he would still take occasion to show that the subtlest detail might be compassed without sacrifice of breadth; and so produced the Christ of the Tribute Money."

Crowe and Cavalcaselle say, "Vasari reflects an opinion which holds to this day, that the 'head of Christ is stupendous and miraculous.'" It was considered by all the artists of his time as the most perfect and best handled of any that Titian ever produced; but for us it has qualities of a higher merit than those of mere treatment. Single as the subject is, the thought which it embodies is very subtle.

"Christ turns towards the questioning Pharisee, and confirms with his eye the gesture of his hand, which points to the coin. His face is youthful, its features and short curly beard are finely framed in a profusion of flowing locks. The Pharisee to the right stands in profile before Jesus, holds the coin, and asks the question. The contrast is sublime between the majestic calm and elevation and what Inandt calls the 'Godlike beauty' of Christ, and the low cunning and coarse air of the Pharisee; between the delicate chiselling of the features, the soft grave eye and pure-cut mouth of the Saviour, and the sharp aquiline nose or the crafty glance of the crop-haired, malignant Hebrew....

"The form of Christ was never conceived by any of the Venetians of such ideal beauty as this. Nor has Titian ever done better; and it is quite certain that no one, Titian himself included, within the compass of the North Italian schools, reproduced the human shape with more nature and truth, and with greater delicacy of modelling. Amidst the profusion of locks that falls to Christ's shoulders, there are ringlets of which we may count the hairs, and some of these are so light that they seem to float in air, as if ready to wave at the spectator's breath. Nothing can exceed the brightness and sheen or the transparent delicacy of the colors. The drapery is admirable in shade and fold, and we distinguish with ease the loose texture of the bright red tunic, and that of the fine broadcloth which forms the blue mantle. The most perfect easel picture of which Venice ever witnessed the production, this is also the most polished work of Titian."

In 1511 Titian was called to Padua and Vicenza, where he executed some frescos, principally from the life of St. Anthony, returning to Venice in 1512.

He was now famous, and Pope Leo X naturally desired to draw him to Rome, where Raphael and Michael Angelo were the admired of all. Cardinal Bembo, the secretary of the pope, and the friend of Raphael, importuned Titian; but the Venetian loved his own state and preferred to serve her, sending, May 31, 1513, the following petition to the Council of Ten.

"I, Titian of Cadore, having studied painting from childhood upwards, and desirous of fame rather than profit, wish to serve the Doge and Signori, rather than his highness the pope and other Signori, who in past days, and even now, have urgently asked to employ me. I am therefore anxious, if it should appear feasible, to paint in the Hall of Council, beginning, if it please their sublimity, with the canvas of the battle on the side towards the Piazza, which is so difficult that no one as yet has had the courage to attempt it."

For this work Titian asked a moderate compensation, and the first vacant brokership for life, all of which the government granted. He moved into a studio in the old palace of the Duke of Milan, at San Samuele on the Grand Canal, where he remained for sixteen years.

It seemed now as though comfort were guaranteed to the hard-working artist. But unfortunately rivalries arose. The Bellinis had worked in this Hall of Council in the Ducal Palace, till they felt the position to be theirs by right. After long discussions, Titian was successful, receiving from the Fondaco an annuity of one hundred ducats as a broker, and the privilege of exemption from certain taxes, while, on the other hand, he had to paint the Doge's portrait.

Titian was now painting the following works for Alfonso d'Este, Duke of Ferrara, who had married the handsome and celebrated Lucretia Borgia:—

The "Venus Worship," now in the Museum of Madrid, represents the goddess standing on a marble pedestal, with two nymphs at her feet, while winged cupids pluck the apples sacred to Venus, from the branches of great trees, "climbing boughs like boys, dropping down from them like thrushes, loading baskets, throwing and catching, tumbling, fighting, and dancing."

This picture was a favorite study for artists, and it is said that Domenichino wept when he heard that it had been carried to Spain.

"The Three Ages," now in the collection of Lord Ellesmere, has been frequently copied. A cupid steps on two sleeping children: a beautiful girl sits near her lover, "the holy feeling of youthful innocence and affection charmingly expressed in both:" an old man contemplates two skulls on the ground. "To the children, as to the lovers, the forms appropriate to their age are given; and the whole subject is treated with such harmony of means as to create in its way the impression of absolute perfection."

The "Virgin's Rest, near Bethlehem," now in the National Gallery, shows the mother with the infant Christ on her lap, taking a bunch of flowers from St. John. The "Noli Me Tangere," also in the National Gallery, represents Christ with Mary Magdalene on her knees before him. "One cannot look without transport on the mysterious calm of this beautiful scene, which Titian has painted with such loving care, yet with such clever freedom. The picture is like a leaf out of Titian's journal, which tells us how he left his house on the canals, and wandered into the country beyond the lagoons, and lingered in the fresh sweet landscape at eventide, and took nature captive on a calm day at summer's end."

While painting these pictures, besides various portraits of the poet Ariosto, Alfonso, and others, Titian was producing what is generally regarded as his masterpiece, "The Assumption of the Virgin," a colossal picture, now in the Academy of Arts at Venice. It was painted for Santa Maria di Frari, and was shown to the public, March 20, 1518, on St. Bernardino's Day, when all the public offices were closed by order of the Senate, and a great crowd thronged the church.

"The gorgeous blue and red of Mary's tunic and mantle stand out brilliant on the silvery ether, vaulted into a dome, supported by countless cherubs. The ministry of the angels about her is varied and eager. One raises the corner of the mantle, some play the tabor, others hold the pipes, or sing in choir, whilst others again are sunk in wonderment, or point at the Virgin's majesty; and the rest fade into the sky behind, as the sound of bells fades sweetly upon the ear of the passing traveller.... All but the head and arms of the Eternal is lost in the halo of brightness towards which the Virgin is ascending. He looks down with serene welcome in his face, an angel on one side ready with a crown of leaves; an archangel swathed in drapery, on the other, eagerly asking leave to deposit on the Virgin's brow the golden cincture in his hands."

Titian was at once declared to be the foremost painter in Venice, and was, indeed, the idol of the people.

He now painted the "Annunciation" for the Cathedral of Treviso, and executed several frescos. Meantime, the Venetian Government threatened that unless he went forward with the work in the Ducal Palace it should be finished by others at his expense. Pressed on every hand for pictures, he still neglected the Palace, and painted the brilliant "Bacchanal," now at Madrid, for Duke Alfonso.

Ariadne reposes on the ground, insensible from wine, while a company of Menads sport about her as Theseus sails away in the distance. The most beautiful Menad, with white muslin tunic and ruby-red bodice and skirt, has the exquisite face and form of Violante, with a violet or pansy on her breast. The painter was now over forty, and still seemed to bear Violante on his heart.

Ariadne, daughter of Minos, King of Crete, according to the legend, fell in love with Theseus, when he came to Crete to kill the Minotaur, and gave him a thread by means of which he found his way out of the labyrinth. In gratitude he offered her his hand. She fled with him, and he deserted her on the Island of Naxos, where Bacchus found her and married her. On the "Bacchanal" a couplet shows its motive,—

"Who drinks not over and over again,
Knows not what drinking is."

Alfonso d'Este was delighted with this gay picture. Although Lucretia Borgia, whom he never loved, had been dead but a few months, he had married a girl in humble station, Laura Dianti, whom he loved tenderly, and who kept his fickle heart true till his death. She must have been a person of gentle and lovely nature, for the duke became kinder to everybody, and more devoted to art, literature, and the refining influences of life.

It is believed that the famous picture in the Louvre called "Titian and his Mistress" represents Laura and Alfonso. "The girl stands behind a table or slab of stone, dressing her hair, whilst a man in the gloom behind her holds, with his left hand, a round mirror, the reflection of which he catches with a square mirror in his right. Into the second of these the girl gently bends her head to look, eagerly watched by her lover, as she twists a long skein of wavy golden hair. Over the white and finely plaited linen that loosely covers her bosom, a short green bodice is carelessly thrown, and a skirt of the same stuff is gathered to the waist by a sash of similar color. The left side of the girl's head is already dressed; she is finishing the right side, and a delightful archness and simplicity beam in the eyes as they turn to catch the semblance in the mirror. The coal-black eye and brow contrast with the ruddy hair; the chiselled nose projects in delicate line from a face of rounded, yet pure contour; and the lips, of a cherry redness, which

Titian alone makes natural, are cut with surprising fineness. The light is concentrated with unusual force upon the face and bust of the girl, whilst the form and features of the man are lost in darkness. We pass with surprising rapidity from the most delicate silvery gradations of sunlit flesh and drapery, to the mysterious depths of an almost unfathomable gloom, and we stand before a modelled balance of light and shade that recalls Da Vinci, entranced by a chord of tonic harmony, as sweet and as thrilling as was ever struck by any artist of the Venetian school."

Tired with his constant labor, Titian journeyed to Conegliano, at the foot of the Venetian Alps, and painted, at his leisure, a series of frescos on the front of the Scuola di Santa Maria Nuova, in return for which he received the gift of a house, where he rested ever after, when on his way to Cadore.

In 1522 the great altar-piece of the "Resurrection" was finished for Brescia, and placed on the high altar of St. Nazaro e Celso, where it long remained an object of study by artists. Titian thought the martyrdom of St. Sebastian, in this picture, the best thing he had ever done.

Seven years had now passed since he had received the commission to paint the Hall of the Great Council. His property was to be taken from him, and, alarmed at the prospect, he worked vigorously for several weeks on the "Battle of Cadore" or the other great painting, "The Humiliation of the Emperor Barbarossa by Pope Alexander III."

Duke Alfonso was urging the overworked master for a new picture, the "Bacchus and Ariadne," now in the National Gallery of England: a picture five feet nine inches by six feet three inches. The scene is taken from the classic poem of Catullus, when Ariadne, near the shore of Naxos, flees from the presence of Bacchus, whose chariot is drawn by leopards. He was the son of Jupiter by Semele, whose death being caused by Juno, the god of the vintage was reared by nymphs in Thrace. He taught men the cultivation of the vine and the art of wine-making.

Concerning this picture, Crowe and Cavalcaselle say, "Centuries have robbed the canvas of its freshness, and restorers have done their best to remove its brightest surfaces; yet no one who looks at it even now can fail to acknowledge the magic of its enchantment. Rich harmony of drapery tints and soft modelling, depth of shade and warm flesh, all combine to produce a highly colored glow; yet in the midst of this glow the form of Ariadne seems incomparably fair. Nature was never reproduced more kindly or with greater exuberance than it is in every part of this picture. What subtlety there is in the concentration of light on Ariadne, which alone gives a focus to the composition. What splendor in the contrasts of color, what wealth and diversity of scale in air and vegetation; how infinite is the space, how varied yet mellow the gradations of light and shade.

"There is not a single composition by Titian up to this time in which the scene and the dramatis personæ are more completely in unison; and, looking at these groves and cliffs and seas, or prying into the rich vegetation of the foreground, we are startled beyond measure to think that they were worked out piecemeal, that the figures were put in first and the landscape last. Nor is it without curiosity that we inquire where Titian got that landscape, where he studied that foreground; and we are forced to conclude that he forsook the workshop on the Grand Canal, where there certainly was no vegetation, even in the sixteenth century, and went to Ferrara, and there reproduced with 'botanical fidelity' the iris, the wild rose and columbine, which so exquisitely adorn the very edge of the ground on which the Satyrs tread." This picture has been copied by Rubens, Poussin, and other noted artists.

About this time the "Flora" of the Uffizi was painted, a beautiful woman with the Violante face. "She is not yet dressed, but her hair is looped up with a silken cord so as to shape the most charming puffs above the ears, falling in short and plaited waves to the bosom, leaving bare the whole of the face, the neck, and throat. No one here holds the mirrors, yet the head is bent and the eyes are turned as if some one stood by to catch the glance, and stretch a hand for the flowers; for whilst with her left Flora strives by an intricate and momentary play of the fingers, to keep fast the muslin that falls from her shoulder and the damask that slips from her form, with the other she presents a handful of roses, jessamines, and violets to an unseen lover. The white dress, though muslin-fine and gathered into minute folds, is beyond measure graceful in fall, and contrasts in texture as well as harmonizes in color with the stiffer and more cornered stuff of the rose-tinged cloth which shows such fine damask reflexes on the left arm."

At this time, also, Titian painted one of his most exquisite creations, the "Sleeping Venus," now at Darmstadt, a graceful nude figure asleep on a red couch strewn with roses, her arm under her head. The face is delicate, innocent, pensive, and refined—still the face of Violante,—one of the most beautiful, it seems to me, which an artist has ever put upon canvas. There are several replicas in England and elsewhere. The figure is not more perfect, perhaps, than the Venus of the Uffizi, painted later for the Duke of Urbino, or the Venus of Madrid; but the face is one which I have always felt an especial pleasure in possessing.

Taine says of Titian, "He was endowed with that unique gift of producing Venuses who are real women, and colossi who are real men, a talent for imitating objects closely enough to win us with the illusion and of so profoundly transforming objects as to enkindle reverie. He has at once shown in the same nude beauty a courtesan, a patrician's mistress, a listless and voluptuous fisherman's daughter, and a powerful ideal figure, the masculine force of a sea-goddess, and the undulating forms of a queen of the empyrean....

"The infinite diversities of nature, with all her inequalities, are open to him; the strongest contrasts are within his range; each of his works is as rich as it is novel. The spectator finds in him, as in Rubens, a complete image of the world around him, a history, a psychology, in an epitomized form."

The Venus Anadyomene, now in Lord Ellesmere's collection, rising new-born but full-grown from the sea, wringing her long hair, has the features of a new model, not Violante, but the same which Titian used in his famous Magdalen. This represents a woman of about twenty-five, "with finely rounded limbs and well-modelled figure, handsome face, and streaming golden hair, and the white splendor of the entire form thrown into bold relief by a dark and lonely background. The Magdalen is distinguishable from Venus only by her upturned face and tearful eyes."

Who was this new model? Could it possibly have been Cecilia, the lady whom Titian married about this time? In 1525, a son, Pomponio, was born to him, who became a lifelong sorrow, and before 1530 two other children, Orazio and Lavinia. The happiness of this married life was of short duration, for on the fifth of August, 1530, after the birth of Lavinia, with a mournful heart, he buried Cecilia. One of his friends wrote to the warder of Mantua, "Our master, Titian, is quite disconsolate at the loss of his wife, who was buried yesterday. He told me that in the troubled time of her sickness he was unable to work at the portrait of the Lady Cornelia, or at the picture of the 'Nude,' which he is doing for our most illustrious lord."

Left with three helpless children, Titian sent to Cadore for his sister Orsa, who came and cared for his household as long as she lived. He had grown tired of his home on the Grand Canal, and, longing for the open country, hired a house in the northern suburbs. A little later he took a piece of land adjoining, which extended to the shore, and which became famous in after years for its beauty as a garden and for the distinguished people who gathered there.

Mrs. Jameson says, "He looked over the wide canal which is the thoroughfare between the city of Venice and the Island of Murano; in front, the two smaller islands of San Cristoforo and San Michele; and beyond them Murano, rising on the right, with all its domes and campanili like another Venice. Far off extended the level line of the mainland, and in the distance the towering chain of the Friuli Alps, sublime, half defined, with jagged snow-peaks soaring against the sky; and more to the left, the Euganean hills, Petrarch's home, melting like visions, into golden light. There, in the evening, gondolas filled with ladies and cavaliers, and resounding with music, were seen skimming over the crimson waves of the Lagoon, till the purple darkness came on rapidly—not, as in the north, like a gradual veil, but like a gemmed and embroidered curtain, suddenly let down over all. This was the view from the garden of Titian; so unlike any other in the world that it never would occur to me to compare it with any other. More glorious combinations of sea, mountain, shore, there may be—I cannot tell; like, it is nothing that I have ever beheld or imagined."

Who does not recall such beautiful scenes in silent Venice! And yet one longs, while there, for the sound of the feet of horses, and the zest of a nineteenth-century city; one feels as though life were going by in a dream, and is anxious to awake and be a part of the world's eager, stirring thought. Gondolas and moonlight evenings delight one for a time, but not for long!

Titian was now fifty-four. He had painted the "Entombment of Christ," which was a favorite with Van Dyck, and helped to form his style—a picture four feet and four inches by seven feet, now in the Louvre; the Madonna of San Niccolò di Frari, now in the Vatican, which Pordenone is reported to have said was "not painting, but flesh itself;" the "Madonna di Casa Pesaro," which latter especially won the heartiest praise. St. Peter, St. Francis, and St. Anthony of Padua implore the intercession of the Virgin in favor of the members of the Pesaro family.

Crowe and Cavalcaselle thus speak of it: "High up on a spray of clouds that inwreathe the pillars of the temple, two angels playfully sport with the cross; and, with that wonderful insight which a painter gets who has studied cloud form flitting over Alpine crags, Titian has not only thrown a many-toned gradation of shade on the vapor, but shown its projected shadow on the pillar. The light falls on the clouds, illumines the sky between the pillars, and sheds a clear glow on the angels, casting its brightest ray on the Madonna and the body of the infant Christ.... Decompose the light or the shadow, and you find incredible varieties of subtlety, which make the master's art unfathomable. Both are balanced into equal values with a breadth quite admirable, the utmost darks being very heavy and strong without losing their transparency; the highest lights dazzling in brightness, yet broken and full of sparkle. Round the form of the infant Christ the play of white drapery is magic in effect....

"To the various harmonizing elements of hue, of light, and of shade, that of color superadded brings the picture to perfection; its gorgeous tinting so subtly wrought, and so wonderfully interweaving with sun and darkness and varied textures as to resolve itself with the rest into a vast and incomprehensible whole, which comes to the eye an ideal of grand and elevated beauty, a sublime unity, that shows the master who created it to have reached a point in art unsurpassed till now, and unattainable to those who come after him."

"The Martyrdom of St. Peter Martyr," completed in 1529, where Titian "reproduced the human form in its grandest development," has been studied by generations of artists, from Benvenuto Cellini and

Rubens to Sir Joshua Reynolds. So valued was it by Venice that the Signoria threatened with death any one who should dare to remove it. Unfortunately it was destroyed by fire in 1867, together with the chapel which contained it.

The "Madonna del Coniglio," at the Louvre, is also much valued. "We ask ourselves, indeed, when looking at this picture, whether an artist with only fleeting ties could have created such a masterpiece; and the answer seems to be that nature here gushes from the innermost recesses of a man's heart who has begun to know the charms of paternity, who has watched a young mother and her yearling child, and seized at a glance those charming but minute passages which seldom or never meet any but a father's eye."

In 1533 a most fortunate thing happened to Titian. Charles V. had come to Bologna, to receive the homage of Italy. The great emperor was an enthusiastic lover of art, had seen Titian's work, and desired a portrait from his hand. The artist hastened thither and painted Charles in armor, bare-headed. He used to say of himself that he was by nature ugly, but being painted so often uglier than he really was, he disappointed favorably many persons, who expected something most unattractive.

Another portrait of him which Titian painted, now at Madrid, shows him in splendid gala dress, with red beard, pale skin, blue eyes, and protruding lower lip.

The sculptor Lombardi was so anxious to look upon the emperor that he carried Titian's paintbox at the sittings, and slyly made a relief portrait of Charles on a tablet in wax, which he slipped into his sleeve. The emperor detected him, asked to see the work, praised it, and had Lombardi put it in marble for him.

Charles was so pleased with the portraits by Titian that he would never sit to any other artist. He called him the Apelles of his time, and paid him one thousand scudi in gold for each portrait. He created Titian a Count of the Lateran Palace, of the Aulic Council, and of the Consistory; with the title of Count Palatine, and all the advantages attached to those dignities. His children were thereby raised to the rank of Nobles of the Empire, with all the honors appertaining to families with four generations of ancestors. He was also made a Knight of the Golden Spur, with the right of entrance to Court.

The Cadorine youth had reached the temple of fame, unaided save by his skilful hand and inventive brain. He sat daily from morning till night at his easel, often ill from overwork, yet urged on by that undying aspiration which we call genius.

He painted the beautiful portrait of the young Cardinal Ippolito de' Medici, now in the Pitti Palace, whom Michael Angelo so tenderly loved, and whose untimely death by poison at the hand of his cup-bearer, at Itri, caused general sorrow. Ippolito sat to Titian at Bologna "in the red cap and variegated plumes of a Hungarian chief. His curved sabre hung from an Oriental sash wound round a red-brown coat with golden buttons, and he wielded with his right the mace of command. It appeared as if the burning sun of the Danube valley had bronzed the features of the chieftain, whose skin seemed to glow with a tropical heat, whilst its surface was smooth and burnished as that of the Bella Gioconda." Ippolito urged Titian to come to Rome; Francis I wished him to visit France; but Titian loved his Venice gardens and his mountain resort at Cadore, and could not be induced to leave them. His father, Gregorio Vecelli, had died in 1527, three years before the death of Cecilia, and Francesco, the dearly loved artist brother, had gone to care for the Cadore home, where he often welcomed with enthusiastic admiration his famous brother, Titian.

The next paintings from the great artist were the "Rape of Proserpina;" portraits of the Duke and Duchess of Urbino, Isabella d'Este Gonzaga, the beautiful Eleonora Gonzaga, the twelve Cæsars for Duke Federigo Gonzaga of Mantua; the "Annunciation," for which he received two thousand scudi from the Emperor; "La Bella di Titiano," now in the Pitti, and the "Venus" of the Uffizi. "The face of the 'Bella' was so winning that it lurked in Titian's memory, and passed as a type into numerous canvases, in which the painter tried to realize an ideal of loveliness. The head being seen about two-thirds to the left, whilst the eyes are turned to the right, the spectator is fascinated by the glance in whatever direction he looks at the canvas. The eye is grave, serene, and kindly, the nose delicate and beautifully shaped, the mouth divine. Abundant hair of a warm auburn waves along the temples, leaving a stray curl to drop on the forehead. The rest is plaited and twisted into coils round a head of the most symmetrical shape. A gold chain falls over a throat of exquisite model, and the low dress, with its braided ornaments and slashed sleeves alternately tinted in blue and white and purple, is magnificent. One hand, the left, is at rest; the other holds a tassel hanging from a girdle. Nothing can exceed the delicacy and subtlety with which the flesh and dress are painted, the tones being harmonized and thrown into keeping by a most varied use and application of glazings and scumblings."

Of the Uffizi "Venus," Crowe and Cavalcaselle say, "What the painter achieves, and no other master of the age achieves with equal success, is the representation of a beauteous living being, whose fair and polished skin is depicted with enamelled gloss, and yet with every shade of modulation which a delicate flesh comports: flesh not marbled or cold, but sweetly toned, and mantling with life's blood, flesh that seems to heave and rise and fall with every breath. Perfect distribution of space, a full and ringing harmony of tints, atmosphere both warm and mellow, are all combined in such wise as to bring us in contact with something that is real; and we feel, as we look into the canvas, that we might walk into that apartment and find room to wander in the gray twilight into which it is thrown by the summer sky that shows through the coupled windows."

At the feet of Venus a little dog lies curled up on the couch. In the Venus of Madrid, she pats the back of a dog, while her lover plays an organ at the foot of the couch.

It is interesting to learn how Titian produced such effects by his brush. Says Palma Giovine, "Titian prepared his pictures with a solid stratum of pigment, which served as a bed or fundament, upon which to return frequently. Some of these preparations were made with resolute strokes of a brush heavily laden with color, the half-tints struck in with pure red earth, the lights with white, modelled into relief by touches of the same brush dipped into red, black, and yellow. In this way he would give the promise of a figure in four strokes. After laying this foundation, he would turn the picture to the wall, and leave it there perhaps for months, turning it round again after a time, to look at it carefully, and scan the parts as he would the face of his greatest enemy.

"If at this time any portion of it should appear to him to have been defective, he would set to work to correct it, applying remedies as a surgeon might apply them, cutting off excrescences here, super-abundant flesh there, redressing an arm, adjusting or setting a limb, regardless of the pain which it might cause. In this way he would reduce the whole to a certain symmetry, put it aside, and return again a third or more times, till the first quintessence had been covered over with its padding of flesh. It was contrary to his habit to finish at one painting, and he used to say that a poet who improvises cannot hope to form pure verses. But of 'condiments,' in the shape of last retouches, he was particularly fond. Now and then he would model the light into half-tint with a rub of his finger, or with a touch of his thumb he would dab a spot of dark pigment into some corner to strengthen it; or throw in a reddish stroke—a tear of blood, so to speak—to break the parts superficially. In fact, when finishing, he painted much more with his fingers than with his brush." Titian used to say, "White, red, and black, these are all the colors that a painter needs, but one must know how to use them." Titian painted rapidly. One of his best friends said that "he could execute a portrait as quickly as another could scratch an ornament on a chest."

In 1537 the Council of Ten, angered at Titian's delays in frescoing the ducal palace, gave a portion of the work to the noted artist Pordenone, took away his brokership, and decreed that he should refund his revenues from that source for the past twenty years. In dismay, Titian left his orders from emperors and princes, and went to work in the great halls. Two years later his broker's patent was restored, and, Pordenone having died in 1538, the patronage of the Republic came again into his hands.

Titian now painted the "Angel and Tobit," of San Marciliano at Venice, and the "Presentation in the Temple," now at the Venice

Academy, the latter "the finest and most complete creation of Venetian art since the 'Peter Martyr,' and the 'Madonna di Casa Pesaro.'"

This picture is one of the largest of the master's works, being twenty-five feet long. "Mary, in a dress of celestial blue, ascends the steps of the temple in a halo of radiance. She pauses on the first landing-place, and gathers her skirts to ascend to the second. The flight is in profile before us. At the top of it the high-priest, in Jewish garments, yellow tunic, blue undercoat and sleeves, and white robe, looks down at the girl with serene and kindly gravity, a priest in cardinal's robes at his side, a menial in black behind him, and a young acolyte in red and yellow holding the book of prayer. At the bottom there are people looking up, some of them leaning on the edge of the step, others about to ascend."

Titian painted several portraits of himself, one now at Berlin, another at Madrid, still another in Florence, and others. They show a bold, high forehead, finely cut nose, penetrating eyes, and much dignity of bearing.

Duke Alfonso of Ferrara and Duke Federigo Gonzaga of Mantua, his noble patrons, had both died; but Pope Paul III now became an ardent admirer of Titian's work, invited him to Rome, where he spent several months lodged in the Belvedere Palace, and sat to him for a portrait. It is said, after the picture of Paul was finished and set to dry on the terrace of the palace, that the passing crowd doffed their hats, thinking that it was the living pope.

While in Rome, Titian painted many portraits in the pontiff's family, and a "Danaë receiving the Golden Rain," now in the museum of Naples, for Ottavio Farnese, grandson of Paul III, who was married to Margaret, daughter of Emperor Charles V. Danaë was the daughter of Acrisius, king of Argos. An oracle had predicted that her son would one day kill Acrisius; therefore, to prevent the fulfilment of the prophecy, Danaë was shut up in a brazen tower. But Jupiter transformed himself into a shower of gold, and descended through the roof of her tower. She became the mother of Perseus, and she and her son were put into a chest and cast into the sea. Jupiter rescued them, and Perseus finally killed his grandfather.

Titian was now sixty-eight years of age,—growing old, but never slacking in energy or industry. He had painted for the Church of San Spirito "Abraham's Sacrifice of Isaac," "The Murder of Abel," "David's Victory over Goliath," "The Descent of the Holy Spirit," "The Four Christian Fathers," and "The Four Evangelists." "His figures are not cast in the supernatural mould of those of Michael Angelo at the Sistine, they are not shaped in his sculptural way, or foreshortened in his preternatural manner. They have not the elegance of Raphael, nor the conventional grace of Correggio; but they are built up, as it were, of flesh and blood, and illumined with a magic effect of light and shade and color which differs from all else that was realized elsewhere by selection, outline, and chiaroscuro. They form pictures peculiar to Titian, and pregnant with his, and only his, grand and natural originality." The "Ecce Homo," twelve feet by eight, in the gallery of Vienna, was painted for Giovanni d' Anna, a wealthy merchant. When Henry III. passed through Venice in 1574, he saw this picture, and offered eight hundred ducats for it. When Sir Henry Wotton was English envoy at Venice in 1620, he bought the painting for the Duke of Buckingham, who refused thirty-five thousand dollars offered for it by the Earl of Arundel.

In 1546, on the return of the artist from Rome to his home, Casa Grande, in Venice, he painted the portraits of his lovely daughter Lavinia, now in the Dresden Museum, and in the Berlin gallery. "From the first to the last this beautiful piece (in Dresden) is the work of the master, and there is not an inch of it in which his hand is not to be traced. His is the brilliant flesh, brought up to a rosy carnation by wondrous kneading of copious pigment; his the contours formed by texture, and not defined by outline; his again the mixture of sharp and blurred touches, the delicate modelling in dazzling light, the soft glazing, cherry lip, and sparkling eye. Such a charming vision as this was well fitted to twine itself round a father's heart.

"Lavinia's hair is yellow, and strewed with pearls, showing a pretty wave, and irrepressible curls in stray locks on the forehead. Earrings, a necklace of pearls, glitter with gray reflections on a skin incomparably fair. The gauze on the shoulders is light as air, and contrasts with the stiff richness of a white damask silk dress and skirt, the folds of which heave and sink in shallow projections and depressions, touched in tender scales of yellow or ashen white. The left hand, with its bracelet of pearls, hangs gracefully as it tucks up the train of the gown, whilst the right is raised no higher than the waist, to wave the stiff, plaited leaf of a palmetto fan."...

Lavinia, at Berlin, "is dressed in yellowish flowered silk, with slashed sleeves, a chiselled girdle round her waist, and a white veil hanging from her shoulders. Seen in profile, she raises with both hands, to the level of her forehead, a silver dish piled with fruit and flowers. Her head is thrown back, and turned so as to allow three-quarters of it to be seen, as she looks from the corners of her eyes at the spectator. Auburn hair is carefully brushed off the temples, and confined by a jewelled diadem, and the neck is set off with a string of pearls."

The Titian home had joys and sorrows in it like other homes. Pomponio, the eldest child, though a priest, was dissolute and a spendthrift, constantly incurring debts which his devoted father paid to mitigate the disgrace. Orazio, a noble son, had become an artist, his father's assistant and confidant. He had married and brought his young wife to Casa Grande. Lavinia, a beauty, the only daughter, was about to be married to Cornelio Sarcinella of Serravalle, receiving from her father a dowry of fourteen hundred ducats, a regal sum for a painter.

In January of 1548, Titian, now past seventy, was summoned to Augsburg, where Charles V. had convened the Diet of the Empire. He painted the portrait of Charles on the field of Muhlberg "in burnished armor-inlaid with gold, his arms and legs in chain mail, his hands gauntleted, a morion with a red plume, but without a visor, on his head. The red scarf with gold stripes—cognizance of the House of Burgundy—hung across his shoulders, and he brandished with his right hand a sharp and pointed spear. The chestnut steed, half hid in striped housings, had a head-piece of steel topped by a red feather similar to that of its master."

Titian also painted, while at Augsburg, King Ferdinand, the brother of Charles, Queen Mary of Hungary, "Prometheus," "Sisyphus," "Ixion," and "Tantalus" at her request, besides many other pictures. Charles so honored Titian that once when the artist dropped his brush the emperor picked it up and handed it to him, saying that "Titian was worthy of being served by Cæsar."

On a second visit to Augsburg Titian painted a portrait of Philip II of Spain, the son of Charles. This was sent to Queen Mary of England, when Philip was her suitor, and quite won her heart, presumably more than the man himself when he afterwards became her husband. When Titian parted from his patron, Charles gave him a Spanish pension of five hundred scudi. He returned to Venice "rich as a prince instead of poor as a painter."

Philip II was as much a patron of art as his father, and was constantly soliciting paintings from Titian. It is best, probably, that most of us are worked to our utmost capacity, for work rarely kills people; worry frequently destroys both body and brain.

For Philip he painted a "St. Margaret," now in the museum at Madrid; a "Danaë," where an old woman sits beside the couch and gathers Jupiter's golden shower in her apron; a "Perseus and Andromeda," the princess bound to a rock, and Perseus saving her; and a "Venus and Adonis," now at Madrid. For the enfeebled Emperor Charles he painted "The Grieving Virgin," now in the Madrid Museum, which represents the mother lamenting over the sufferings of the Saviour, and the "Trinity," now at Madrid, showing the Virgin interceding before the Father and Son for the imperial family,—a picture upon which the emperor used to gaze with intense feeling when he had retired to die in the Convent of Yuste. Thither he carried nine of Titian's paintings for his consolation. He died in 1558, with his eyes resting lovingly upon a picture of the emperor painted by Titian, and upon "The Trinity." "Christ appearing to the Magdalen" was sent to Queen Mary of Hungary.

Titian was now seventy-nine years of age, honored and loved by many countries. While his life had been one of almost unceasing labor, he had found time to receive at Casa Grande, poets and artists, dukes and kings, at his delightful garden-parties. Henry III of France came to see him, and received as a gift any pictures in the studio of which he asked the price. When Cardinal Granvelle and Pacheco came to dine at Casa Grande, Titian flung a purse to his steward, and bade him prepare a feast, since "all the world was dining with him."

Titian attached to himself a few most devoted friends: Aretino, a writer, who had many faults, but must have had some virtues to have been loved by Titian for thirty years; Sansovino, an architect; Speroni, a philosopher, and a few others who met frequently for cultured conversation and good-fellowship at Casa Grande. It is said by historians that at some of these garden parties the still beautiful Violante was to be seen among the distinguished guests. Had she been married to another, all these years? or was the old affection renewed in these latter days?

In 1556 Aretino died, and Titian deeply lamented the man who had been an almost inseparable companion; three years later his beloved brother, Francesco, died at Cadore, and two years after this his beautiful daughter Lavinia, leaving six little children.

Still the man past eighty painted on: "The Martyrdom of St. Lawrence," now in the Jesuits' Church at Venice, and "Christ Crowned with Thorns," now in the Louvre, where, "with undeniable originality, he almost attained to a grandeur of composition and bold creativeness equal to those of Buonarotti, whilst he added to his creations that which was essentially his own—the magic play of tints and lights and shadows which mark the true Venetian craftsman."

At eighty-two he painted for Philip II "Diana and Calisto," "Diana and Actæon," and "The Entombment of Christ." The Dianas are now in the Bridgewater collection at London, for which they were purchased for twelve thousand five hundred dollars.

"Titian," says Crowe, "was never more thoroughly master of the secrets of the human framework than now that he was aged. Never did he less require the model. What his mind suggested issued from his hand as Minerva issued from the brain of Jove. His power was the outcome of years of experience, which made every stroke of his brush both sure and telling.... But the field of the earlier time, take it all in all, is sweeter and of better savor than that of the later period. Rich, exuberant, and bright the works of the master always were; but there is something mysterious and unfathomable in the brightness and sweetness of his prime which far exceeds in charm the cleverness of his old age."

With loving care he painted Irene of Spilimberg, who died at twenty, and whose fame in classic learning, in music, painting, and poetry, was celebrated in sonnets and prose at her death. She was a pupil of Titian, a fit representative of an age which produced among learned men such women as Vittoria Colonna and Veronica Gambara. Irene is painted "almost at full length and large as life, in a portico, from which a view is seen of a landscape, with a shepherd tending his flock, and a unicorn to indicate the lady's maiden condition. Her head is turned to the left, showing auburn hair tied with a string of pearls. Round her throat is a necklace of the same. Her waist is bound with a chain girdle, and over her bodice of red stuff a jacket of red damask silk is embroidered with gold, and fringed at the neck with a high standing muslin collar. A band hanging from the shoulders and passing beneath one arm is held in the right hand, whilst the left is made to grasp a laurel crown, and 'Si fata tulissent' is engraved on the plinth of a pillar."

The "Epiphany," now in Madrid, was sent to Philip II., in 1560; a "Magdalen," now in the Hermitage, in 1561; "Christ in the Garden," "Europa and the Bull," and "Jupiter and Antiope," in 1562. Titian wrote to Philip, "I had determined to take a rest for those years of my old age which it may please the majesty of God to grant me; still ... I shall devote all that is left of my life to doing reverence to your Catholic Majesty with new pictures."

"Europa," says Sweetser, "is a lovely and scantily clad maiden sitting on the back of a flower-garlanded white bull, who is swimming proudly through the green sea, throwing a line of foaming surge before his breast. In the air are flying Cupids, and the nymphs on the distant shore bewail the loss of their companion."

"Jupiter and Antiope," now in the Louvre, formerly called the "Venus of Pardo," is very celebrated. "Though injured by fire, travels, cleaning, and restoring," says Crowe, "the masterpiece still exhibits Titian in possession of all the energy of his youth, and leads us back involuntarily to the days when he composed the Bacchanals. The same beauties of arrangement, form, light, and shade, and some of the earlier charms of color, are here united to a new scale of effectiveness due to experience and a magic readiness of hand. Fifty years of practice were required to bring Titian to this mastery. Distribution, movement, outline, modelling, atmosphere and distance, are all perfect."

The following year, 1563, Titian sent to Philip "The Last Supper," with thirteen life-sized figures, upon which he had worked for six years. When it was carried to the Escurial, in spite of the protests of the painter Navarrete, the monks cut off a large piece of the upper part of the canvas, to make it the size of the wall of the refectory!

In 1565 he painted "The Transfiguration," in the San Salvadore at Venice, the "Annunciation" for the same church; "St. James of Compostella," in the Church of San Leo, and the "Cupid and Venus" of the Borghese Palace, the Queen of Love and two Graces teaching Cupid his vocation.

"Venus is seated in front of a gorgeous red-brown drapery; her head is crowned with a diadem, and her luxuriant hair falls in heavy locks on her neck. Her arms are bare, but her tunic is bound with a sash, which meets in a cross at her bosom and winds away under the arms, whilst a flap of a blue mantle crosses the knees. With both hands she is binding the eyes of Eros leaning on her lap, whilst she turns to listen to the whispering of another Eros resting on her shoulder. A girl with naked throat and arm carries Cupid's quiver, whilst a second holds his bow. Behind the group a sky overcast with pearly clouds lowers over a landscape of hills.... Light plays upon every part," says Crowe, "creating, as it falls, a due projection of shadow, producing all the delicacies of broken tone and a clear silvery surface full of sparkle, recalling those masterpieces of Paolo Veronese, in which the gradations are all in the cinerine as opposed to the golden key."

In 1566, the aged artist, now verging on ninety, heretofore exempt from taxation, was obliged to give a list of his property. He owned several houses, pieces of land, sawmills, and the like, and has been blamed because he did not state the full value of his possessions.

Vasari, who visited him at this time, writes,—"Titian has enjoyed health and happiness unequalled, and has never received from heaven anything but favor and felicity. His house has been visited by all the princes, men of letters, and gentlemen who ever come to Venice. Besides being excellent in art, he is pleasant company, of fine deportment and agreeable manners.... Titian, having decorated Venice, and, indeed, Italy and other parts of the world, with admirable pictures, deserves to be loved and studied by artists, as one who has done and is still doing works deserving of praise, which will last as long as the memory of illustrious men."

When he was ninety-one he sent to Philip II. a "Venus," the "Martyrdom of St. Lawrence," a large "Tarquin and Lucretia," and "Philip Presenting his Son to an Angel," now in the Madrid Museum. He also painted for himself "Christ Crowned with Thorns," a powerful work, now in Munich, which Rubens, Rembrandt, and Van Dyck carefully studied as a model. Tintoretto hung it later in his atelier, to show what a painting ought to be.

His "Adam and Eve," now at Madrid, which Rubens greatly admired and copied, was painted at this time.

In 1576, when Titian was ninety-nine, he began his last picture, the "Christ of Pity," for the Franciscans of the Frari, with whom he had bargained for a grave in their chapel. The Saviour rests in death on the lap of the Virgin.

"We may suppose," says Donald G. Mitchell, "that a vision of Lavinia—long gone out of his household—of Cecilia, still longer gone—of Violante, a memory of his young days—may have flitted on his mind as he traced the last womanly face he was to paint."

"On marble plinths at the sides of the niche are statues of Moses and the Hellespontic Sibyl, and on a scutcheon at the Sibyl's feet we see the arms of Titian, a set square sable on a field argent, beneath the double eagle on a field or. A small tablet leaning against the scutcheon contains the defaced portraits of Titian and his son Orazio, kneeling before a diminutive group of the 'Christ of Pity.'... It is truly surprising," says Crowe, "that a man so far advanced in years should have had the power to put together a composition so perfect in line, so elevated in thought, or so tragic in expression.... We see the traces of a brush manipulated by one whose hand never grew weary, and never learned to tremble.... In the group of the Virgin and Christ—a group full of the deepest and truest feeling—there lies a grandeur comparable in one sense with that which strikes us in the 'Pietà' of Michael Angelo. For the sublime conventionalism by which Buonarotti carries us into a preternatural atmosphere, Titian substitutes a depth of passion almost equally sublime, and the more real as it is enhanced by color."

Titian did not live to complete this work, which was done by his pupil, Palma Giovine, who placed conspicuously upon it this touching inscription: "That which Titian left unfinished, Palma reverently completed, and dedicated the work to God."

Age did not spoil the skill of the master. Aretino said, on looking at a portrait of a daughter of the rich Strozzio, "If I were a painter, I should die of despair.... But certain it is that Titian's pencil has waited on Titian's old age to perform its miracles."

Tullia said, "I hold Titian to be not a painter—his creations not art, but his works to be miracles, and I think that his pigments must be composed of that wonderful herb which made Glaucus a god when he partook of it; since his portraits make upon me the impression of something divine, and, as heaven is the paradise of the soul, so God has transfused into Titian's colors the paradise of our bodies."

In the summer of this year, 1576, Venice was stricken by a plague which destroyed fifty thousand people out of one hundred and ninety thousand; more than a quarter of the whole population. There was a general panic, the sick were left to die unattended, and a law was passed that no victims of the scourge should be buried in the churches.

As the plague swept on it carried off Orazio, the son of Titian, and then the idol of Venice, Titian himself. He died suddenly August 27, 1576. The law of burial was quickly set aside by the supreme authorities, and, despite the fear of contagion, the canons of St. Mark bore his body in solemn procession to his grave in the Church of the Frari. In 1852, nearly three centuries later, the Emperor of Austria erected a magnificent mausoleum over his tomb. It is a vast canopy covering a statue of Titian, seated, with one hand resting on the Book of Art, while the other lifts the veil of Nature. Surrounding him are figures representing painting, wood-carving, sculpture, and architecture, while on the wall behind him are bas-reliefs of three of his greatest works, the "Assumption," the "Martyrdom of St. Lawrence," and the "Martyrdom of St. Peter." Two angels bear the simple inscription,—

"Titiano Ferdinandus I. MDCCCLII."

Wonderful old man! self-made, a poet by nature, a marvel of industry, working to the very last on his beloved paintings, rich, tender to his family, true in his friendships. "The greatest master of color whom the world has known."

MURILLO

In the picturesque city of Seville, "the glory of the Spanish realms," the greatest painter of Spain, Bartolomé Estéban Murillo, was born, probably on the last day of the year 1617. He was baptized on New Year's Day, 1618, in the Church of La Magdalena, destroyed in 1810 by the French troops under Marshal Soult.

His father, Gaspar Estéban, was a mechanic, renting a modest house which belonged to a convent, and keeping it in repair for the use of it. His mother, Maria Perez, seems to have been well connected, as her brother, Juan de Costillo, was one of the leaders of art in Seville. It is said that the family were once wealthy and distinguished, but now they were very poor.

The boy, Bartolomé, was consecrated to the church, with the fond hope of his mother that he would become a priest. However, he soon exhibited such artistic talent that this project was abandoned. One day when the mother went to Church, leaving the child at home, he amused himself by taking a sacred picture, "Jesus and the Lamb," and painting his own hat on the Infant Saviour's head, and changing the lamb into a dog.

Probably the reverent mother was shocked, but she thereby gained a knowledge of the genius of her only son. In school, the boy used to make sketches on the margins of his books and on the walls.

Before he was eleven years old, both father and mother died, leaving him to the care of a surgeon, Juan Agustin Lagares, who had married his aunt, Doña Anna Murillo. Probably from this family name the boy derived his own. A little sister, Teresa, was also left an orphan.

He was soon apprenticed to his uncle, Juan del Castillo, who taught him carefully all the details of his art,—correct drawing, how to prepare canvas, mix colors, and study patiently. The lad was very industrious, eager to learn, extremely gentle and amiable, and soon attached himself to both teacher and pupils.

From this it is easy to judge that he had had a lovely mother, one who encouraged, who preserved a sweet nature in her son because sweet herself. How often have I seen a parent lose the confidence of a child by too often reproving, by over-criticism, by disparagement! Praise seldom harms anybody. We usually receive and give too little commendation all our lives.

One of my most precious memories is the fact that my widowed mother made it her life-rule not to find fault with her two children. She loved us into obedience. She told us her wishes and her hopes for us, and the smile with which she spoke lingers in my heart like an exquisite picture. Long ago I learned that no home ever had too much love in it.

For nine years the Spanish lad worked in his uncle's studio,

100

studying nature as well as art, as shown in his inimitable "Beggar Boys" and other dwellers in the streets of Seville. When he was twenty, he painted two Madonnas, "The Virgin with St. Francis," for the Convent of Regina Angelorum, and the "Virgin del Rosario with San Domingo," for the Church of St. Thomas.

It was natural that the young artist, loving the Catholic faith, should paint as one of his first pictures the "Story of the Rosary." Mrs. Jameson, in her "Legends of the Monastic Orders," thus gives the history of St. Dominick: "His father was of the illustrious family of Guzman. His mother, Joanna d'Aza, was also of noble birth.... Such was his early predilection for a life of penance that when he was only six or seven years old he would get out of his bed to lie on the cold earth. His parents sent him to study theology in the university of Valencia, and he assumed the habit of a canon of St. Augustine at a very early age.

"Many stories are related of his youthful piety, his self-inflicted austerities, and his charity. One day he met a poor woman weeping bitterly, and when he inquired the cause she told him that her only brother, her sole stay and support in the world, had been carried into captivity by the Moors. Dominick could not ransom her brother; he had given away all his money, and even sold his books, to relieve the poor; but he offered all he could,—he offered up himself to be exchanged as a slave in place of her brother. The woman, astonished at such a proposal, fell upon her knees before him. She refused his offer, but she spread the fame of the young priest far and wide....

"He united with himself several ecclesiastics, who went about barefoot in the habit of penitents, exhorting the people to conform to the Church. The institution of the Order of St. Dominick sprang out of this association of preachers, but it was not united under an especial rule, nor confirmed, till some years later, by Pope Honorius, in 1216.

"It was during his sojourn in Languedoc that St. Dominick instituted the Rosary. The use of a chaplet of beads, as a memento of the number of prayers recited, is of Eastern origin, and dates from the time of the Egyptian Anchorites. Beads were also used by the Benedictines, and are to this day in use among the Mohammedan devotees. Dominick invented a novel arrangement of the chaplet, and dedicated it to the honor and glory of the Blessed Virgin, for whom he entertained a most especial veneration. A complete rosary consists of fifteen large and one hundred and fifty small beads; the former representing the number of Paternosters, the latter the number of Ave Marias.... The rosary was received with the utmost enthusiasm, and by this single expedient Dominick did more to excite the devotion of the lower orders, especially of the women, and made more converts, than by all his orthodoxy, learning, arguments, and eloquence.

"St. Dominick, in the excess of his charity and devotion, was accustomed, while preaching in Languedoc, to scourge himself three times a day,—once for his own sins; once for the sins of others; and once for the benefit of souls in purgatory." He preached in all the principal cities of Europe, and died at Bologna in 1221.

In 1640, when Murillo was twenty-two, the Castilli home was broken up, the uncle Juan going to Cadiz to reside. Without fame and poor, the youth was thrown upon his own resources. There were many artists in the city of Seville, and Murillo, shy and retiring, could not expect much patronage. He decided to go to the Feria, a weekly market, held in front of the Church of All Saints, and there, in the midst of stalls where eatables, old clothes, and other wares were sold, he set up his open-air studio, and worked among the gypsies and the muleteers.

Rough, showy pictures were painted to order and sold to those who frequented the market-place. For two long years he lived among this humble class, earning probably but a scanty subsistence. Here, doubtless, he learned to paint flower-girls and squalid beggars. "There was no contempt," says Sweetser, "in Murillo's feelings towards these children of nature; and his sentiments seemed to partake almost of a fraternal sympathy for them. No small portion of his popularity among the lower classes arose from the knowledge that he was their poet and court painter, who understood and did not calumniate them. Velasquez had chosen to paint superb dukes and cardinals, and found his supporters in a handful of supercilious grandees; but Murillo illustrated the lives of the poorest classes on Spanish soil, and was the idol of the masses. With what splendor of color and mastery of design did he thus illuminate the annals of the poor! Coming forth from some dim chancel or palace-hall in which he had been working on a majestic Madonna-picture, he would sketch in, with the brush still loaded with the colors of celestial glory, the lineaments of the beggar crouching by the wall or the gypsy calmly reposing in the black shadow of the archway. Such versatility had never before been seen west of the Mediterranean, and commanded the admiration of his countrymen.

"We do not find in his pictures the beggar of Britain and America, cold, lowering, gloomy, and formidable; but the laughing child of the sunlight, full of joy and content, preferring to bask rather than to work, yet always fed somehow, and abundantly; crop-haired, brown-footed, clad in incoherent rags, but bright-eyed, given to much joviality, and with an affluence of white teeth, often shown in merry moods; not so respectable as the staid burghers of Nuremberg and Antwerp, but far more picturesque and perhaps quite as happy."

But for Murillo's life of poverty he could not have had this sympathy with the poor. Doubtless every experience is given us with a purpose, that either through the brush or the pen, or by word or deed, we may the better do our part for the elevation of mankind.

In 1642, Murillo had a new inspiration. A fellow-pupil in Castillo's school, Pedro de Moya, after joining the Spanish army and campaigning in Flanders, had spent six months in London under Van

Dyck. Now he came back to Seville aglow with his delights in travel and the wonders of the Flemish painters.

Murillo was fired with ambition. He too would see famous painters and renowned cities, and become as great as his young friend Moya. But how? He had no money and no influential friends. He would make the effort. He might stay forever at the Feria, and never be heard of beyond Seville.

He bought a piece of linen, cut it into pieces of various sizes, and, in some obscure room, painted upon them saints, flowers, fruit, and landscapes. Then he sallied forth to find purchasers. One wonders whether the young man did not sometimes become discouraged in these years of toil; if he did not sometimes look at the houses of the grandees and sigh because he was not rich or because he was homeless and unknown?

He sold most of his pictures to a ship-owner, by whom they were sent to the West Indies and other Catholic portions of America. Then he started on foot over the Sierras,—a long and tedious journey to Madrid. In the Spanish capital he could find the works of art which he wished to study.

He had no money nor friends when he arrived in the great city, but he had courage. He had learned early in life a most valuable lesson,—to depend on himself. To whom should he go? Velasquez, formerly of Seville, was at the height of his fame, the favorite of the king, the friend of the wealthy and the distinguished. Murillo determined to seek the great artist in his own home; at least he could only be refused admittance.

Velasquez kindly received the young man, who told him how he had come on foot over the mountains to study. There was no jealousy in the heart of the painter, no fear of rivalry. He was pleased with the modesty, frankness, and aspiration of the youth, and, strange to say, took him into his own home to reside. What a contrast to painting in the Feria, and living in a garret!

Murillo at once began to study in the royal galleries where Philip II and his father Charles V. had gathered their Titians, their Rubenses, and their Van Dycks. For three years, through the kindness of Velasquez, he met the leading Spanish artists and the prominent people of the court. The king admired his work, and greatly encouraged him. Murillo was fortunate,—yes; but Fortune did not seek him, he sought her! Ambition and action made him successful.

Early in 1645, Murillo returned to Seville. Velasquez offered to give him letters of introduction to eminent artists in Rome, but he preferred to go back to his native city. Probably he longed for the old Cathedral, with La Giralda, the Alcazar, the Moorish palaces, and the Guadalquivir.

The Alcazar, says Hare, in his "Wanderings in Spain," begun in 1181, was in great part rebuilt by Pedro the Cruel, 1353-64. "The history of this strange monarch gives the Alcazar its chief interest. Hither he fled with his mother as a child from his father, Alonzo XI, and his mistress, Leonora de Guzman. They were protected by the minister, Albuquerque, at whose house he met and loved Maria de Padilla, a Castilian beauty of noble birth, whom he secretly married. Albuquerque was furious, and, aided by the queen-mother, forced him into a political marriage with the French princess, Blanche de Bourbon. He met her at Valladolid; but three days after his nuptials fled from the wife he disliked to the one he loved, who ever after held royal court at Seville, while Queen Blanche,—a sort of Spanish Mary Stuart,—after being cruelly persecuted and imprisoned for years, was finally put to death at Medina-Sidonia.

"In this Alcazar, Pedro received the Red King of Granada, with a promise of safe-conduct, and then murdered him for the sake of his jewels, one of which—a large ruby—he gave to the Black Prince after Navarete, and which is 'the fair ruby, great like a rachet-ball,' which Elizabeth showed to the ambassador of Mary of Scotland, and now adorns the royal crown of England....

"It was in the Alcazar, also, that Pedro murdered his illegitimate brother, the master of Santiago, who had caused him much trouble by a rebellion. Maria de Padilla knew his coming fate, but did not dare to tell him, though from the beautiful ajimez window over the gate she watched for his arrival, and tried to warn him by her tears. Six years after, this murder was avenged by Henry of Trastamare, the brother of the slain, who stabbed Pedro to the heart. But Maria de Padilla was already dead, and buried with queens in the royal chapel, when Pedro publicly acknowledged her as his lawful wife, and the marriage received the sanction of the Spanish Church....

"Within the Alcazar all is still fresh and brilliant with light and color. It is like a scene from the 'Arabian Nights,' or the wonderful creation of a kaleidoscope.... The Hall of Ambassadors is perfectly glorious in its delicate lace-like ornaments and the rich color of its exquisite azulejos."

"The cathedral," says Hare, "stands on a high platform, girdled with pillars, partly brought from Italica and partly relics of the mosques, of which two existed on this site. The last, built by the Emir Yusuf in 1184, was pulled down in 1401, when the cathedral was begun, only the Giralda, the Court of Oranges, and some of the outer walls being preserved. The chapter, when convened for the building of the cathedral, determined, like religious Titans, to build 'one of such size and beauty that coming ages should proclaim them mad for having undertaken it.'...

"Far above houses and palaces, far above the huge cathedral itself, soars the beautiful Giralda, its color a pale pink, incrusted all over with delicate Moorish ornament, so high that its detail is quite lost as you gaze upward; so large that you may easily ride on horseback to the summit, up the broad roadway in the interior....

"In the interior everything is vast, down to the Paschal candle, placed in a candlestick twenty-five feet high, and weighing twenty-five hundred pounds, of wax, while the expenditure of the chapter may be estimated by the fact that eighteen thousand seven hundred and fifty litres of wine are consumed annually in the sacrament. Of the ninety-three stained windows many are old and splendid. Their light is undimmed by curtains, for there is an Andalusian proverb that the ray of the sun has no power to injure within the bounds in which the voice of prayer can be heard. In the centre of the nave, near the west door, surrounded by sculptured caravelas, the primitive ships by which the New World was discovered, is the tomb of Ferdinand Columbus, son of the great navigator (who himself rests in Havanna), inscribed,—

"'A Castilla y á Leon
Mundo nuevo dio Colon.'

At the opposite end of the church is the royal chapel, where St. Ferdinand, who was canonized in 1627, 'because he carried fagots with his own hands for the burning of heretics,' rests beneath the altar, in a silver sarcophagus. Here also are his Queen, Beatrix, his son Alonzo el Sabio, father of our Queen Eleanor, and Maria de Padilla, the beautiful Morganatic wife of Pedro the Cruel....

"Many of the services in this church reach a degree of splendor which is only equalled by those of St. Peter's; and the two organs, whose gigantic pipes have been compared to the columns of Fingal's Cave, peal forth magnificently. But one ceremony, at least, is far more fantastic than anything at Rome."

Frances Elliot, in her "Diary of an Idle Woman in Spain," thus describes this remarkable ceremony: "To the left, within the bars, I am conscious of the presence of a band of stringed instruments,—not only violins and counter-bass, but flutes, flageolets, and hautboys, even a serpent, as they call a quaint instrument associated with my earliest years, forthwith all beginning to play in a most ancient and most homely way, for all the world like a simple village choir, bringing a twang of damp, mouldy, country churches to my mind, sunny English afternoons, and odors of lavender and southern-wood.

"As they play—these skilled musicians—a sound of youthful voices comes gathering in, fresh, shrill, and childlike, rising and falling to the rhythm.

"All at once the music grows strangely passionate, the voices and the stringed instruments seem to heave and sigh in tender accents, long-drawn notes and sobs wail out melodious cries for mercy and invocations for pardon, growing louder and intenser each moment.

"Then, I know not how, for the great darkness gathers round

even to the gates of the altar, a band of boys, the owners of the voices, appears as in a vision in the open space between the benches on which the chapter sits, and, gliding down the altar steps, move in a measure fitting in softly with the music.

"How or when they begin to dance, singing as if to the involuntary movement of their feet, I know not; at first 'high-disposedly,' their bodies swaying to and fro to the murmur of the band, which never leaves off playing a single instant, in the most heavenly way. Then, as the music quickens and castanets click out, the boys grow animated, and move swifter to and fro, raising their arms in curves and graceful interlacing rounds. Still faster the music beats, and faster and faster they move, crossing and recrossing in mazy figures, the stringed instruments following them with zeal, the castanets, hautboys, and flutes, their interlacing forms knotting in a kind of ecstasy, yet all as grave and solemn as in a song of praise, a visible rejoicing of the soul at Christmas time and the Divine birth. As David danced before the ark for joy, so do these boys dance now with holy gladness.

"I made out something of their costume,—broad Spanish hats, turned up with a panache of blue feathers, the Virgin's color, a flowing mantle of the same hue over one shoulder, glittering in the light, white satin vests, and white hose and shoes.

"The dance is most ancient, archi-old, as one may say—of an origin Phœnician or Arab, sanctified to Christian use. The music, like the dance, quaint and pathetic, with every now and then a solo so sweet it seems as if an angel had come down unseen to play it. I have inquired on all hands what is the origin of this singular rite, which takes place twice a year, at Advent and Easter, but no one can tell me. About two centuries ago an Archbishop of Seville objected to the dance as giddy and mundane, and forbade it in his cathedral, causing a terrible scandal. The Sevillians were enraged; their fathers had loved the dance, and their fathers before them, and they were ready to defend it with swords and staves.

"As the Archbishop was inexorable, an appeal was made to Rome. The Pope of that day, a sensible man, replied that he could give no judgment without seeing the dance himself; so the whole troop— stringed instruments, castanets, serpent, cavalier hats and cloaks, and the boys who wore them—were carried off to Rome at the expense of rich citizens. Then the measure was tried before the Pope in the Vatican, and he approved. 'Let the citizens of Seville have their dance,' the Pope said; 'I see no harm in it. As long as the clothes last it shall continue.'

"Need I add that those clothes never wore out, but, like the widow's curse, renewed themselves miraculously, to the delight of the town, and that they will continue to last fresh and new as long as the gigantic walls of the cathedral uprear themselves, and the sun of Andalusia shines on the flat plains!"

Murillo loved this old cathedral, and later he painted for it some of his wonderful pictures, among them "The Guardian Angel," in which "a glorious seraph with spreading wings leads a little, trustful child by the hand, and directs him to look beyond earth into the heavenly light," and "St. Anthony of Padua visited by the infant Saviour." The saint is kneeling with outstretched arms, looking above to the child, who descends through a flood of glory filled with cherubs, drawn down by the prayers of the saint. On the table beside him is a vase of white lilies, which many persons averred were so natural that the birds flew down the cathedral aisles to peck at the flowers. For this picture the cathedral clergy paid ten thousand reals. Mrs. Jameson declares this the finest work ever executed in honor of St. Anthony, a subject chosen by Titian and scores of other artists.

When the nephew of Murillo's first master, Castillo, looked upon this work, he exclaimed, "It is all over with Castillo! Is it possible that Murillo, that servile imitator of my uncle, can be the author of all this grace and beauty of coloring?"

The canons told M. Viardot that the Duke of Wellington offered to pay for this picture as many gold pieces as would cover its surface of fifteen feet square, about two hundred and forty thousand dollars. In 1874 the figure of St. Anthony was cut out, stolen, and sold to a Mr. Schaus, a picture-dealer of New York, for two hundred and fifty dollars. He turned his purchase over to the Spanish consul, who restored it to the cathedral.

St. Anthony was a Portuguese by birth, and taught divinity in the universities of Bologna, Toulouse, Paris, and Padua. Finally he became an eloquent preacher among the people. It is said that when they refused to listen he preached to the dwellers in the sea, "and an infinite number of fishes, great and little, lifted their heads above water, and listened attentively to the sermon of the saint!"

Very many miracles are attributed to him. He restored to life by his prayers Carilla, a young maiden who was drowned; also a young child who was scalded to death; renewed the foot of a young man who had cut it off because the saint rebuked him for having kicked his brother; caused the body of a murdered youth to speak, and acquit an old man who had been accused of his death; made a glass cup remain whole when thrown against a marble slab, while the marble was shivered.

"The legend of the mule," says Mrs. Jameson, "is one of the most popular of the miracles of St. Anthony, and is generally found in the Franciscan churches. A certain heretic called Bovidilla entertained doubts of the real presence in the sacrament, and, after a long argument with the saint, required a miracle in proof of this favorite dogma of the Roman Catholic Church. St. Anthony, who was about to carry the host in procession, encountered the mule of Bovidilla, which fell down on its knees at the command of the saint, and, although its heretic master endeavored to tempt it aside by a sieve full of oats, remained kneeling till the host had passed."

After Murillo's return from the house of Velasquez to Seville, he worked incessantly for nearly three years upon eleven paintings for the convent of the Franciscans near Casa del Ayuntamiento. The cloisters contained three hundred marble columns. For the decoration of a minor cloister the priests offered so small an amount that no leading artist in Seville would attempt it. But Murillo, still poor, and not well known, gladly accepted the work. It was a laborious undertaking, with perhaps scarcely enough compensation to provide for his daily needs; but it made him famous. Henceforward there was neither poverty nor obscurity for the great Spanish master.

The first picture for the Franciscans represented "St. Francis, on an iron bed, listening to an angel who is playing on a violin." The second portrayed "St. Diego blessing a pot of broth," which he is about to give to a group of beggars at the gate of his convent. Another picture, called, "The Angel Kitchen," now in the Louvre, represents a monk who fell in a state of ecstasy whilst cooking for the convent, and angels are doing his work. Still another represents a Franciscan praying over the dead body of a friar, as if to restore it to life. This is now owned by Mr. Richard Ford, of Devonshire, England.

The finest picture of the series represents "The Death of St. Clara of Assisi." She was the daughter of a noble knight of great wealth, and much sought in marriage. Desiring to devote herself to a religious life, she repaired to St. Francis for counsel, who advised her to enter a convent. She fled from her home to where St. Francis dwelt, and he with his own hands cut off her luxuriant golden tresses, and threw over her his own penitential habit of gray wool. Her family sought to force her away, but later her sister Agnes and mother Ortolana joined her in the convent.

On the death of her father, St. Clara gave all her wealth to the poor. She went, like the others of her order, barefoot or sandalled, slept on the hard earth, and lived in silence. The most notable event of her life was the dispersion of the Saracens. Emperor Frederic ravaged the shores of the Adriatic. In his army were a band of infidel Saracens, who attacked the Convent of San Damiano. The frightened nuns rushed to the side of "Mother Clara," who had long been unable to rise from her bed. At once she arose, took from the altar the pyx of ivory and silver which contained the Host, placed it on the threshold, knelt, and began to sing. The barbarians were overcome with fear, and tumbled headlong down their scaling-ladders.

Mrs. Jameson says, "The most beautiful picture of St. Clara I have ever seen represents the death of the saint, or, rather, the vision which preceded her death, painted by Murillo.... St. Clara lies on her couch, her heavenly face lighted up with an ecstatic expression. Weeping nuns and friars stand around; she sees them not, her eyes are fixed on the glorious procession which approaches her bed: first, our Saviour, leading his Virgin-mother; they are followed by a company of virgin-martyrs, headed by St. Catharine, all wearing their crowns and bearing their palms, as though they had come to summon her to their paradise of bliss. Nothing can be imagined more beautiful, bright, and elysian than these figures, nor more divine with faith and transport than the head of St. Clara."

These paintings of Murillo were the one topic of conversation in Seville. Orders for pictures came from every side; artists crowded to the convent to study works so unlike their own; the chief families of the city made the hitherto unknown young man a welcome guest at their palaces; fame and position had come when he was only thirty years old.

For one hundred and seventy years these pictures were the pride of the convent, when they were taken by Marshal Soult under Napoleon, and eventually scattered through Northern Europe. The convent was destroyed by fire soon afterwards.

The old adage that "blessings never come singly" was realized in the case of Murillo, for at this time he married a wealthy lady from a family of high renown, Doña Beatriz de Cobrera y Sotomayor, who dwelt at Pilas, about five leagues from Seville. It is said that he first saw her when painting an altar-piece in the Church of San Geronimo at Pilas, and portrayed her as an angel in his picture while he was winning her love.

Their married life seems to have been an eminently happy one. Their home became a centre for artists and the best social circles of the city. Three children were born to them: Gabriel, who went to the West Indies; Francisca, who became a nun; and Gaspar, afterwards a canon of Seville Cathedral.

Murillo's manner of painting changed now from what the Spanish call frio, or his cold style, to cálido, or his warm style, where the outlines were less pronounced, the figures rounder, and the coloring more luminous and tender. "The works of the new manner," says Sweetser, "are notable for graceful and well-arrayed drapery, skilfully disposed lights, harmonious tints, soft contours, and a portrait-like naturalness in the faces, lacking in idealism, but usually pure and pleasing. His flesh-tints were almost uniformly heightened by dark gray backgrounds, and were so amazingly true that one of his critics has said that they seemed to have been painted with blood and milk (con sangre y leche)."

Many of the Madonnas which Murillo painted were evidently from the same sweet, pure-faced model, and it is believed that they are the likeness of his wife. His boys were his models for the infants Jesus and John.

His first work in the so-called warm manner was "Our Lady of the Conception," a colossal picture for the Brotherhood of the True Cross. The monks were at first displeased, thinking that the finishing was not sufficiently delicate; but when Murillo caused it to be hung in the dome, for the high position for which it was intended, they were greatly delighted. Murillo, however, made them pay double the original price for their fault-finding.

"Saints Leander and Isidore," two archbishops of Seville, in the sixth and seventh centuries, who fought the Arian heresy, was his next picture, followed by the "Nativity of the Virgin,"—a much admired work,—a group of women and angels dressing the new-born Mary.

In 1656, for one of the canons of Santa Maria la Blanca, Murillo painted four large semicircular pictures, the "Immaculate Conception," where the Virgin is adored by several saints, "Faith," and two pictures, "The Dream" and "The Fulfilment," to illustrate Our Lady of the Snow, the two latter now in the Academy of San Fernando at Madrid.

According to a fourth-century legend, the Virgin appeared by night to a wealthy Roman senator and his wife, commanding them to build a church in her honor on a certain spot on the Esquiline Hill, which they would find covered with August snow. They went to Pope Liberius, and, after obtaining his blessing, accompanied by a great concourse of priests and people, sought the hill, found the miraculous snow in summer, and gave all their possessions to build the church.

One picture of Murillo represents the senator in a black velvet costume, asleep in his chair, while his wife reposes on the floor, the Madonna and Holy Child above them; the other picture shows them telling their dream to the Pope. Viardot calls these paintings the "miracles of Murillo." These were painted in the last of the three manners of Murillo, the method usually adopted in his Madonnas,—the "vapory" style, "with soft and tender outlines, velvety coloring, and shadows which are only softened lights."

In 1660, Murillo founded an academy of art in Seville, of which he was president for two years. The students were required to abstain from swearing and ill behavior, and to give assent to the following: "Praised be the most Holy Sacrament and the pure conception of our Lady."

Murillo was a most gentle and encouraging teacher. His colored slave, Sebastian Gomez, who had listened to the teaching which he gave to others, finished the head of the Virgin which his master had left on the easel. Murillo exclaimed on seeing it, "I am indeed fortunate, Sebastian; for I have created not only pictures, but a painter!" Many of the works of Gomez, whom Murillo made free, are still preserved and prized in Seville.

During the next ten years, Murillo did much work for the cathedral clergy; eight oval, half-length pictures of saints, Justa, Rufina, Hermengild, Sidon, Leander, Archbishops Laureano and Pius, and King Ferdinand; the "Repose in Egypt;" the infants Christ and John for the Antigua Chapel, and other works.

Saints Justa and Rufina were daughters of a potter, whom they assisted. Some women who worshipped Venus came to the shop to buy vessels for idolatrous sacrifice. The sisters declared that they had nothing to sell for such purposes, as all things should be used in the service of God. The Pagan women were so incensed that they broke all the earthenware in the place. The sisters then broke the image of Venus, and flung it into a kennel. For this act the populace seized them, and took them before the Prefect. Justa expired on the rack, and Rufina was strangled. These two saints have always guarded the beautiful tower Giralda. They are said to have preserved it from destruction in 1504, in a terrific thunder-storm. When Espartero bombarded Seville in 1843, the people believed that Giralda was encompassed by angels led by these sisters, who turned aside the bombs.

Murillo was now fifty-two years old, in the prime of life, famous and honored. He was named by his admiring contemporaries "a better Titian," and it was asserted that even Apelles would have been proud to be called "the Grecian Murillo." He lived in a large and handsome house, still carefully preserved, near the Church of Santa Cruz, not far from the Moorish wall of the city. "The courtyard contains a marble fountain, amidst flowering shrubs, and is surrounded on three sides by an arcade upheld by marble pillars. At the rear is a pretty garden, shaded by cypress and citron trees, and terminated by a wall whereon are the remains of ancient frescos which have been attributed to the master himself. The studio is on the upper floor, and overlooks the Moorish battlements, commanding a beautiful view to the eastward, over orange-groves and rich corn-lands, out to the gray highlands about Alcalá."

Murillo's only sister, Teresa, had married a noble of Burgos, a knight of Santiago, judge of the royal colonial court, a man of great cultivation, and later chief secretary of state at Madrid. The artist was also urged by King Charles II. to enter the royal service at Madrid, especially since a picture of the Immaculate Conception, exhibited during a festival of Corpus Christi, had awakened the greatest enthusiasm among the people. But he loved Seville, and would not leave it. And the Sevillians equally loved the man so generous that he gave all he earned to the poor; so diligent at his work that he had no time for evil speaking; with so much tact and sweetness and vital piety that he left no shadow upon his name.

In 1670, Murillo began his great works for La Caridad, or the Hospital of St. George. The Brotherhood of Holy Charity built a church about 1450, but it had fallen into ruin. In 1661, Don Miguel Manura Vicentelo de Leca determined to restore and beautify the church and its adjacent buildings, and secured over half a million ducats for this purpose. His history was a strange one.

Frances Elliot says of this dissolute man, "Returning at midnight from a revel given by some gallants, in the now ancient quarter of the Macarena, Don Miguel falls in with a funeral procession with torches and banners. Some grandee of high degree, doubtless, there are so many muffled figures, mutes carrying silver horns, the insignia of knighthood borne upon shields, a saddled horse led by a shadowy page, and the dim forms of priests and monks chanting death dirges.

"Don Miguel can recall no death at court or among the nobles, and this is plainly a corpse of quality. Nor can he explain the midnight burial, a thing unknown except in warfare or in time of plague; so, advancing from the dark gateway where he had stood to let the procession pass, he addresses himself to one of the muffled figures, and asks, 'Whose body are they carrying to the Osario at this time of night?'

"'Don Miguel de Mañara,' is the answer; 'a great noble. Will you follow us and pray for his sinful soul?'

"As these words are spoken, the funeral procession seems to pause, and one advances who flings back the wreaths and flowers which shroud the face, and lo! Don Miguel gazes on his own visage.

"Spellbound, he seems to join the ghostly throng which wends its slow way into the Church of Santa Inez, where spectral priests appear to meet it, and carry the bier into the nave, where, next morning, Don Miguel is found, by the nuns coming to matins, insensible upon the stones."

He at once reformed his vicious life, erected a great cloistered hospital, with one of the most beautiful churches in Seville, and endowed it, so that a large company of priests, sisters of charity, physicians, and domestics could be provided for. Don Miguel caused this inscription to be cut on the façade of the hospital: "This house shall stand as long as God shall be feared in it, and Jesus Christ be served in the persons of His poor. Whoever enters here must leave at the door both avarice and pride."

The noble was buried at the church door, so that all who passed in might trample upon his grave. The monumental slab bears the perhaps not inappropriate words, dictated by himself: "To the memory of the greatest sinner that ever lived, Don Miguel de Mañara."

Murillo painted for the new Church of St. George eight pictures for the side walls, and three for the altars, for which he received over seventy-eight thousand reals. The "Annunciation," the "Infant Saviour," and the "Infant St. John" were destined for the side altars; the remaining eight, "Moses striking the Rock," the "Prodigal's Return," "Abraham receiving the Three Angels," the "Charity of San Juan de Dios," the "Miracle of the Loaves and Fishes," "Our Lord healing the Paralytic at the Pool of Bethesda," "St. Peter released from Prison by the Angel," and "St. Elizabeth of Hungary tending the Sick," were intended for the walls. Only three of these eight are left at La Caridad,—"Moses," the "Loaves and Fishes," and "San Juan,"—the rest having been carried to France by Marshal Soult.

Of these three, "San Juan" is considered the "most spirited and powerful." This saint was the founder of the Hospitallers or Brothers of

Charity. Born of very poor parents, at nine years of age he ran away from home with a priest, who deserted him on the road to Madrid, at a little village near Oropesa, in Castile. He hired himself to a shepherd; later he entered the wars between Charles V. and Francis I., and became a brave but profligate soldier. He was about to be hanged for allowing some booty to be carried off, over which he had been placed as sentinel. The rope was already around his neck, when an officer, touched with pity, interfered to save his life, on condition that he should quit the camp.

After various wanderings, he returned to his native town, only to find that both his father and mother had died of grief in consequence of his flight. He nearly lost his reason through remorse, became converted, and began to devote his life to the poor and the sick. To the deserted shed which served for his home, he brought the starving and wretched whom he found in the streets, and worked for them and begged for them. He finally obtained a large building, where, in the winter, he kept a great fire to warm homeless travellers.

"Thus passed ten years of his life," says Mrs. Jameson, "without a thought of himself; and when he died, exhausted in body, but still fervent and energetic in mind, he, unconsciously as it seemed, bequeathed to Christendom one of the noblest of all its religious institutions.

"Under how many different names and forms has the little hospital of Juan de Dios been reproduced throughout Christian Europe, Catholic and Protestant! Our houses of refuge, our asylums for the destitute; the brotherhood of the 'Caridad,' in Spain; that of the 'Misericordia,' in Italy; the 'Maisons de Charité,' in France; the 'Barmherzigen Brüder,' in Germany,—all these sprang out of the little hospital of this poor, low-born, unlearned, half-crazed Juan de Dios! I wonder if those who go to visit the glories of the Alhambra, and dream of the grandeur of the Moors, ever think of him.

"The only representation of this good saint which can rank high as a work of art is a famous picture by Murillo, painted for the Church of the Caridad, at Seville. In a dark, stormy night, Juan is seen staggering—almost sinking—under the weight of a poor dying wretch, whom he is carrying to his hospital. An angel sustains him on his way. The dark form of the burden and the sober gray frock of the bearer are dimly seen in the darkness, through which the glorious countenance of the seraph, and his rich yellow drapery, tell like a burst of sunshine."

Of the five pictures removed by Marshal Soult, the "St. Elizabeth of Hungary," called "El Tiñoso," now in the Madrid Academy, is considered one of Murillo's finest works. It represents her dressed in her royal robes, washing the head of a leprous boy, while around her are beggars and the ladies of her court.

"The St. Elizabeth," says John Hay, in his "Castilian Days," "is a triumph of genius over a most terribly repulsive subject. The wounds

113

and sores of the beggars are painted with unshrinking fidelity, but every vulgar detail is redeemed by the beauty and majesty of the whole. I think in these pictures of Murillo (his Madonnas and others) the last word of Spanish art was reached. There was no further progress possible in life, even for him. 'Other heights in other lives, God willing.'"

Of Murillo's "Marys of the Conception, that fill the room with light and majesty," Colonel Hay beautifully says: "They hang side by side, so alike and yet so distinct in character. One is a woman in knowledge and a goddess in purity; the other, absolute innocence, startled by the stupendous revelation, and exalted by the vaguely comprehended glory of the future. It is before this picture that the visitor always lingers longest. The face is the purest expression of girlish loveliness possible to art. (Supposed to be the face of his daughter, Francesca.) The Virgin floats, up-borne by rosy clouds; flocks of pink cherubs flutter at her feet, waving palm branches. The golden air is thick with suggestions of dim, celestial faces, but nothing mars the imposing solitude of the Queen of Heaven, shrined alone, throned in the luminous azure. Surely no man ever understood or interpreted, like this grand Andalusian, the power that the worship of woman exerts on the religions of the world. All the passionate love that has been poured out in all the ages at the feet of Ashtaroth and Artemis and Aphrodite and Freya found visible form and color at last on that immortal canvas, where, with his fervor of religion, and the full strength of his virile devotion to beauty, he created, for the adoration of those who should follow him, this type of the perfect feminine,—

"'Thee! standing loveliest in the open heaven!
Ave Maria! only heaven and Thee!'"

The story of St. Elizabeth is both touching and beautiful. The daughter of Andreas II., King of Hungary, born in 1207, she was betrothed, in her childhood, to Duke Louis of Thuringia. She early developed the most generous and spiritual character, giving to the poor, praying much, even at midnight, on the bare, cold earth, winning for herself the hatred of a fashionable court and the adoration of her subjects. Various legends are told of her.

"When Elizabeth was ministering to her poor at Eisenach," says Mrs. Jameson, "she found a sick child cast out from among the others because he was a leper, and so loathsome in his misery that none would touch him or even go nigh him; but Elizabeth, moved with compassion, took him in her arms, carried him up the steep ascent to the castle, and, while her attendants fled at the spectacle, and her mother-in-law, Sophia, loaded her with reproaches, she laid the sufferer in her own bed. Her husband was then absent, but shortly afterwards his horn was heard to sound at the gate. Then his mother, Sophia, ran out to meet him, saying, 'My son, come hither! See with whom thy wife shares her bed!' And she led him up to the chamber, telling him what had happened. This time, Louis was filled with impatience and disgust; he rushed to the bed and snatched away the coverlid; but behold! instead of the leper, there lay a radiant infant, with the features of the New-born in Bethlehem; and while they stood amazed, the vision smiled, and vanished from their sight.

"Elizabeth, in the absence of her husband, daily visited the poor, who dwelt in the suburbs of Eisenach and in the huts of the neighboring valleys. One day, during a severe winter, she left her castle with a single attendant, carrying in the skirts of her robe a supply of bread, meat, and eggs for a certain poor family; and, as she was descending the frozen and slippery path, her husband, returning from the chase, met her, bending under the weight of her charitable burden. 'What dost thou here, my Elizabeth?' he said. 'Let us see what thou art carrying away?' and she, confused and blushing to be so discovered, pressed her mantle to her bosom; but he insisted, and, opening her robe, he beheld only red and white roses, more beautiful and fragrant than any that grow on this earth, even at summer-tide; and it was now the depth of winter!

"Then he was about to embrace his wife, but, looking in her face, he was overawed by a supernatural glory, which seemed to emanate from every feature, and he dared not touch her; he bade her go on her way and fulfil her mission; but, taking from her lap one of the roses of Paradise, he put it in his bosom, and continued to ascend the mountain slowly, with his head declined, and pondering these things in his heart.

"In 1226, a terrible famine afflicted all Germany; but the country of Thuringia suffered more than any other. Elizabeth distributed to the poor all the corn in the royal granaries. Every day a certain quantity of bread was baked, and she herself served it out to the people, who thronged around the gates of the castle, sometimes to the number of nine hundred. Uniting prudence with charity, she so arranged that each person had his just share, and so husbanded her resources that they lasted through the summer; and when harvest-time came round again, she sent them into the fields, provided with scythes and sickles, and to every man she gave a shirt and a pair of new shoes. But, as was usual, the famine had been succeeded by a great plague and mortality, and the indefatigable and inexhaustible charity of Elizabeth was again at hand.

"In the city of Eisenach, at the foot of the Wartburg, she founded an hospital of twenty beds, for poor women only; and another, called the Hospital of St. Anne, in which all the sick and poor who presented themselves were received; and Elizabeth herself went from one to the other, ministering to the wretched inmates with a cheerful countenance, although the sights of misery and disease were often so painful and so disgusting that the ladies who attended upon her turned

115

away their heads, and murmured and complained of the task assigned to them.

"She also founded a hospital especially for poor children. It is related by an eye-witness that whenever she appeared among them they gathered round her, crying 'Mutter! Mutter!' clinging to her robe and kissing her hands. She, mother-like, spoke to them tenderly, washed and dressed their ulcerated limbs, and even brought them little toys to amuse them. In these charities, she not only exhausted the treasury, but she sold her own robes and jewels, and pledged the jewels of the state. When the landgrave (her husband) returned, the officers and councillors went out to meet him, and, fearing his displeasure, they began to complain of the manner in which Elizabeth, in their despite, had lavished the public treasures. But Louis would not listen to them; he cut them short, repeating, 'How is my dear wife? how are my children? are they well? Let her give what she will, so long as she leaves me my castles of Eisenach, Wartburg, and Naumburg!' Then he hurried to the gates, and Elizabeth met him with her children, and threw herself into his arms, and kissed him a thousand times, and said to him tenderly, 'See! I have given to the Lord what is his, and he has preserved to us what is thine and mine!'"

Louis was soon after killed in the Crusades, and she and her children were driven out of Thuringia by his brothers, Henry and Conrad. Later, some of her possessions were restored to her. She spun wool to earn more money to give away, and wore ragged clothes that she might help the destitute. She died at twenty-four, singing hymns, her sweet voice murmuring, "Silence!" at the last.

"No sooner had Elizabeth breathed her last breath than the people surrounded her couch, tore away her robe, cut off her hair, even mutilated her remains for relics. She was buried amid miracles and lamentations, and four years after her death she was canonized by Gregory IX"

Murillo's "Abraham receiving the Angels" and "The Prodigal's Return" were purchased of Marshal Soult by the Duke of Sutherland, and are now in Stafford House. "The Healing of the Paralytic" was purchased of Marshal Soult for thirty-two thousand dollars, and is now in the possession of Mr. Tomline of London. The head of the Christ is thought to be Murillo's best representation of our Lord. "The soft violet hue, so dear to Valencian art, of the Saviour's robe, is skilfully opposed to the deep brown of St. Peter's mantle, a rich tint then and still made by Andalusian painters from beef-bones." "The Release of St. Peter" is at the Hermitage, in St. Petersburg.

Before the paintings for La Caridad were finished, Murillo was asked to decorate the new Capuchin church. For three years he worked here, not leaving the convent, it is said, for a single day. Such diligence is most suggestive to those persons who expect to win success without unremitting labor! Of the more than twenty pictures painted here by

116

Murillo, nine formed the retablo of the high altar, and eight were on the side altars. Seventeen of these are now in the Seville Museum.

The immense altar-piece, "The Virgin granting to St. Francis the Jubilee of the Porciuncula," is now in the National Museum of Madrid. This was a feast in honor of the Cavern of St. Francis of Assisi, in which he received a visit from the Virgin and Child. Thirty-three beautiful cherubs are showering the kneeling St. Francis with red and white roses, blossoms from the briers with which he scourged himself. Over the high altar were pictures of "Saints Justa and Rufina," "St. Anthony of Padua," "St. John in the Desert," "St. Joseph," "St. Felix of Cantalicio," the "Veronica," "Saints Leander and Bonaventura," and a gem called "The Madonna of the Napkin."

Murillo had so endeared himself to one of the lay brethren of the convent, a cook, that he begged some token of remembrance from the hand of the great artist. As he had no canvas, Murillo took the napkin which the cook had brought with his food, and, before nightfall, made a most beautiful Virgin, and a Child so natural that it seems, says E. G. Minor, in her life of Murillo, "as if it would spring from its mother's arms. The coloring of this picture, of which innumerable copies and engravings have been made, was never surpassed even by Murillo himself."

St. Veronica was a noble-hearted woman, who, seeing the Saviour pass her door, on his way to Calvary, wiped the perspiration from his brow with her handkerchief or veil. To her surprise and delight, she found an image of the Lord's face upon it. She suffered martyrdom under Nero.

The great pictures on the side altars of the church illustrated "St. Thomas of Villanueva," which the artist himself esteemed the best of all his works; "St. Francis of Assisi, embracing the Crucified Redeemer," "St. Anthony of Padua and the Infant Christ"; the "Vision of St. Felix," the "Annunciation," the "Immaculate Conception," the "Nativity," and the "Virgin with the Head of the Saviour on her Knee."

St. Thomas is represented as at the door of his cathedral, giving alms to beggars. "In the year 1544," says Mrs. Jameson, "Charles V. showed his respect for him by nominating him Archbishop of Valencia. He accepted the dignity with the greatest reluctance. He arrived in Valencia in an old black cassock, and a hat which he had worn for twenty-one years; and as he had never in his life kept anything for himself beyond what was necessary for his daily wants, he was so poor that the canons of his cathedral thought proper to present him with four thousand crowns for his outfit; he thanked them gratefully, and immediately ordered the sum to be carried to the hospital for the sick and poor; and from this time forth we find his life one series of beneficent actions. He began by devoting two-thirds of the revenues of his diocese to purposes of charity.

"He divided those who had a claim on him into six classes: first, the bashful poor who had seen better days, and who were ashamed to beg; secondly, the poor girls whose indigence and misery exposed them to danger and temptation; in the third class were the poor debtors; in the fourth, the poor orphans and foundlings; in the fifth, the sick, the lame, and the infirm; lastly, for the poor strangers and travellers who arrived in the city or passed through it, without knowledge where to lay their heads, he had a great kitchen open at all hours of the day and night, where every one who came was supplied with food, a night's rest, and a small gratuity to assist him on his journey. 'There were few churches or convents on the sunny side of the Sierra Morena without some memorial picture of this holy man,' but the finest beyond all comparison are those of Murillo."

The "St. Francis" represents Christ appearing to the saint in his grotto on Mount Alvernus when he received the stigmata, wounds similar to those of the Saviour in the Crucifixion.

In 1678, Murillo painted for the Hospital de los Venerables, at Seville, an asylum for aged priests, "St. Peter Weeping," the "Virgin and Child enthroned on Clouds," the portrait of his friend Don Justino Neve y Yevenes, and the "Immaculate Conception," now in the Louvre, for which the French government paid, in 1852, at the sale of Marshal Soult's collection, over one hundred and twenty-three thousand dollars. The beautiful Virgin, in her mantle of exquisite blue, over her white robe, floats upward toward the sky, attended by angels, her feet treading upon the crescent, showing her triumph over the other religions of the world. It is a marvel of color and pure saintly expression.

Viardot says: "Murillo comes up, in every respect, to what our imagination could hope or conceive. His earthly daylight is perfectly natural and true; his heavenly day is full of radiance. We find in the attitude of the saints, and the expression of their features, all that the most ardent piety, all that the most passionate exaltation, can feel or express in extreme surprise, delight, and adoration. As for the visions, they appear with all the pomp of a celestial train, in which are marvellously grouped the different spirits of the immortal hierarchy, from the archangel with outspread wings to the bodiless heads of the cherubim. It is in these scenes of supernatural poetry that the pencil of Murillo, like the wand of an enchanter, produces marvels. If in scenes taken from human life, he equals the greatest colorists, he is alone in the imaginary scenes of eternal life. It might be said of the two great Spanish masters, that Velasquez is the painter of the earth, and Murillo of heaven."

His next work was for the Augustinian convent church, the "Madonna appearing to St. Augustine," and "St. Augustine and the little Child on the Seashore," who is trying to fill a hole in the sand with water carried from the ocean in a shell.

About this time, he painted the exquisite "St. John with the

Lamb," now in the National Gallery, for which the government paid ten thousand dollars; "Los Niños de la Concha," the "Children of the Shell," where the Child Jesus holds the shell, filled with water, to the lips of St. John, now in the Prado Museum at Madrid; and "St. Ildefonso receiving the Chasuble from the Virgin," also at Madrid. This saint defended the doctrine of the Immaculate Conception at a time when it had many opponents. In token of her appreciation, the Virgin came to his cathedral, seated herself upon his ivory pulpit, and, with the angels about her, chanted a service from the Psalter. He bowed to the ground, and the Virgin said, "Come hither, most faithful servant of God, and receive this robe, which I have brought thee from the treasury of my Son." He knelt before her, and she threw over him a cassock of heavenly tissue. The ivory chair remained thereafter unoccupied, till the presumptuous Archbishop Sisiberto sat in it, and died a miserable death in consequence.

Besides all this work, Murillo's various "Beggar Boys" are known wherever art is loved; one is in the Louvre, "El Piojoso"; several, in the Pinakothek at Munich; the "Flower-Girl" and a "Boy with a Basket and Dog," at the Hermitage; and others, in London and Madrid. The "Education of the Virgin," Mary kneeling by the side of St. Anna, her mother, the faces portraits, it is believed, of his wife and daughter, is in the Royal Gallery at Madrid. Five large paintings from the life of Jacob, "Isaac blessing Jacob," "Jacob's Dream," "Jacob and Laban's Sheep," "Laban searching for his Gods in the Tent of Rachel," and one other, are in various galleries.

Murillo was now growing old. All the time which he could possibly spare from his work he passed in devotion. He often visited the Church of Santa Cruz, where he spent hours before the altar-piece, "The Descent from the Cross," by Pedro Campaña. When lingering late one night, he was asked by the sacristan why he thus tarried. He replied: "I am waiting till those men have brought the body of our blessed Lord down the ladder."

His last picture, the "Marriage of St. Catharine," was begun in 1680, in the Capuchin Church at Cadiz, when he was sixty-two years of age. He had finished the centre group of the Madonna and Child and St. Catharine, when he fell from the scaffold on which he was climbing to his work, and fatally injured himself. Whether this accident occurred in the chapel at Cadiz, or in his own studio, is not positively known, but he died soon afterward, at Seville, April 3, 1682, in the arms of his friend Canon Neve and his pupil Pedro Nuñez de Villavicencio. His wife was dead, and his daughter had become a nun six years previous, but his second son, Gaspar, stood beside the bed of death.

He was buried with distinguished honors, the bier being carried by two marquises and four knights, and followed by a great concourse of people. At his own request, he was buried beneath his favorite picture, the "Descent from the Cross." His grave was covered with a stone slab on which were carved his name, a skeleton, and the words, "Vive moriturus," "Live as one who is about to die."

During the French occupation, the Church of Santa Cruz was destroyed, and its site is now occupied by the Plaza Santa Cruz. A tablet was placed in the adjacent wall in 1858, stating that Murillo was buried there. A bronze statue of the painter has been erected by the city of Seville, near the Provincial Museum.

More than five hundred of the works of Murillo are scattered through Europe. Self-made, he left a name honored alike for great genius and great beauty of character. Says Emelyn W. Washburn, in "Spanish Masters," "We shall not err when we say that Murillo is the sweetest and richest painter of his day.... He has a glowing fancy, an eye for all beauty of nature and life, and a lofty mind and moral purpose. His magic pencil writes the heart of his saints on the face; none better than he can draw the pure brow of childhood; and, above all, his conceptions suggest a mystery hidden beneath the outward coloring.

"His name recalls Spanish art in the noon of its glory. There is in that series of great and small artists not one who has so won the heart of all time; none depicts so much of that personal beauty which gives life to the past. We approach Zurbaran with somewhat of awe; Velasquez is the grand historical painter. But in Murillo we see the mingling of the two, with a milder grace. In him, we see the sweet singer with the golden harp strung always before him, the man with all the chords of his fine nature touched by the Holy Ghost.

"There is, perhaps, no point where Murillo appears in more winning beauty than in his relations with other painters. He shows the most generous soul, the rarest gentleness, a heart where the struggles of youth have only brought forth the richest fruits. We see the picture of a man too great for little hates. His is a character shaped by the mild spirit of Christ's religion....

"Murillo stands forth as a mind which most faithfully represents Spanish genius, art, religion; who lived a Spaniard of the Spaniards in that brilliant world; who wore the same long cloak and grave dignity as is now met with in the narrow, dirty lanes of Seville; nay, more, who had a living human heart, and who pondered as we now ponder the problems of art and life; who taught a nation and an age."

120

RUBENS

Taine says, in his "Philosophy of Art in the Netherlands": "Rubens is to Titian what Titian was to Raphael, and Raphael was to Phidias. Never did artistic sympathy clasp nature in such an open and universal embrace. Ancient boundaries, already often extended, seem removed purposely to expose an infinite career. He shows no respect for historic proprieties: he groups together allegoric with real figures, and cardinals with a naked Mercury.

"There is no deference to the moral order; he fills the ideal heaven of mythology and of the Gospel with coarse or mischievous characters; a Magdalen resembling a nurse, and a Ceres whispering some pleasant gossip in her neighbor's ear. There is no dread of exciting physical sensibility; he pushes the horrible to extremes, ... all the animal instincts of human nature appear; those which had been excluded as gross he reproduces as true, and in him, as in nature, they encounter the others. Nothing is wanting but the pure and the noble; the whole of human nature is in his grasp, save the loftiest heights. Hence it is that this creativeness is the vastest we have seen, comprehending as it does all types, Italian cardinals, Roman emperors, contemporary citizens, peasants and cowherds, along with the innumerable diversities stamped on humanity by the play of natural forces, and which more than fifteen hundred pictures did not suffice to exhaust.

"For the same reason, in the representation of the body, he comprehended more profoundly than any one the essential characteristic of organic life; he surpasses in this the Venetians as they surpass the Florentines; he feels still better than they that flesh is a changeable substance in a constant state of renewal; and such, more than any other, is the Flemish body, lymphatic, sanguine, and voracious; more fluid, more rapidly tending to accretion and waste than those whose dry fibre and radical temperance preserve permanent tissues.

"Hence it is that nobody has depicted its contrasts in stronger relief, nor as visibly shown the decay and bloom of life; at one time the dull, flabby corpse, a genuine clinical mass, empty of blood and substance; livid, blue, and mottled through suffering, a clot of blood on the mouth, the eye glassy, and the feet and hands clayish, swollen, and deformed because death seized them first; at another, the freshness of living carnations, the handsome, blooming, and smiling athlete, the mellow suppleness of a yielding torso in the form of a well-fed youth, the soft rosy cheeks and placid candor of a girl whose blood was never quickened or eyes bedimmed by thought, flocks of dimpled cherubs and merry cupids, the delicacy, the folds, the exquisite melting rosiness of infantile skin, seemingly the petal of a flower moistened with dew and impregnated with morning light.

"His personages speak; their repose itself is suspended on the verge of action; we feel what they have just accomplished, and what they are about to do. The present with them is impregnated with the past and big with the future; not only the whole face, but the entire attitude conspires to manifest the flowing stream of their thought, feeling, and complete being; we hear the inward utterance of their emotion; we might repeat the words to which they give expression. The most fleeting and most subtle shades of sentiment belong to Rubens; in this respect he is a treasure for novelist and psychologist; he took note of the passing refinements of moral expression as well as of the soft volume of sanguine flesh; no one has gone beyond him in knowledge of the living organism and of the animal man....

"There is only one Rubens in Flanders, as there is only one Shakespeare in England. Great as the others are, they are deficient in some one element of his genius."

This great painter, Peter Paul Rubens, whom Sir Joshua Reynolds called "the best workman with his tools that ever managed a pencil," was born at Siegen, June 29, 1577, on the day commemorating the martyrdom of these saints at Rome, hence the names given to the child. Antwerp and Cologne have claimed his birth, but subsequent historical investigation has shown Siegen as his birthplace. Jans Rubens, the father of Peter, was a distinguished councilman and alderman of Antwerp, having taken his degree of Doctor of Laws at Rome when he was thirty-one. When he was about that age he married Marie Pypelincx, a woman of good family, unusual force of character, and the idol of her son Peter as long as she lived.

Antwerp was now the scene of a desolating war. Charles V., Emperor of Germany and King of Spain, had abdicated, leaving the Netherlands to his son Philip II. Religious dissensions, the presence of Spanish soldiers, and other matters, led to revolts, which the Duke of Alva, with twenty thousand soldiers, was sent to suppress in 1576. Seven thousand of the people of Antwerp were slain, and five hundred houses burned.

Jans Rubens had been accused of Calvinistic tendencies, and thought it prudent to retire to Cologne before the arrival at Antwerp of the Roman Catholic Duke of Alva, placing himself on the side of Prince William of Orange, the Silent, who had married Annie of Saxony. She had quarrelled with her husband, had come to Cologne, and had employed Jans Rubens as one of her counsellors in obtaining her property, which Philip II. had confiscated. Forgetting his high position and his family, Jans Rubens sacrificed his good name and character by his immorality, was arrested and thrown into prison by Count John of Nassau, the brother of Prince William, and Annie was divorced by her husband. By German law Rubens was under the penalty of death. He wrote to his wife, confessing his guilt and imploring her pardon. She determined at once to save his life, if possible. The noble-hearted woman wrote him tenderly—only great souls know how to forgive,—

"How could I push severity to the point of paining you when you are in such affliction that I would give my life to relieve you from it? Even had this misfortune not been preceded by a long affection, ought I to show so much hatred as not to be able to pardon a fault against me?... Be, then, assured that I have entirely forgiven you, and would to Heaven that your deliverance depended on this, for then we should soon be happy again.

"Alas! it is not what your letter announces that affects me. I could scarcely read it. I thought my heart would break. I am so distressed, I hardly know what I write. This sad news so overwhelms me it is with difficulty I can bear it. If there is no more pity in this world, to whom shall I apply? I will implore Heaven with tears and groans, and hope that God will grant my prayer by touching the hearts of these gentlemen, so that they may spare us, may have compassion on us; otherwise, they will kill me as well as you, my soul is so linked to yours that you cannot suffer a pain without my suffering as much as you. I believe that if these good lords saw my tears they would have pity on me, even if they were of stone; and, when all other means fail, I will go to them, although you write me not to do so."

Marie could not reach William the Silent, for he was away in the country, consolidating the Dutch Republic; but she visited in person his mother, and his brother, Count John. All her entreaties availed nothing. It was publicly stated that Jans Rubens had been imprisoned for political treason to Prince William, and must suffer death. Marie was forbidden access to any of William's family, and for two years was not allowed to enter the dungeon where her husband was confined.

At length she declared that the whole truth should be told, and Annie of Saxony be forever disgraced. This threat moved the proud Orange family, and procured the release of Jans Rubens, under bonds of six thousand thalers, that he would never go outside the little town of Siegen. Here he lived for some years, broken in health by his prison life, and under the strict surveillance of Count John. Finally, Marie obtained permission for them to reside in Cologne, where he died in 1587, when his boy Peter was ten years of age.

The next year Marie Rubens returned to their old home at Antwerp, and by her good sense and persistence recovered the estates of her husband, which had been confiscated during the wars, thus placing her family in very comfortable circumstances. Peter entered a Jesuits' college, where he showed great aptitude for languages. In childhood he had been taught Latin by his father, and French by a tutor. Later, he learned Italian, Spanish, German, and English, besides, of course, speaking his native Flemish. His mother had destined him for the law, but it was distasteful to him.

At the age of thirteen, as was often the custom, the frank and handsome boy was made a page in the household of his godmother, the Countess Lalaing, but he took no pleasure in mere fashionable surroundings, and begged his mother that he might become an artist.

This choice did not attract the mother, whose ambitions and hopes centred largely in her enthusiastic Peter, but she had the wisdom to lead rather than to dictate. Parents who break the wills of their children usually have spoiled children as the result.

She placed her boy with Tobias Verhaeght, a landscape painter, from whom the lad learned that close study of nature which made him thereafter a reader of her secrets. Conrad Busken Huet says, in his "Land of Rubens": "Man and nature as the Creator made them were quite sufficient for Rubens's inspiration, no matter where he found them, far from home or close to it. What attracted him most in nature was the unchangeable, the imperishable, and the grand. He knew how to find these everywhere. Artists less gifted and born by the seashore have before now felt the want of sniffing the mountain breeze. Did their cradle stand among the meadows, they longed for running streams and rivers. Rubens's pictures prove that such contrasts had no value for him.

"Within the narrow limits of his native soil, he found every condition necessary to the practice of his art. His imagination had no need of anything more stirring than that presented to him by the recollection of human vicissitudes amidst glebe and glade. The twinkling of the eye sufficed to transform them into battlefields in his productions....

"When the sun shines, he shines everywhere. Such is Rubens's motto. He knows but one moon, but one starry vault, but one gloaming, but one morning dew. Every raindrop on which there falls a ray of light reminds him of a diamond. Each stubble-field whence uprises the lark supplies music to his ears. Each swan to which he flings bread-crumbs on his arrival at 'Steen' (his country home) teaches him to keep the most sublime song of his art for the end."

"It is curious to note that Rubens," says Charles W. Kett, in his "Life of Rubens," "who began with scenes of country life, returned in his last days to his first love, so that when he could no longer cover his huge canvases with heroic figures, he would retire to his château at Steen, and paint landscapes, even though the gout almost incapacitated him from holding his brushes."

After about ten years spent with Verhaeght, young Rubens, thinking that he would devote himself to historical subjects, became a pupil of Adam van Noort, a teacher skilled in drawing, and in the use of brilliant color, with study of light and shade. He is said to have been intemperate and quick-tempered, but for four years Rubens found him a useful teacher.

"It is related," says George H. Calvert, "that one day, when the master was absent, the pupil took a fresh canvas to try what he could do by himself towards representing a weeping Madonna. He worked for hours, and so intently that he did not hear the returning footsteps of the master, who from behind gazed in admiration and wonder at his performance."

The young painter was restless, not an unnatural condition for an ardent, ambitious boy or girl. Such a life, fruitful for good or evil, must be filled with the best activities.

When Rubens was nineteen, he entered the studio of Otto Venius, a kind and learned man, of courtly manners, a free-master of the Guild of St. Luke, and court painter to Archduke Albert of Austria and the Infanta Isabella of Spain. She was the daughter of Philip II., to whom he had ceded the "Spanish Netherlands." They were distinguished patrons of art, and did everything to restore the war-worn country to peace and prosperity. Venius became deeply attached to his pupil, made him acquainted with the Regents Albert and Isabella, and inspired him to go to Italy to study art, the country in which he had studied for seven years.

Rubens had already painted some admirable works: the "Adoration of the Three Kings," a "Holy Trinity," a "Dead Christ in the Arms of the Father," and a portrait of Marie Pypelincx, "the true-hearted wife," says Mr. Kett, "of the faithless Jans, the mother of the artist, the upholder of the family after the death of the father, the educator of his children, and the restorer of the fallen greatness of the name of Rubens. Calmly and beautifully does the pale face still look forth from the canvas as of old. She must have smiled with satisfaction on the rising fame of her youngest surviving son, now going forth into the world to have those talents acknowledged which her maternal heart was assured were in his keeping. Carefully attired, like a matron of good family, in velvet dress, mourning coif, and muslin cuffs, denoting her widowed state, she carries in her face the traits of a shrewd woman of the world, who has battled bravely with the times, and now sees victory crowning her endeavors.

"Her very chair, somewhat similar to the one still preserved in the Academy at Antwerp as the gift of her son, speaks of a home of comfort; her book, held in her still handsome hand, a forefinger marking the page she has not finished reading, tells of a certain amount of learned leisure; and her whole surroundings recall a home whence an artist, a man of culture, and a courteous gentleman might derive those early impressions and first inspirations which would develop, when he came in contact with a larger world, into masterpieces of art."

On May 8, 1600, Rubens, at twenty-three years of age, having said good-by to his fond mother, started for Italy. His first visit was to Venice, where he studied the wonderful colorists, Titian, Paul Veronese, and Tintoretto. He is said to have copied twenty portraits by

Titian, so earnest was he in obtaining the secret of these marvellous tints.

While here he became the friend of a Mantuan, an officer at the court of Vincenzo de Gonzaga, Duke of Mantua. This duke was thirty-seven years old, rich, handsome, somewhat of a poet, the patron of artists and authors, a brilliant and extravagant ruler. Through this friend, and also by letters of introduction from Archduke Albert, Rubens met Gonzaga, who was surprised at the learning of the attractive and distinguished-appearing young artist. Hearing him repeat a passage from Virgil, Gonzaga addressed him in Latin, and was answered in the same language, fluently and correctly. The duke had made a fine collection of paintings and antiques, and these Rubens was glad to study. A most fortunate thing resulted from this acquaintance; Rubens was appointed painter to the court and a member of the ducal household.

This was not the result merely of fortuitous circumstances. Rubens had been a student. He was called later by scholars, "the antiquary and Apelles of our time." He was also a most industrious worker. Philip Rubens, his nephew, says in his life of his uncle, "He never gave himself the pastime of going to parties where there was drinking and card-playing, having always had a dislike for such." So fond was he of reading the best books, that in after years, when he painted, Seneca and Plutarch were often read to him. He had studied the technique of painting since he was thirteen years old. He was especially charming in manner, being free from harshness or censoriousness, and, withal, a person of much tact and consideration. He had prepared himself for a great work, and was ready to embrace his opportunity when it came.

Besides painting several originals for the Duke of Mantua, Rubens was sent to Rome to make copies of some of the masterpieces. He took letters of introduction to Cardinal Alessandro Montalto, the nephew of Sixtus V., very rich, and a great patron of art.

Besides this work for Gonzaga, Rubens painted for the chapel of St. Helena, in the Church of the Holy Cross of Jerusalem, at Rome, at the request of Archduke Albert, formerly its cardinal, three pictures: "St. Helena embracing the Cross," "Christ crowned with Thorns," and a "Crucifixion."

On his return to Mantua, he copied the "Triumph of Julius Cæsar," by Andrea Mantegna; in one of the series, in place of a sheep walking by the side of an elephant, he painted a lion. Dr. Waagen says in his "Life of Rubens": "His love of the fantastic and pompous led him to choose that with the elephant carrying the candelabra, but his ardent imagination, ever directed to the dramatic, could not be content with this; instead of a harmless sheep, which in Mantegna is walking by the side of the foremost elephant, Rubens has introduced a lion and lioness, which growl angrily at the elephant. The latter, on his part, is

126

not idle, but, looking furiously round, is on the point of striking the lion a blow with his trunk. The severe pattern he had before him in Mantegna has moderated Rubens in his taste for very full forms, so that they are here more noble and slender than is usual with him. The coloring, as in his earliest pictures, is more subdued than in the later, and yet more powerful. Rubens himself seems to have set a high value upon this study, for it was among his effects at his death."

In 1603, Rubens was sent by the Duke of Mantua on a pleasant mission to Spain, with costly presents to Philip III., the indolent son of Philip II., and his powerful favorite, the Duke of Lerma. For the king there was a "gorgeous coach and seven beautiful horses, twelve arquebuses, six of whalebone and six variegated, and a vase of rock crystal filled with perfumes." For the Duke of Lerma, "a number of pictures, a silver vase of large dimensions inwrought with colors, and two vases of gold. For the Countess of Lerma, a cross and two candelabra of rich crystal. For the secretary, Pedro Franqueza, two vases of rock crystal, and a complete set of damask hangings, the edges of gold tissue."

After a long journey, with continuous rain for twenty-five days, Rubens and his gifts reached Valladolid. When the paintings were unpacked, they were nearly ruined, from the colors having peeled off. At the request of Iberti, resident at the Court of Madrid from Mantua, Rubens undertook the work of restoration, and, better still, painted two originals for the Duke of Lerma, a "Democritus," and a "Heraclitus," both life-size, now in the gallery of Madrid. He also painted an equestrian likeness of the duke himself, several ladies of the court, for the gallery of beauties possessed by Gonzaga, and probably many other pictures on this first visit, as more than one hundred and twenty of Rubens's paintings are known to have existed in Spain. On his return to Italy he was loaded with gifts from the King of Spain and grandees, so much were his works esteemed and so greatly was the young Fleming admired. Once more in Italy, Rubens painted an altar-piece for the Church of the Holy Trinity at Mantua, in which the mother of the duke was buried; three pictures, the "Baptism of our Saviour," the "Mystery of the Transfiguration," and a central picture, the "Mystery of the Trinity," which latter contained portraits of Duke Vincenzo, his Duchess Leonora, his parents, and his children. When the French took Mantua in 1797, this church was used as a storehouse for food for the horses. A French commissary cut this picture in pieces, the better to carry it, and, when about to send it to France, was prevented by the Academy of Mantua. Some of the pieces have disappeared.

Rubens also painted, for the Church of Santa Maria in Valicella, Rome, an altar-piece, representing the "Madonna and Child," with side pictures of the pope and several saints. In co-operation with his brother Philip, he published, in 1608, a book on Roman antiquities, with six copper-plate illustrations. The pope was so pleased with Rubens that he desired to keep him in Rome permanently.

For the Grand Duke Ferdinand I. of Florence, Rubens painted several pictures, among them a "Hercules between Venus and Minerva." In Spain he executed a series called "The Labors of Hercules," besides three separate ones, representing the slaying of the dragon, the struggle with Antæus, and the combat with a lion. He also copied the celebrated cartoon of Leonardo da Vinci, called "The Battle of the Standard," and made a valuable portrait of himself for the Grand Ducal collection of self-painted heads of artists. At Genoa he made drawings of her remarkable palaces and churches, which he published later in a volume with one hundred and thirty-nine illustrations.

After an absence of eight years in Italy, Rubens was recalled to Antwerp by the illness of his mother. He started homeward October 28, 1608, with a heavy heart. On his way he learned that she had died nine days before he began his long journey.

On reaching Antwerp, he shut himself up for four months in the Abbey of St. Michael's, where she had been buried. He had given her no ordinary affection, and his was no ordinary loss. He met this loss in the silence of his own thoughts in the abbey, and when he had gained the self-control necessary for his work, he came out into the world. Most of us learn to bear our sorrows in our own hearts, without laying our burdens upon others, finding, sooner or later, that the world has enough of its own.

He talked of returning to Italy, but Archduke Albert and Isabella, proud of his genius and his attainments, invited him to court, sat for their portraits, and made him their official painter. One of his first works for them was a "Holy Family," which was so much admired that the Society of St. Ildefonso of Brussels, Archduke Albert being its head, ordered an altar-piece for the Chapel of the order of St. James. "This picture," says Dr. Waagen, "which is at present in the Imperial gallery at Vienna, represents the Virgin Mary enthroned, and putting the cloak of the order on the shoulders of St. Ildefonso. She is surrounded by four female saints. On the interior of the wings are the portraits of Albert and Isabella, with their patron saints. This work, one of the most admirable ever painted by Rubens, displays in a remarkable degree the qualities praised in the one painted for the Archduke."

The association were so pleased that they offered the artist a purse of gold, which, having been made a member, he would not receive, saying that his only desire was to be useful to his brother members.

Lonely from the death of his mother, a new affection came into his heart to sustain and console him. Philip, his brother, now secretary of Antwerp, had taken as his wife Maria de Moy, whose sister, Clara, much older, had married a former secretary of Antwerp, Jan Brandt. Their daughter, Isabella Brandt, was a young woman of attractive face and sweet disposition. Peter naturally met the niece of his brother Philip's wife, loved her, and married her October 13, 1609, in the Abbey Church of St. Michael, when he was thirty-two.

He soon built a house, costing sixty thousand florins, in the Italian style of architecture, with a spacious studio, and a separate building or rotunda, like the Pantheon at Rome, lighted from the top, where he arranged the pictures, marbles, vases, and gems which he had collected in Italy. Adjoining this he laid out a large garden, planted with flowers and choice trees.

"The celebrated picture of Rubens and his first wife," says Mr. Kett, "now in the Pinakothek at Munich, must have been painted within the first few years of their married life, and is a striking example of the painter's manner at this period. His calm serenity and thoughtful expression, combined with beauty and force of character, are well balanced by the placid contentment and happy dignity of his wife, as the pair sit under their own vine and fig-tree, prepared to receive their visitors. There is no affected demonstration of feeling, no bashful restraint. A couple well-to-do and able to enjoy themselves are happy to share their pleasure with others."

In 1611, Rubens met with a severe loss in the death of his greatly beloved brother, Philip. All the seven children of Jans Rubens and Maria Pypelincx were now dead save Peter Paul.

In 1614, Rubens's heart was made glad by the birth of a son, to whom Archduke Albert became godfather, and gave him his own name. Four years later his only other child by Isabella Brandt was born, both of whom survived their father. A beautiful painting of these two children is now in the Liechtenstein Gallery, in Vienna.

The rich and famous painter was now happy, surrounded by his loved ones, busy constantly with his work, which poured in upon him. In summer he rose at four o'clock, heard mass, and went to work early. Says Dr. Waagen, "This was the time when he generally received his visitors, with whom he entered willingly into conversation on a variety of topics, in the most animated and agreeable manner. An hour before dinner he always devoted to recreation, which consisted either in allowing his thoughts to dwell as they listed on subjects connected with science or politics, which latter interested him deeply, or in contemplating his treasures of art. From anxiety not to impair the brilliant play of his fancy, he indulged but sparingly in the pleasures of the table, and drank but little wine. After working again till the evening, he usually, if not prevented by business, mounted a spirited Andalusian horse, and rode for an hour or two.

"This was his favorite exercise; he was extremely fond of horses, and his stables generally contained some of remarkable beauty. On his return home, it was his custom to receive a few friends, principally men of learning or artists, with whom he shared his frugal meal, and afterwards passed the evening in instructive and cheerful conversation.

This active and regular mode of life could alone have enabled Rubens to satisfy all the demands that were made upon him as an artist, and the astonishing number of works that he completed, the genuineness of which is beyond all doubt, can only be accounted for by this union of extraordinary diligence with his unusually fertile powers of production."

In building his home, Rubens encroached a little on land owned by the Company of Arquebusiers of Antwerp. A lawsuit was threatened, but finally a compromise was effected whereby Rubens agreed to paint a triptych, that is, a picture in three parts, of their patron St. Christopher, to be hung in the cathedral. In fulfilment of this contract, he painted the renowned "Descent from the Cross," now in the south end of the transept of the cathedral, with St. Simon on one wing of the triptych, and "The Visitation" on the other, with St. Christopher in person.

Says Huet: "Playing upon the name of a patron saint, he has represented a threefold 'bearing of Christ'; Christ borne from the Cross in the centre; Christ borne by old Simon on the right; Christ borne "neath his mother's heart' on the left wing.... There is no need to insist as to how Rubens acquitted himself of his task in the centre piece. Da Vinci's 'Last Supper' and Rubens's 'Descent from the Cross' are the two most popular altarpieces of Christianity, admired alike by Protestant and Catholic. For the history of Flemish art this 'Descent' possesses as much value as does Goethe's 'Faust' for the history of German literature. No one has succeeded in painting subsequent to Rubens a 'Descent from the Cross' without paying toll to the master.... It is the triumph of human sympathy expressed in accordance with the theory of line and color. The painter had no other aim than to limn a perfect group of loving people, occupied in taking down the body of Christ. He does not portray your sorrow, but theirs. What he tenders us is sentiment, not sentimentality; emotion, not intellect. The allusion to St. Christopher must be disinterred from encyclopædias; the recollection of John in his red cloak, carrying his burden, of the fair-haired Mary Magdalen, of the disciple with the winding-sheet betwixt his teeth, has become immortal.

"The lovely mother-virgin of the left-hand side leaf deserves particular attention.... I know of no more fascinating female figure from Rubens's brush; none which in its Flemish guise is so original, so wholly his. The 'Descent from the Cross' itself one might still believe to be the work of one of the great Italians. No such mistake is possible with the side leaf. What excites our wonder in Goethe is his succeeding in raising a Leipzig girl of the lower classes to the rank of a tragic heroine, the very mention of whose name suffices to remind us of an imperishable type. Rubens's pregnant Mary is an honorable Gretchen. He created her out of the most hidden depths of human nature, where blood and soul, mind and matter, melt into one. When Jordaens wishes to paint fertility, he resorts to the allegory of the schools. To Rubens life itself is the best of all allegories. Mary's clinging for support to the railing of the staircase, as she ascends it, is a hymn in honor of maternity. In the course of ages pictorial art has produced many beautiful works, none more beautiful than that scene."

About this time Rubens painted some of his greatest works. "Our Saviour giving the Keys to St. Peter" was originally placed in the Cathedral of St. Gudule; it was sold in 1824 to the Prince of Orange, for one hundred and twenty-five thousand dollars. An "Elevation of the Cross," an immense picture, executed for the Church of St. Walburg, at Antwerp, is now in the north transept of the cathedral. He painted an "Adoration of the Magi" for the choir of the Abbey Church of St. Michael, dear to him from the burial of his mother and his own marriage, and a similar picture for the Church of St. John at Malines.

Of an "Adoration of the Magi" in the Museum at Antwerp, Eugène Fromentin says: "It is truly a tour de force, especially if one recalls the rapidity of this work of improvisation. Not a gap, not a strain; a vast, clear half-tint and lights without excess envelop all the figures, supporting one the other; all the colors are visible and multiply values the most rare, the least sought and yet the most fit, the most subtle and yet the most distinct. By the side of types that are very ugly swarm superior types. With his square face, his thick lips, his reddish skin, big eyes strongly lighted up, and his stout body girt in green pelisse with sleeves of peacock blue, this African among the Magi is a figure entirely new, before which, assuredly, Tintoretto, Titian, Veronese would have clapped their hands.

"On the left stand in dignified solemnity two colossal cavaliers of a singular Anglo-Flemish style, the most extraordinary piece of color in the picture, with its dull harmony of black, greenish blue, of brown and white. Add the profile of the Nubian camel-drivers, the supernumeraries, men in helmets, negroes, the whole in the most ample, the most transparent, the most natural of atmospheres. Spider-webs float in the framework, and quite low down the head of the ox,—a sketch achieved by a few strokes of the brush in bitumen,—without more importance and not otherwise executed than would be a hasty signature. The Child is delicious; to be cited as one of the most beautiful among the purely picturesque compositions of Rubens, the last word of his knowledge as to color, of his skill as to technique, when his sight was clear and instantaneous, his hand rapid and careful, and when he was not too exacting, the triumph of rapture and science—in a word, of self-confidence."

Rubens had courage. He used to say: "Every one according to his gift; my talent is such that never yet has an undertaking, however extraordinary in size or diversity of subjects, daunted my courage."

The "Assumption of the Virgin" in the Antwerp Cathedral, Dr. Waagen says, "may be said to produce the same effect as a symphony, in which the united sounds of all the instruments blend together joyously, divinely, mightily. No other painter has ever known how to produce such a full and satisfactory tone of light, such a deep chiaroscuro united with such general brilliancy."

"St. Theresa pleading for the Souls in Purgatory," "St. Anne instructing the Virgin," and the "Dead Saviour laid on a Stone," are now at Antwerp. Five of the above pictures and three others, "Christ on the Cross," "The Resurrection of our Saviour," and "The Adoration of the Shepherds," were painted in eighteen days, Rubens receiving as compensation fifty dollars per day, his usual price.

For a magnificent church built by the Jesuits, Rubens painted two works for the high altar, pictures for two other altars, and thirty-nine ceilings with Bible scenes, including the "Assumption" and "Coronation of the Virgin," the "Translation of Elijah," and the "Archangel Michael triumphing over the Serpent." These works with the church were all destroyed by fire, caused by lightning, in 1718.

With all this prosperity it was not strange that envy and jealousy should now and then confront Rubens. One of his rivals invited him to paint a picture on some chosen subject, and allow umpires to decide which was the better work. Rubens replied to the challenge: "My attempts have been subjected to the scrutiny of connoisseurs in Italy and Spain. They are to be found in public collections and private galleries in those countries; gentlemen are at liberty to place their works beside them, in order that the comparison be made."

The great artist used to say, "Do well, and people will be jealous of you; do better, and you confound them."

He employed several pupils to help him constantly. He would make sketches and superintend the work, adding the finishing touches. Having been asked to paint for the Cathedral of Malines a "Last Supper," Rubens made the drawing and sent it to one of his pupils, Juste van Egmont, to lay on the ground color. The canon of the cathedral said to Van Egmont, "Why did your master not come himself?" "Don't be uneasy," was the reply. "He will, as is his custom, finish the picture."

Egmont went on with the work, when finally the canon, in a rage, ordered him to stop, while he wrote to Rubens: "'Twas a picture by your own hand I ordered, not an attempt by an apprentice. Come, then, and handle the brush yourself: or recall your Juste van Egmont, and tell him to take with him his sketch; my intention being not to accept it, you can keep it for yourself."

Rubens wrote back: "I proceed always in this way; after having made the drawing, I let my pupils begin the picture, finish even, according to my principles; then I retouch it, and give it my stamp. I shall go to Malines in a few days; your dissatisfaction will cease." Rubens came, and the canon was satisfied.

Mr. Kett says: "Rubens's method of painting was his own. Some of his fellow-countrymen, who were jealous of him, said he did not use paints, but colored varnishes, and that his pictures would not last; of the latter point we are the better judges. He used light grounds, almost, if not quite white; his outlines were drawn with a brush in color (often red for the flesh), and very transparent glazes were laid over all the shadows, the lights being sometimes, not always, painted thicker. He exposed his pictures to the sun for short spaces of time, between the paintings, to dry out the oil. They received several coats of color, and then, finally, he put in the stronger touches himself, the light ones now thick. All his works, however, do not seem to have been done in this way, but many have solid painting from the first."

Rubens had become both rich and famous. When an alchemist visited him, urging that he furnish a laboratory and apparatus for the process of transmutation of metals, and share the profits, the painter replied: "You have come twenty years too late; I found out the secret long ago;" and then, pointing to his palette and brushes, he added, "Everything I touch with these turns to gold."

A new honor was now conferred upon Rubens. Marie de' Medici, the sister of the Duchess Leonora of Mantua, wished to adorn her palace of the Luxembourg, in Paris, with great magnificence. Henry, Baron Vicq, the ambassador of the Archduke Albert and Isabella, spoke to Queen Marie of Rubens. She must have known of his work, also, when he was the court painter of Mantua. He was summoned to Paris, and took the order for twenty-two immense pictures, illustrative of her life. These are now in the Louvre, full of vigor, brilliant in imagery, and rich in color.

In the first picture the three Fates spin the fortunes of Marie de' Medici; the second represents her birth at Florence, in 1575, Lucina, the goddess of births, being present with her torch, while Florentia, the goddess of the city, holds the new-born infant; the third, her education, conducted by Minerva, Apollo, and Mercury; fourth, Love shows the princess the portrait of Henry IV., whom she married in 1600, after he had been divorced from Margaret of Valois, in the preceding year; above are Jupiter and Juno; beside the king appears Gallia; fifth shows the nuptials; the Grand Duke Ferdinand of Tuscany acts as proxy for his niece's husband; sixth, the queen lands at Marseilles; seventh, the wedding festival, at Lyons, with Henry IV. as Jupiter, and Marie as Juno; eighth, the birth of Louis XIII., in 1601, with Fortuna behind the queen; ninth, Henry IV. starting on his campaign against Germany, in 1610, when he makes the queen regent; tenth, coronation of the queen at St. Denis; eleventh, apotheosis of Henry IV., who was stabbed by Ravaillac, it is said, not against the queen's wishes, who, nevertheless, in the picture is enthroned in mourning robes between Minerva and Wisdom; twelfth, regency of the queen under the protection of Olympus; Mars, Apollo, and Minerva drive away the hostile powers, while Juno and Jupiter cause the chariot of France to be drawn by

133

gentle doves; thirteenth, the queen in the field during the civil war in France; fourteenth, treaty between France and Spain; fifteenth, prosperity during the regency, the queen bearing the scales of justice with Minerva, Fortuna, and Abundantia on the right, Gallia and Time on the left, while below are Envy, Hatred, and Stupidity; sixteenth, the queen commits the rudder of the Ship of State, rowed by the Virtues, to Louis XIII., who certainly must have deserted these virtues early in his career; seventeenth, flight of the queen, in 1619, to Blois, where the wily Cardinal Richelieu joined her as a pretended friend; eighteenth, Mercury presents himself to the queen as a messenger of peace; nineteenth, the queen is conducted into the temple of peace; twentieth, Marie and Louis XIII. on Olympus, with the dragon of rebellion below them; twenty-first, the king giving his mother a chaplet of peace; twenty-second, portrait of Marie; followed by portraits of her parents, Grand Duke Francis and Johanna, Grand Duchess of Tuscany.

Fortunately, Rubens could not paint the sad future of Marie de' Medici. She died in a poor apartment at Cologne, deserted by her family. The queen was delighted with Rubens's pictures, taking lessons of him in drawing, and often conversing with him while he made the sketches, the painting being done by himself and his pupils in his studio at Antwerp, in about two years and a half.

The queen had intended to adorn another gallery at the Luxembourg with the life of Henry IV., but the project was abandoned in consequence of the quarrel between Marie and Cardinal Richelieu.

Rubens painted other pictures while at work on the Medici allegory: "Susannah and the Elders," "Lot's Daughters," a beautiful "Virgin and Child" for Baron de Vicq, who had recommended him to Marie de' Medici, and several other works.

In his "Kermess" now in the Louvre, a peasant festival in Flanders, "in front of a village inn about fourscore persons of both sexes are depicted, intermingled in varieties of groups, in the full swing of boisterous enjoyment after a better meal than peasants are used to, singing, dancing, talking, shouting, gambolling, love-making. A large, serious dog tries to get his share by prying into a pail half filled with empty platters. An abounding scene of rustic revelry, in the groups and individuals a character and expression which only warm genius animating rich intellectual resources could give."

Rubens delighted in painting animals. "It is related," says Calvert, "that he caused to be brought to his house a very fine and powerful lion that he might study him in his various attitudes. But what he had still greater delight in painting than animals was children. Here, too, as with animals, and in a higher form, he had what a healthy, juicy mind like his revelled in, nature unsophisticated. It may have been in front of one of his canvases glowing with the luminous rosiness of half a dozen of these happy soul-buds that Guido exclaimed, 'Does Rubens mix blood with his paint?' The mobility of children, their naturalness, their unveiled life and innocence, humanity in its heavenly promise, laughing incarnations of hope, all appealed to his liveliest sympathies, as to his artistic preferences."

He was skilled, also, in portraits. Mr. Kett says the picture of his mother, in the Dulwich Gallery, the "Spanish Hat," in the National Gallery, and the portrait called "General Velasquez" "are three that could scarcely be excelled by any master of any time."

Dr. Waagen says of "Le Chapeau de Poil" ("The Spanish Hat"), "No picture justifies more than this the appellation which Rubens has obtained of 'The Painter of Light.' No one who has not beheld this masterpiece of painting can form any conception of the transparency and brilliancy with which the local coloring in the features and complexion, though under the shadow of a broad-brimmed Spanish beaver hat, are brought out and made to tell, while the different parts are rounded and relieved with the finest knowledge and use of reflected lights. The expression of those youthful features, beaming with cheerfulness, is so full of life, and has such a perfect charm, that one is inclined to believe the tradition that Rubens fell in love with the original (a young girl of the Lunden family, at Antwerp) whilst she was sitting to him."

Mrs. Jameson says, "The picture as a picture is miraculous, all but life itself.... Rubens, during his life, would never part with this picture.... After the death of his widow, it passed into the possession of the Lunden family, whose heir, M. Van Havre, sold it in 1817, for sixty thousand francs, to another descendant of the family, M. Stier d'Artselaer. At his death, in 1822, it was sold by auction and purchased by M. Niewenhuys for seventy-five thousand francs, and brought to England, where, after being offered in vain to George IV., it was bought by Sir Robert Peel for three thousand five hundred guineas...."

"To venture to judge Rubens, we ought to have seen many of his pictures. His defects may be acknowledged once for all. They are in all senses gross, open, palpable; his florid color, dazzling and garish in its indiscriminate excess; his exaggerated, redundant forms; his coarse allegories; his historical improprieties; his vulgar and prosaic versions of the loftiest and most delicate creations of poetry; let all these be granted, but this man painted that sublime history (a series of six pictures), almost faultless in conception and in costume, the 'Decius' in the Liechtenstein Gallery. This man, who has been called unpoetical, and who was a born poet, if ever there was one, conceived that magnificent epic, the 'Battle of the Amazons;' that divine lyric, the 'Virgin Mary' trampling sin and the dragon, in the Munich Gallery, which might be styled a Pindaric Ode in honor of the Virgin, only painted instead of sung; and those tenderest moral poems, the 'St. Theresa' pleading for the souls in Purgatory, and the little sketch of 'War,' where a woman sits desolate on the black, wide heath, with dead bodies and implements of war heaped in shadowy masses around her, while, just seen against the lurid streak of light left by the setting sun, the battle rages in the far distance....

"Though thus dramatic in the strongest sense, yet he is so without approaching the verge of what we call theatrical. With all his flaunting luxuriance of color, and occasional exaggeration in form, we cannot apply that word to him. Le Bran is theatrical; Rubens, never. His sins are those of excess of daring and power; but he is ever the reverse of the flimsy, the artificial, or the superficial. His gay magnificence and sumptuous fancy are always accompanied by a certain impress and assurance of power and grandeur, which often reaches the sublime, even when it stops short of the ideal."

A few months after the paintings were finished for Marie de' Medici, a great sorrow came to the Rubens mansion. Isabella Brandt, his wife, died in the middle of the year 1626, leaving two sons, Albert and Nicholas, twelve and eight years of age. She was buried with much display in the Abbey Church of St. Michael, where she had been married,—in the same tomb with his mother and his brother Philip, and her husband dedicated a beautiful "Virgin and Child" to her memory. He wrote to a friend, sadly, in regard to her whom he had lost, as one "not having any of the vices of her sex. She was without bad temper or feminine frivolity, but was in every way good and honorable—in life loved on account of her virtues, and since her death universally bewailed by all. Such a loss seems to me worthy of sympathy, and because the true remedy for all evils is forgetfulness, the daughter of time, one must without doubt hope for relief; but I find the separation of grief for the departed from the memory of a person whom I ought to revere and honor whilst I live, to be very difficult."

Partly to distract his mind from his grief, and partly to assist his own country, to which he was devotedly attached, to keep peace with the powers at war, which made Belgium their battle-ground, at the request of the Infanta Isabella he visited Holland on a diplomatic mission, and, a little later, Spain and England. The King of Spain had already ennobled Rubens. "Regard being had to the great renown which he has merited and acquired by excellence in the art of painting, and rare experience in the same, as also by the knowledge which he has of histories and languages, and other fine qualities and parts which he possesses, and which render him worthy of our royal favor, we have granted and do grant to the said Peter Paul Rubens and his children and posterity, male and female, the said title and degree of nobility." In consequence of this, Isabella had made him "gentleman of her household."

In this his second visit to Spain, he is said to have painted forty pictures in nine months. Rubens and Velasquez became intimate friends, although the former was fifty-one, and the latter twenty-eight.

A little later he was sent by Philip IV. of Spain, who had appointed Rubens secretary to his privy council, on a mission to

England. Here he was discovered by a courtier, one morning, busy at his painting. "Ho!" said the courtier, "does his Most Catholic Majesty's representative amuse himself with painting?"

"No," answered Rubens, "the artist sometimes amuses himself with diplomacy."

Rubens painted for King Charles I., "Diana and her Nymphs surprised by Satyrs," and "Peace and Plenty," which latter, after remaining in Italy for a century, was finally bought by the Marquis of Stafford, for fifteen thousand dollars, and by him presented to the National Gallery. Rubens also made nine sketches for pictures ordered by the king to decorate the ceiling of the throne-room of Whitehall, illustrating the deeds of James I. These cost fifteen thousand dollars.

King Charles knighted the famous painter, and after the ceremony presented him with the sword, a handsome service of plate, a diamond ring, and a rich chain to which was attached a miniature of the king; this he ever afterwards wore round his neck.

At Cambridge University he was received by Lord Holland, the Chancellor, and admitted to the honorary degree of Master of Arts.

As a diplomatist, M. Villoamil says, "Rubens had great tact, was prudent, active, forbearing, and patient to the last degree, and, above all, throwing aside all personality, how exclusively careful he was neither to exceed nor fall short of the line laid down to him from Spain, softening, when it seemed harsh, what the Count Duke (Olivarezs) had charged him to communicate, and even taking on himself faults and errors which he had not committed, when by such assumption he could advance his objects and gain the ends he had in view in the service of Spain."

How few in this world learn the beauty and the power of being "patient to the last degree!" How few learn early in life to avoid gossip, to speak well of others, and to make peace!

In 1630, four years after the death of Isabella Brandt, Rubens married her sister's daughter, Helena Fourment, a wealthy girl of sixteen, while the painter was fifty-three. He seems to have thought her beautiful, as she appears in nearly all his subsequent paintings. At Blenheim are two portraits of the fair Helena: one, representing himself and his wife in a flower garden with their little child, Dr. Waagen regards as one of the most perfect family pictures in the world.

In the Belvidere, Vienna, is a magnificent portrait of Helena Fourment. She bore to Rubens five children in the ten remaining years of his life.

He soon bought a lovely country home, the Château de Steen at Elewyt, which was sold at his death for forty thousand dollars. "It was," says Huet, "a feudal castle, surrounded on all sides with water. Rubens, though nothing need have prevented him from demolishing the castle and erecting an Italian villa on its site, respected its mediæval architecture. One may take it that the mediæval turrets and the mediæval moat made up, according to him, an agreeable whole with the sylvan surroundings. An imagination like his felt at home everywhere. The principal charm of 'Steen' lay in its being but a day's journey from Antwerp,—that there wife and children could breathe the beneficent country air in unstinted draughts, and the artist himself could indulge his leisure and find new subjects. It is all but certain that the idyl of 'The Rainbow' and the bacchanalia of 'The Village Fair' were painted nowhere else but at Steen....

"Though the two centuries and a half that have elapsed since then have altered the means of locomotion and communication so thoroughly as to make them difficult of recognition, it needs no great effort of the imagination to follow the Rubens family from stage to stage on its flitting to the summer quarters. We can fancy him sitting one of those splendid horses he so magnificently bestrode. A team of four or six less costly, but well-fed, well-groomed, and well-equipped cattle drags through the loose sand or heavy clay the still heavier coach, where, between children and nursemaids, thrones the mistress of the house, not very securely; for she, like the rest, is considerably jolted. She wears the large hat with feathers, beneath which the charming face meets the spectators, as in the picture in the Louvre. A solid train with provisions for the long journey brings up the rear of the procession. Proud of his young wife, anxious as to her every want, the great artist, whose hair and beard are plentifully besprinkled with gray, does not leave the carriage door by her side."

During the last years of his life Rubens suffered much from gout, but, with the help of his pupils, he accomplished a great amount of work. Many of his scholars became famous: Van Dyck, Jordaens, Snyders, Teniers, and others.

Van Dyck was twenty-two years younger than Rubens, and entered his studio when he was seventeen. In four years his works began to be almost as much esteemed as those of his master. It is said that one day, during the absence of Rubens from his studio, the pupils, crowding around a freshly painted picture, pushed against it, thus effacing the arm and chin of a Virgin. They were greatly distressed over the matter, when Van Hoeck cried out: "Van Dyck is the handiest; he must repair the mischief." The restoration was so deftly made that Rubens did not observe the accident.

Later, when Van Dyck came back from Italy, after five years of study there, he found little sale for his pictures, and was depressed. Rubens went to his studio, comforted him, and bought all his paintings which were finished. He did the same thing with a rival who had maligned him because he was not as successful as the great painter. When Rubens died, he owned in his gallery over three hundred pictures, many by Titian, Paul Veronese, Tintoretto, and Van Dyck, and ninety by his own hand.

In 1635, when Philip IV of Spain had appointed as governor of the Netherlands his own brother, the Cardinal Infanta Ferdinand, Sir Peter Paul Rubens was deputed to design the triumphal arches and ornamental temples for his solemn entry into Antwerp. These beautiful designs were afterwards engraved and published, with a learned Latin description by his friend Gevaerts, though they were not ready for the press till the year after Rubens's death. On the day when Ferdinand entered Antwerp, Rubens was ill at his house, but the new governor showed his appreciation of his talent and learning by calling upon him in his own home, as Queen Marie de' Medici, the Infanta Isabella, and other famous persons had done.

His last piece of work was the "Crucifixion of St. Peter," for St. Peter's Church at Cologne. He asked for a year and a half to complete the picture, but death came before it was finished. It represents the apostle nailed to the cross with his head downwards, surrounded by six executioners. "He has proved," says Gustave Planche, "over and over again that he knew all the secrets of the human form, but never has he proved it so clearly as in the Crucifixion of Peter."

May 30, 1640, Antwerp was in mourning for her world-renowned painter. He was buried at night, as was the custom, a great concourse of citizens, all the artistic and literary societies, and sixty orphan children with torches, following his body to the grave. It was temporarily placed in the vault of the Fourment family, and March 4, 1642, was removed to a special chapel built by his wife in the Church of St. James in Antwerp. At his own request, made three days before his death, a "Holy Family," one of his best works, was hung above his resting-place. In the picture, St. George is a portrait of himself, St. Jerome of his father, an angel of his youngest son, and Martha and Mary of Isabella and Helena, his two wives. "A group of tiny angels, floating in the air, crown the Holy Child with a wreath of flowers."

The learned nephew of Rubens, Gevaerts, wrote the following epitaph, in Latin, now inscribed on his monument:—

"Here lies Peter Paul Rubens, knight, and Lord of Steen, son of John Rubens, a senator of this city. Gifted with marvellous talents, versed in ancient history, a master of all the liberal arts and of the elegancies of life, he deserved to be called the Apelles of his age and of all ages. He won for himself the good will of monarchs and of princely men. Philip IV., King of Spain and the Indies, appointed him secretary of his Privy Council, and sent him on an embassy to the King of England in 1629, when he happily laid the foundation of the peace that was soon concluded between those two sovereigns. He died in the year of salvation 1640, on the 30th of May, aged sixty-three years."

The wife of Rubens afterwards married John Baptist Broechoven, Baron van Bergeyck, an ambassador in England in the reign of Charles II.

Rubens left his large collection of sketches to whichever of his sons might become an artist, or whichever of his daughters might marry an artist, but not one fulfilled the conditions.

Two hundred years after Rubens's death, in 1870, a monument was erected to his memory in one of the public squares of Antwerp, and in 1877 a memorial festival was held in his honor in the same city.

REMBRANDT

Edmondo De Amicis, that wonderful word-painter, says in his "Holland and its People:" "However one may be profane in art, and have made a vow never more to offend in too much enthusiasm, when one is in the presence of Rembrandt van Rhijn, one can but raise a little, as the Spaniards say, the key of one's style. Rembrandt exercised a particular prestige. Fra Angelico is a saint, Michael Angelo a giant, Raphael an angel, Titian a prince; Rembrandt is a supernatural being. How otherwise shall we name that son of a miller? Born in a windmill, rising unheralded, without master, without examples, without any derivation from schools, he became a universal painter, embraced all the aspects of life, painted figures, landscapes, marine views, animals, saints in paradise, patriarchs, heroes, monks, wealth and misery, deformity and decrepitude, the ghetto, the tavern, the hospital, death; made, in short, a review of heaven and earth, and rendered all things visible by a light from the arcana of his own imagination.

"It was said that the contrast of light and shadow corresponded in him to diverse movements of thought. Schiller, before beginning a work, heard within himself a harmony of indistinct sounds, which were like a prelude to inspiration; in like manner, Rembrandt, when in the act of conceiving a picture, had a vision of rays and shadows, which spoke to his soul before he animated them with his personages. There is in his pictures a life, and what may almost be called a dramatic action, quite apart from the human figures. Vivid rays of light break into the darkness like cries of joy; the darkness flies in terror, leaving here and there fragments of shadow full of melancholy, tremulous reflections that seem like lamentations; profound obscurity full of dim threatenings; spurts of light, sparkles, ambiguous shadows, doubtful transparencies, questionings, sighs, words of a supernatural language, heard like music, and not understood, and remaining in the memory like the vague relics of a dream.

"And in this atmosphere he plants his figures, of which some are clothed in the dazzling light of a theatrical apotheosis, others veiled like phantoms, others revealed by one stroke of light upon the face; dressed in habits of luxury or misery, but all with something strange and fantastic; without distinctness of outline, but loaded with powerful colors, sculptural reliefs, and bold touches of the brush; and everywhere a warmth of expression, a fury of violent inspiration, the superb, capricious, and profound imprint of a free and fearless genius."

This strange, great painter, Rembrandt, was born, not in a windmill, as Amicis says, but in Leyden, Holland, July 15, 1607. His father, Gerrit Harmen van Rhijn, a miller, was then forty years old, in easy circumstances, married to the daughter of the baker Willems van

141

Snydtbrouck, then thirty-five, a vigorous, strong-charactered woman, whom the boy, in after years, loved to paint, over and over again.

Of their six children, Adriaen, who became a miller, Gerrit, Machteld, Cornelis, Willem, who became a baker, and Rembrandt, the latter was destined for the law. He was early taught Latin, as a preparation for the Leyden Academy, but before he was twelve he showed such decided taste for painting and designing that his parents removed the lad from school, and placed him with a relative, who was an artist, Jacob van Swanenburg. He had returned from study in Italy in 1617, and Rembrandt entered his studio, probably in 1620, the year in which our forefathers left Holland.

For three years the boy bent himself closely to the work he loved. He made such remarkable progress that, at the end of this time, he was sent to the well-known painter, Pieter Lastman of Amsterdam. He remained there but six months, and then returned to his home in Leyden.

From the age of seventeen to twenty, while in his Leyden home, we know little of the youth, save that he studied nature with loving fidelity, wandered over the low, picturesque country with its canal and windmills, and observed people and skies and landscapes.

The first work attributed to Rembrandt was painted in 1627, when he was twenty years old, "St. Paul in Prison," showing care in detail and richness in color. During the next two years, he made etchings of himself and of his mother, who appears to have been his ideal.

His first oil paintings were done in 1630; one, now lost, showing a philosopher in a grotto; and the "Bust of an Old Man," which, says Prof. John W. Mollett of France, in his Life of Rembrandt, "is the most interesting of all the Rembrandts in the Cassel Gallery, from the fact that it first displayed his knowledge of the great secret, which he subsequently so wonderfully developed, of concentrating light upon the heads of his portraits. He painted other old men's heads at the same date, and all are remarkable for indefatigable elaboration and care. In this same year, Rembrandt produced more than thirty etchings."

After several years passed at Leyden, Rembrandt removed his studio to Amsterdam, a rich and flourishing city of one hundred thousand people at that time, whither his fame had preceded him. He hired apartments over a shop on the Bloemgracht, a quay in the western part of the city, where numerous pupils soon came to him, and commissions from the wealthy. One of his first principal works was "The Presentation in the Temple," now in the museum at the Hague. "The picture," says Mr. Sweetser, "presents a great temple interior, with groups of citizens and prelates, and, in the centre, massed under a bright light, the Holy Family, with the richly robed Simeon adoring the child Jesus. It is full of the strong shades and contrasting brightness of the new school of art, replete with poetic power and fresh personality, warm in golden lights, and in certain parts showing a rare minuteness of finish in detail. This subject was always a favorite with Rembrandt, and several other paintings thereof are preserved, together with numerous sketches and engravings, showing the venerable Simeon in the Temple at Jerusalem.

"The 'Susannah' was executed during the same year, and is now at the Hague. The shrinking, naked figure of the fair bather, though lacking in statuesque beauty and symmetry, is thoroughly natural and tender, palpitating with life, and lighted with a warm and harmonious glow. This, also, was a favorite theme with Rembrandt, and conveniently replaced the Diana and Actæon of the classical painters with a subject not less alluring, and perhaps more permissible."

Rembrandt also painted "St. Jerome," now at Aix-la-Chapelle, the lost pictures of "Lot and his Daughters," and the "Baptism of the Eunuch;" "The Young Man," now at Windsor; the "Prophetess Anna," in the Oldenbourg Gallery; the "Portrait of a Man," in the Brunswick Museum; and about forty etchings, among them two portraits of his mother, several of himself; the "Bath of Diana," and the Meeting of "Danaë and Jupiter."

In 1632, Rembrandt painted his famous "School of Anatomy," now at the Hague, for which the Dutch government, two centuries later, gave thirty-two thousand florins.

"This picture represents the celebrated anatomist, Nicolaus Tulp, a friend and patron of Rembrandt, in a vaulted saloon, engaged in explaining the anatomy of the arm of a corpse. He wears a black cloak with a lace collar, and a broad-brimmed soft hat. With his half-raised left hand, he makes a gesture of explanation, while with his right he is dissecting a sinew of the arm of his subject. The corpse lies on a table before him. To the right of Tulp is a group of five figures; and two other men are sitting at the table in front. These listeners are not students, but members of the guild of surgeons of Amsterdam, as shown by a paper held by one of them. They are attending to the lecture with very various expressions.

"They are all bare-headed, dressed in black, and with turned-over collars except one, who still wears the old-fashioned upright ruff. There are, perhaps, other persons present in the hall, as Tulp appears to be looking beyond the picture, as if about to address an audience not visible to the spectator; and it is here worthy of remark that Rembrandt's compositions are never imprisoned in their frames, but convey an idea of a wide space beyond them. It is somewhat singular that the spectator seems hardly to notice the corpse lying before him at full length, the feet of which he can almost touch, although it is strongly lighted in contrast to the surrounding black garments, and most faithfully presents the peculiar hue of a dead body, leaving no doubt that it was painted from nature, as well as the living heads. The admirable art of the composition consists in its power of riveting the attention to the living in the presence of death."

Amicis says: "It is difficult to express the effect produced by this picture. The first feeling is that of horror and repulsion from the corpse. The forehead is in shadow, the eyes open with the pupils turned upwards, the mouth half open as if in astonishment, the chest sunken, the legs and feet stiff, the flesh livid, and looking as if, should you touch it with your hand, it would feel cold. With this rigid body a powerful contrast is produced by the vivacious attitudes, the youthful faces, the bright, attentive eyes, full of thought, of the disciples, revealing in different degrees the avidity for knowledge, the joy of learning, curiosity, wonder, the strength of intelligence, the suspense of the mind. The master has the tranquil face, the serene eye, and the almost smiling lip of one who feels the complacency of knowledge. There is in the complexion of the group an air of mystery, gravity, and scientific solemnity, which inspires reverence and silence.

"The contrast between the light and shadow is as marvellous as that between life and death. It is all done with extraordinary finish; one can count the folds of the ruffs, the lines of the face, the hairs of the beards. It is said that the foreshortening of the corpse is wrong, and that in some points the finish runs into dryness, but universal judgment places the 'Lesson in Anatomy' among the greatest triumphs of human genius.

"Rembrandt was only twenty-six years old when he painted this picture, which, therefore, belongs to his first manner, in which there are not yet apparent that fire and audacity, that sovereign security in his own genius, which shine in the works of his maturer years: but there is already that luminous potency, that marvellous chiaroscuro, that magic of contrasts, which form the most original trait of his genius."

I remember, in standing before this picture, to have had the same "repulsion" of which Amicis speaks. How differently one feels before that other marvel of the Hague, Paul Potter's "Bull," so at one with nature, so tender, so restful! What wonder that it once hung in the Louvre, beside the "Transfiguration" of Raphael, the "St. Peter Martyr," of Titian, and the "Communion of St. Jerome" by Domenichino?

During this year, 1632, Rembrandt executed several portraits of men; the "Rape of Proserpine," in the Berlin Gallery; "Moses saved from the Nile;" "Christ and Nicodemus;" the "Oriental Standing," in the gallery of the King of Holland; the "Betrothed Jewess;" the "Rape of Europa;" and portraits of six women. His etchings this year were, "Man on Horseback," "Cottage with White Palings" his first landscape, "Seller of Rat's Poison," "Jesus being carried to the Tomb," and the "Resurrection of Lazarus."

In the following year he painted "Susannah Surprised by the Elders," which is now in Russia; "The Boat of St. Peter," a powerful conception, showing dark storm-shadows surrounding the sea-tossed bark, with a high light thrown on the nearer mountain-like waves and on the men at the sails; "The Elevation of the Cross," and "The Descent from the Cross," bought by Prince Frederick Henry of Holland, and now in Munich; "The Good Samaritan," now in Sir Richard Wallace's collection; "The Philosophers in Meditation," two delicate pictures, now in the Louvre; "The Master Shipbuilder and his Pipe," now at Buckingham Palace, sold for sixteen thousand five hundred francs, in 1810; portraits of Madame Grotius, a youth at Dresden, another in the Pourtales Collection, sold for seven thousand dollars in 1865; and no less than sixteen others, besides many etchings. One of these portraits, that of a young boy, was bought by J. de Rothschild, in 1865, for five thousand dollars; and a portrait of Saskia, now at Cassel, for ten thousand dollars.

Of the picture of Saskia in the Dresden Museum, painted this year, Professor Mollett says: "The head in this portrait is slightly inclined, the long chestnut curls are covered by a cherry-colored bonnet ornamented with white feathers. The light falling on the figure from above illuminates the rim of the bonnet and the lower part of the face, while the forehead is covered by the shadow thrown by the hat."

Of the large portrait in the Cassel Gallery, painted the same year, he says: "In this picture Saskia is very richly dressed, and covered with a profusion of pearls and precious stones. The face, a delicate profile of a bright, fresh color, drawn against a dark brown background, is entirely in the light, almost without shadows."

The portrait of her in the late Fesch Gallery, says Sweetser, "displays the maiden's snowy complexion, great deep eyes, rosy lips, and rich auburn hair, adorned with white and green plumes, and wearing pearls on her neck, and a chain of gold on her green silk mantilla."

Who was Saskia? The lovely and beautiful woman whose life was to Rembrandt like the transcendent light he threw into his pictures; whose death left him forever in the shadow of shadows, which he, of all painters, knew best how to paint.

Saskia van Ulenburgh was the orphan daughter of Rombertus Ulenburgh, a Frisian lawyer of high standing, envoy from Friesland to the court of William of Orange. She was wealthy, of lovely character, and attractive in face and in manner. Her brother-in-law, the painter Nijbrand de Geest, was a man of influence, and her cousin, Hendrik Ulenburgh, was the publisher of Rembrandt's engravings. They therefore naturally met each other. She was young and of distinguished family; the young artist, who fell in love with her, had his genius alone to offer her.

The devoted love of Rembrandt won the happy-hearted, refined Saskia. They were married June 5, 1634, when she was twenty-one and

Rembrandt twenty-seven, and went to live in his pleasant home in Amsterdam.

The next eight years were given to arduous work, blessed by the well-nigh omnipotent influence of a seemingly perfect love. In his marriage year he painted "Queen Artemisia," now in Madrid; "The Incredulity of St. Thomas," now at the Hermitage; "Repentance of Peter," "Judas and the Blood Money;" a larger "Descent from the Cross," now at St. Petersburg; "Rev. Mr. Ellison and Wife of the English Church at Amsterdam," sold in London, in 1860, for about nine thousand dollars; several portraits of himself and several of Saskia. In the large "Jewish Wife," in "Bathsheba receiving David's Message," in the long lost "Vertumnus and Pomona," Saskia, the beloved Saskia, is always the model.

At the same time were made five sketches and sixteen engravings, the most notable being "The Annunciation to the Shepherds." "This," says Professor Mollett, "is a night effect, with a mass of trees on the right hand, and a distance in which a city is seen, with its factories and bridges in a nest of foliage, and fires reflected in water. In the foreground the shepherds and their flocks are alarmed by the sudden appearance of the celestial glory, in the luminous circles of which thousands of cherubim are flying; an angel is advancing, and, with the right hand raised, is announcing the news to the shepherds. The whole composition is wonderful for the energy it displays, and appears as if it had been thrown on the copper with swift, nervous, inspired touches, but always accurate and infallible."

In 1635 a son was born to Rembrandt and Saskia, named Rombertus, after her father, but the child soon died, the first shadow in the famous artist's home. This year he painted "Samson menacing his Father-in-law," now in the Berlin Museum; the "Rape of Ganymede," now at Dresden; "Christ driving out the Money-changers;" "The Martyrdom of St. Stephen;" in all, eight portraits, seven other paintings, nine designs, and twenty-three etchings. One of the most attractive of the pictures about this time is Rembrandt at home, with Saskia, life-size, and full of happiness, seated upon his knee.

Three scenes from the history of Tobias follow. The first, the blind father awaiting his son's return, is in the Berlin Museum; the second contains Tobias and his wife seated in a chamber; the third illustrates Tobias restoring sight to his father.

In 1636 he painted "The Entombment," "The Resurrection," and "The Ascension," companion pictures to the "Crucifixion" painted for Prince Frederick Henry four years previously; "The Repose in Egypt," now at Aix-la-Chapelle; "The Ascension," in the Munich Pinakothek; "Samson blinded by the Philistines, with Delilah in Flight;" and "St. Paul," in the Vienna Belvidere, besides three portraits and ten etchings.

The finest etching of this period was "Ecce Homo," a marvellous composition, consisting of an immense number of figures admirably disposed. Our Lord is seen in front standing, surrounded by guards. His eyes are raised to heaven, his hands are manacled and clasped together, and on his head is the crown of thorns. "It is," says Mollett, "one of the painter's grandest works."

"The 'Ecce Homo,'" says Wilmot Buxton, "to say nothing of the splendor, the light and shade and richness of execution, has never been surpassed for dramatic expression; and we forgive the commonness of form and type, in the expression of touching pathos in the figure of the Saviour; nor would it be possible to express with greater intensity the terrible raging of the crowd, the ignobly servile and cruel supplications of the priests, or the anxious desire to please on the part of Pilate."

The following year, "The Lord of the Vineyard," now in the Hermitage, was painted, representing the master in a chamber flooded with light, listening to the complaints of the laborers; "Abraham sending away Hagar and Ishmael;" and several portraits of himself and Saskia. Now she is seated at a table face to face with her husband, her blue eyes looking pleased and happy into his; now they walk hand in hand in a beautiful landscape.

In July, 1638, a second child gladdened the Rembrandt household, this time a daughter, named Cornelia after the artist's mother. In less than four weeks she passed out of Saskia's arms, leaving them again childless. Rembrandt's father had died six years before, and of his brothers and sisters, Gerrit, Machteld, and Cornelis were dead also. Still the painter worked on bravely, for did he not have the one inspiration that gave almost superhuman power to overcome obstacles, and made work a pleasure,—the love of his blue-eyed Saskia?

During this year some lawsuits occurred in the family over her property, and Rembrandt sued some of her relatives for slander, because they had insinuated that Saskia "has squandered her heritage in ornaments and ostentation." How little the Friesland people knew of the poetry of the painter's heart, which, for the love he bore Saskia, decked, with his rich imagination, every picture of her with more than royal necklaces, and covered her robes with priceless gems, because she was his idol!

This year, 1638, he painted the great picture "The Feast of Ahasuerus," or "The Wedding of Samson," now at Dresden, where at the middle of the table sits the joyous queen, Esther or Delilah, robed in white silk, and richly jewelled, of course with Saskia's face; "Christ as a Gardener," long owned by the Prince of Hesse-Cassel, presented to Josephine at Malmaison, and bought by George IV. for Buckingham Palace, where it still remains; "Joseph telling his Dream;" "The Little Jewish Bride," representing St. Catherine and her wheel of martyrdom (the hair, the pearls, the face are all Saskia's), and other works.

The next year among his many superb portraits are three of his mother: one in Vienna, painted a year before her death, in a furred cloak, resting her folded hands on a staff; another with a red shawl on her head; and still another seated, with her hands joined;—both the latter in the Hermitage. He also finished "The Entombment" and "The Resurrection," begun three years before. He said, "These two pieces are now finished with much of study and of zeal, ... because it is in these that I have taken care to express the utmost of naturalness and action; and this is the principal reason why I have been occupied so long on them." He urged that they be hung in a strong light, for he said, "A picture is not made to be smelt of. The odor of the colors is unhealthy."

He etched "The Death of the Virgin," "The Presentation," "Youth surprised by Death," and others.

The next year, 1640, a baby's voice was again heard in the handsome Rembrandt home, a little daughter named, for the second time, Cornelia, but in a few short months the household was again stricken by death.

Rembrandt's activity was now marvellous. In the next two years he painted "Le Doreur," a portrait of his artist friend Domer, which was sold in 1865 for over thirty thousand dollars; it is also called "The Gilder," and is now in the Metropolitan Museum of Art in New York; the portrait of an aged woman, purchased in 1868 for the Narishkine Collection, for eleven thousand dollars; "Woman with the Fan," of Buckingham Palace; the mysterious "Witch of Endor," Schönborn Gallery in 1867, for five thousand dollars; "The Carpenter's Household," now in the Louvre, representing Joseph at work, with the tender mother nursing her child; "The Salutation," in the Grosvenor Gallery; "Susannah at the Bath;" "The Offering of Manoah," at the Dresden Museum, showing Manoah and his wife prostrate before the altar, from which an angel crowned with flowers is ascending; a magnificent portrait of himself at thirty, in the National Gallery, in a black cap and fur robe, his arms crossed on a window-sill; sixteen fine etchings, among them three lion-hunts, the preacher Anslo and his wife seated at a book-laden table; several exquisite portraits of ladies, and two of the beloved Saskia: one is full of life and health, with the sweetest expression, and carefully finished; the other, in 1642, is richly dressed, but the face is delicate and dreamy, like that of one who may have received a message from the unseen world.

Professor Mollett says of these, "The first represents Saskia in all the freshness of her beauty, seen through the prism of love and art; in her rich dress, fresh color, and bright smile, bearing a strong resemblance to the Saskia on her husband's knee. It is difficult to imagine a more charming and amiable face, or a portrait more happy in color and expression. The work is very carefully finished without being minute, the tone profound, the touch broad and melting. No greater contrast can be conceived to this picture bathed in light, radiant with happiness and health, than the 'Saskia' of Antwerp. This portrait has an indefinable charm. The very soul of the painter seems to have entered into the picture, to which a melancholy interest is attached. It bears the same date as the year of Saskia's death, 1642. The face no longer shows the serene beauty of youth and strength, but its etherealized and delicate features have a thoughtful and dreamy expression. It was probably painted from memory, after Saskia's death."

In September, 1641, a son was born to Saskia, Titus, named for her sister Titia van Ulenburgh. The latter died the same year. On the 19th of the next June, Saskia was buried from the Oude Kerk in Amsterdam, leaving her son, not a year old, and her husband, to whom her loss was irreparable.

This year he had completed his greatest work, "The Night Watch," now in the Amsterdam Museum, and stood at the very zenith of his fame. From this time, while he did much remarkable work, he seems like a man on a mountain top, looking on one side to sweet meadows filled with flowers and sunlight, and on the other to a desolate landscape over which a clouded sun is setting. With Saskia died the best of Rembrandt. Before her death he had painted various pictures of himself, all joyous, even fantastic, sometimes as a warrior, sometimes with jewelled robes and courtly attire. Now for five years he made no portrait of himself, and then one simple and stern, like a man who lives and does his work because he must.

"The Night Watch," or the "Sortie of the Banning Cock Company," represents Captain Frans Banning Cock's company of arquebusiers emerging from their guild-house on the Singel. Amicis says of it, "It is more than a picture; it is a spectacle, and an amazing one. All the French critics, to express the effect which it produces, make use of the phrase, 'C'est écrasant!' ('It is overpowering!') A great crowd of human figures, a great light, a great darkness—at the first glance this is what strikes you, and for a moment you know not where to fix your eyes in order to comprehend that grand and splendid confusion.

"There are officers, halberdiers, boys running, arquebusiers loading and firing, youths beating drums, people bowing, talking, calling out, gesticulating—all dressed in different costumes, with round hats, pointed hats, plumes, casques, morions, iron gorgets, linen collars, doublets embroidered with gold, great boots, stockings of all colors, arms of every form; and all this tumultuous and glittering throng start out from the dark background of the picture and advance towards the spectator.

"The two first personages are Frans Banning Cock, Lord of Furmerland and Ilpendam, captain of the company, and his lieutenant, Willem van Ruijtenberg, Lord of Vlaardingen, the two marching side by side. The only figures that are in full light are this lieutenant, dressed in a doublet of buffalo-hide, with gold ornaments, scarf, gorget, and white plume, with high boots; and a girl who comes behind, with blond hair ornamented with pearls, and a yellow satin dress; all the other figures are in deep shadow, excepting the heads, which are illuminated. By what light? Here is the enigma. Is it the light of the sun? or of the moon? or of the torches?

"There are gleams of gold and silver, moonlight, colored reflections, fiery lights; personages which, like the girl with blond tresses, seem to shine by a light of their own; faces that seem lighted by the fire of a conflagration; dazzling scintillations, shadows, twilight, and deep darkness, all are there, harmonized and contrasted with marvellous boldness and insuperable art.... In spite of censure, defects, conflicting judgments, it has been there for two centuries triumphant and glorious; and the more you look at it, the more it is alive and glowing; and, even seen only at a glance, it remains forever in the memory, with all its mystery and splendor, like a stupendous vision."

Charles Blanc says of the picture: "To tell the truth, this is only a dream of night, and no one can decide what the light is that falls on the groups of figures. It is neither the light of the sun nor of the moon, nor does it come from torches; it is rather the light from the genius of Rembrandt."

The home of the artist at that time, of brick and cut stone, four stories high, on one of the quays of the river Amstel, must have been most attractive and happy until the death of Saskia.

Says Mr. Sweetser: "The house still stands, and, by the aid of an existing legal inventory (dated 1656), we can even refurnish it as it was in the days of Rembrandt. Entering the vestibule, we find the flagstone paving covered with fir-wood, with black-cushioned Spanish chairs for those who wait, and to amuse their leisure several busts and twenty-four paintings—four each by Brouwer and Lievens, the rest mostly by Rembrandt.

"The ante-chamber, or saloon, was a large room furnished with seven Spanish chairs upholstered in green velvet, a great walnut table covered with Tournay cloth, an ebony-framed mirror, and a marble wine-cooler. The walls were covered with thirty-nine pictures, many of which were in massive and elegant frames. There were religious scenes, landscapes, architectural sketches, works of Pinas, Brouwer, Lucas van Leyden, and other Dutch masters; sixteen pictures by Rembrandt; and costly paintings by Palma Vecchio, Bassano, and Raphael.

"The next room was a perfect little museum of art, containing a profusion of the master's pictures, with rare works of Van Leyden, Van Dyck, Aartgen, Parsellis, Seghers, and copies from Annibale Caracci. The oaken press and other furnishings indicated that the marvellous etchings of our artist were engraved and printed here.

"The next saloon was the gem of the establishment, and was equipped with a great mirror, an oaken table with an embroidered cloth, six chairs with blue coverings, a bed with blue hangings, a cedar-wood wardrobe, and a chest of the same wood. The walls even here showed the profound artistic taste of the occupant, for they were overlaid with twenty-three pictures by Aartgen, Lievens, Seghers, and other northern painters; The 'Concordi,' 'Resurrection,' and 'Ecce Homo' of Rembrandt; a Madonna by Raphael; and Giorgione's great picture of 'The Samaritan.'

"On the next floor the master had his studio and museum. The great art-chamber contained materials for weeks of study; the walls were covered with rich and costly bric-à-brac—statuettes in marble, porcelain, and plaster; the Roman emperors; busts of Homer, Aristotle, and Socrates: Chinese and Japanese porcelains and drawings; Venetian glass; casts from nature; curious weapons and armor, with a shield attributed to Quentin Matsys; minerals, plants, stuffed birds, and shells; rare fans, globes, and books. Another feature was a noble collection of designs, studies, and engravings, filling sixty leather portfolios, and including specimens of the best works of the chief Italian, German, and Dutch artists and engravers."

To gain this beautiful collection of works of art, Rembrandt spared no money, paying eighty-six dollars for a single engraving of Lucas van Leyden's, and fourteen hundred florins for fourteen proofs from the same painter.

After Saskia died, the tide of fortune seemed to turn. Several artists who had studied in Italy returned to Holland, and popularized the Italian style, so that the works of Rembrandt seemed to fade somewhat from the public gaze. With pride and sorrow he went on painting, but he must have been deeply wounded.

In 1643 and '44, he painted "Bathsheba at the Bath." "The nude figure of Bathsheba," says Professor Mollett, "stands out in a dazzling effect of light from a background of warm, confused shadows. The figure is not beautiful to a sculptor's eye, nor in the Italian style; but in animation, in the flesh color, and in the modelling it is superb. The harmony of the tints and of the general tone is very beautiful; tints of bronze and gold combine with shades of violet, brown, green, and yellow ochre into a warm, poetic, and mysterious gamut. 'This picture should be hung in a strong light, that the eye may penetrate into the shadows,' said Rembrandt."

The other works of this time were the "Diana and Endymion" of the Liechtenstein Gallery at Vienna; "Philemon and Baucis;" the "Old Woman Weighing Gold," now in the Dresden Museum; "The Woman taken in Adultery," which brought thirty thousand dollars at public sale, and is now in the English National Gallery; a portrait of Jan Cornelis Sylvius, which was sold in 1872 for nearly eight thousand dollars, and the "Burgomaster Six" for six thousand dollars. The latter was the portrait of Jan Six, a young patrician, an enthusiastic student and poet, married to Margaret the daughter of the famous surgeon Dr. Tulp.

Other pictures in the next few years were "The Tribute Money;" the "Burgomaster Pancras giving a Collar of Pearls to his Wife," now owned by Queen Victoria; "Abraham receiving the Three Angels;" two

151

paintings of the "Adoration of the Shepherds," one now in Munich and one in the National Gallery; "The Good Samaritan," and "The Pilgrims of Emmaus," now in the Louvre; and "The Peace of the Land," celebrating the peace of Westphalia, now in the Boymans Museum at Rotterdam. "It represents the enclosure of a fortress, the walls of which are visible in the right-hand background, where cannons are blazing and a group of soldiers fighting; the right-hand foreground is entirely occupied by a group of horsemen, of remarkable vigor and truth; on the left are two thrones, on one of which leans a figure of Justice, clasping her hands as if in supplication. The centre, which is in the light, is occupied by a couchant lion growling, his one paw on a bundle of arrows, the symbol of the United Provinces. The lion is bound by two chains, the one attached to the thrones, the other fastened to an elevation, bearing on a shield the arms of Amsterdam, surrounded by the words, 'Soli Deo Gloria.'"

"Samuel taught by his Mother," "Christ appearing to Mary," "The Prophetess Anna," "Jesus blessing Little Children," purchased for the National Gallery for thirty-five thousand dollars;—"The Bather," in the National Gallery, of which Landseer says: "It is the most artful thing ever done in painting, and the most unsophisticated;" a likeness of Rembrandt's son Titus, now twelve years old, were his next works. Fifty-seven etchings were made between 1649 and 1655, the most celebrated being the "Hundred-Guilder Print," or "Jesus healing the Sick."

"The subject of this etching is taken from the words, 'And Jesus went about all Galilee, preaching the gospel of the kingdom, and healing all manner of sickness and all manner of disease among the people.' The serene and calm figure of Jesus stands out from the shadow of the background, preaching to the people around him. By a superb antithesis, the Pharisees and Sadducees, the priests and the curious and unbelieving, are standing on Christ's right hand, bathed in light, while from the shadows that envelop the left side of the picture are coming the sick, the possessed, and unfortunates of all kinds. The composition is full of feeling, drawn and executed with a rare genius, the details revealing a world of expression and character: the lights and shadows, disposed in large masses, are of wonderful softness. The etching, commenced with aqua-fortis, is finished with the dry point, the silvery neutral tints of Christ's robe and the soft shadows being produced in this manner."

Frederick Wedmore says in his "Masters of Genre-Painting," "I should be thankful for the 'Hundred-Guilder Print,' were it only because of the half-dozen lines in which Rembrandt has etched one figure, to me the central one, a tall man, old and spare, and a little bent, with drooped arms, and hands clasped together in gesture of mild awe and gently felt surprise, as of one from whose slackened vitality the power of great surprise or of very keen interest has forever gone. On his face there is the record of much pain, of sufferings not only his own, not only of the body, but of saddening experiences which have left him quelled and forever grave."

The name arose from the fact that a Roman merchant gave Rembrandt for one engraving seven Marc Antonio engravings, which were valued at a hundred guilders, and the artist would never sell any of these pictures below this price. Only eight impressions of the first plate are in existence; two are in the British Museum, one is in Paris, one in Amsterdam, one in Vienna, one in the collection of the Duke of Buccleuch, one in Mr. Holford's, and one owned by M. Eugene Dutuit of Rouen, sold in 1867 for about six thousand dollars.

When Saskia died, she left her property—she had brought Rembrandt forty thousand florins—to her infant son Titus, with the condition that her husband should have the use of the money until his death or his second marriage. If the boy died, Rembrandt was to receive the whole estate, save in case of a second marriage, when half should go to her sister.

Already Saskia's friends saw the money passing away from the artist, and they brought suits for Titus's sake, to recover it. Finally, in 1656, he transferred his house and land to Titus, with the privilege of remaining there during the pleasure of Saskia's relatives.

Matters did not improve, and the following year all the rich collection of art works and household goods were sold by auction to meet the demands of creditors. The next year his engravings and designs were sold in the same way, and the year following the house was disposed of, Rembrandt being allowed to remove two stoves only and some screens. These must have been bitter days for the once happy artist. It was fortunate that Saskia did not live to see such a direful change.

During all the struggle and disgrace Rembrandt kept on working. In 1656 and '57 he painted for the Surgeons' Guild, a large picture, "Lesson on Anatomy of Joan Deyman," containing the portraits of nine celebrated doctors; "St. John the Baptist Preaching," a canvas with over one hundred small figures; "The Adoration of the Magi," now in Buckingham Palace and greatly admired; "Joseph accused by Potiphar's Wife," and "Jacob blessing Ephraim and Manasseh."

Professor Mollett says that the "Jacob" "belongs as much to all times and all nations as the masterpieces of Greek sculpture. This touching scene, which is simply rendered with all the power of Rembrandt's art, represents the aged patriarch extending his hands, which Joseph is guiding, towards the boys, who are kneeling before him. Behind the bed stands their mother, Asenath, with clasped hands. The light falling from behind Jacob, on the left, leaves his face in the shade. His head is covered by a yellowish cap, bordered with clear-colored fur; the sleeve of the right arm is of a beautiful gray; the hand

153

painted with large, broad touches. The bed is covered with a sheet and a counterpane of pale red and fawn color.

"Joseph wears a turban, and his wife a high cap, long veil, and robe of gray and fawn-colored brown. The fair child has a yellow vest; and his head, bright with reflected lights, is very fine in tone, and of extreme delicacy. We see the colors here employed are gray and fawn-colored brown, which, in the highest notes, only reach subdued red or yellow. The whole bears a mysterious air; in a fine and luminous light, filled with tones and half-tones that are indefinable. The touch is of such surpassing boldness and ease, that, when viewed in detail, the picture might be called a sketch, if the harmony and completeness of the whole did not indicate the maturity and profundity of the work."

After Rembrandt's home was sold, he hired a house on the Rosengracht, a retired but respectable part of the city, two blocks away from the Bloemgracht, where he began life with his beloved Saskia. Here, as elsewhere, he gathered admiring pupils about him, and kept diligently at his work. It is probable that he was married at this time, or later, for in 1663 he painted a picture known as "Rembrandt and his Family," now in the Brunswick Museum, where a rosy and smiling lady is seated with a child on her lap, while two little girls of perhaps five and seven stand by her. The man with brown hair stands on the left, giving a flower to one of the girls.

Rembrandt's chief works now were "Moses descending from Sinai, and breaking the Tables of the Law," "Jacob wrestling with the Angels," a striking picture of "Ziska and his Adherents swearing to avenge the Death of Huss," and "The Syndics of the Guild of Clothmakers," now in the Amsterdam Museum.

Professor Springer writes concerning the latter picture, the "School of Anatomy," and "The Night Watch:" "Art has never again created a greater wealth of stirring imagery or poetry of color so entrancing as these three pictures reveal to us. Unconsciously our thoughts return to Shakspeare's familiar creations, and we recognize in these two mighty art champions of the north kindred natures and a corresponding bent of fancy."

In 1668, Titus, now twenty-seven years old,—he studied painting, but became a merchant,—was married to his cousin Magdalena van Loo, one of the Frisian families, and died in September of the same year. The next March, his widow bore a daughter who received the name of Titia, for her dead father. Magdalena died in the same year in which her child was born. Thus frequently did sorrow shadow the path of the great master of shadows.

This year, Rembrandt painted several portraits of himself. "In that of the Pitti Palace, we see him wrapped in fur, a medal is hung about his neck, and he is wearing a close-fitting cap, from which his ample white hair escapes. His face is furrowed with age, but the brightness of the eye is not diminished....

"In the splendid portrait in the Double Collection at Rouen, he again stands before us, with bending attitude and slightly inclined head, in theatrical costume, with his maulstick in his hand, laughing heartily. And this is Rembrandt's farewell! His face is wrinkled across and across by time and care, but it is no gloomy misanthrope crushed by evil fortune whom we see, but the man who opposed to all fortunes the talisman of Labor, and thus paints the secret of his life in his final portrait of himself, in the midst of his work, scorning destiny."

A year after Titus died, death came to Rembrandt, at sixty-two. He was buried simply in the West Church, so simply that the registered expense of his burial is fifteen florins!

His power of work was marvellous. He painted over six hundred and twenty pictures, executed three hundred and sixty-five etchings, besides two hundred and thirty-seven variations of these, with hundreds of drawings and sketches scattered over Europe. Among the best known etchings are "Rembrandt's Portrait with the Sword," "Lazarus rising from the Dead," the "Hundred-Florin Plate," "Annunciation," "Ecce Homo," "The Good Samaritan," "The Great Descent from the Cross," the landscape with the mill, and that with the three trees.

That he was a man of great depth of feeling is shown by his love of his mother, his worship of Saskia, and his tenderness to his brothers and sisters after they had lost their fortunes. He was also passionately fond of nature and of animals. Sweetser tells this incident: "One day he was making a portrait group of a notable family, when he was informed that his favorite monkey had died. The grieving artist caused the body to be brought to the studio, and made its portrait on the same canvas on which he was engaged. The family, aforesaid, was naturally incensed at such an interpolation, and demanded that it should be effaced; but Rembrandt preferred to keep the whole work himself, and let his patrons seek a more accommodating artist."

Taine pays Rembrandt this glowing tribute in his "Art in the Netherlands:" "Rembrandt, constantly collecting his materials, living in solitude and borne along by the growth of an extraordinary faculty, lived, like our Balzac, a magician and a visionary in a world fashioned by his own hand, and of which he alone possessed the key. Superior to all painters in the native delicacy and keenness of his optical perceptions, he comprehended this truth and adhered to it in all its consequence,—that, to the eye, the essence of a visible object consists of the spot (tache), that the simplest color is infinitely complex, that every visual sensation is the product of its elements coupled with its surroundings, that each object on the field of sight is but a single spot modified by others, and that in this wise the principal feature of a picture is the ever-present, tremulous, colored atmosphere into which figures are plunged like fishes in the sea....

"Free of all trammels and guided by the keen sensibility of his organs, he has succeeded in portraying in man not merely the general structure and the abstract type which answers for classic art, but again that which is peculiar and profound in the individual, the infinite and indefinable complications of the moral being, the whole of that changeable imprint which concentrates instantaneously on a face the entire history of a soul, and which Shakespeare alone saw with an equally prodigious lucidity.

"In this respect he is the most original of modern artists, and forges one end of the chain of which the Greeks forged the other; the rest of the masters, Florentine, Venetian, and Flemish, stand between them; and when, nowadays, our over-excited sensibility, our extravagant curiosity in the pursuit of subtleties, our unsparing search of the true, our divination of the remote and the obscure in human nature, seeks for predecessors and masters, it is in him and in Shakespeare that Balzac and Delacroix are able to find them."

SIR JOSHUA REYNOLDS

In Plympton, Devonshire, July 16, 1723, the great English painter, Sir Joshua Reynolds, was born. His father, Samuel, and his grandfather, John, were both ministers, while his mother and grandmother were both daughters of clergymen.

Samuel Reynolds was a gentle, kindly man, master of the grammar school at Plympton, supporting his eleven children on the meagre income of seven hundred and fifty dollars a year. He had married Theophila Potter, when she was twenty-three, the lovely daughter of a lovely young mother, Theophila Baker, who, marrying against the consent of her father, was disinherited by him, and at the early death of her devoted husband wept herself blind, and died broken-hearted.

Joshua, the seventh child of Samuel and Theophila, was a thoughtful, aspiring boy, who cared more for drawing than for Ovid, and spent his early years in copying the illustrations from "Plutarch's Lives" and Jacob Cats's "Book of Emblems," which his grandmother, on his father's side, had brought with her from Holland. His sisters were also fond of drawing, and as pencils and paper could not be afforded in the minister's family, they drew on the whitewashed walls of a long passage, with burnt sticks. The boy's sketches were the poorest, and he was therefore nicknamed "the clown."

On the back of a Latin exercise, the lad drew a wall with a window in it. Under it, the not highly delighted father, who wished his boy to be a learned doctor, wrote: "This is drawn by Joshua in school, out of pure idleness." But when in his eighth year the boy made a fine sketch of the grammar school with its cloister, having studied carefully the Jesuit's "Treatise on Perspective," the astonished father said, "Now, this exemplifies what the author of the 'Perspective' says in his preface, 'that, by observing the rules laid down in this book, a man may do wonders;' for this is wonderful."

Joshua was fond of literary composition, and early composed some rules of conduct for himself, which influenced him through life. He said, "The great principle of being happy in this world is not to mind or be affected with small things," a maxim which he carried out in his peaceful, self-poised, and remarkably happy life.

"If you take too much care of yourself, nature will cease to take care of you," he said, and thus without excessive self-consciousness he did his great work and reaped his great reward.

A book did for Joshua what a book has often done before, became an inspiration, and therefore led to grand results. He read Richardson's "Theory of Painting," wherein was expressed the hope and belief that there was a future for England in art. "No nation under

157

heaven so nearly resembles the ancient Greeks and Romans as we. There is a haughty courage, an elevation of thought, a greatness of taste, a love of liberty, a simplicity and honesty amongst us which we inherit from our ancestors, and which belong to us as Englishmen; and 'tis in these this resemblance consists.... A time may come when future writers may be able to add the name of an English painter.... I am no prophet, nor the son of a prophet, but, considering the necessary connection of causes and effects, and upon seeing some links of that fatal chain, I will venture to pronounce (as exceedingly probable) that if ever the ancient, great, and beautiful taste in painting revives, it will be in England; but not till English painters, conscious of the dignity of their country and of their profession, resolve to do honor to both by Piety, Virtue, Magnanimity, Benevolence, and a contempt of everything that is really unworthy of them.

"And now I cannot forbear wishing that some younger painter than myself, and one who has had greater and more early advantages, would practise the magnanimity I have recommended, in this single instance of attempting and hoping only to equal the greatest masters of whatsoever age or nation. What were they which we are not or may not be? What helps had any of them which we have not?"

The boy Joshua was electrified by these words. Perhaps he could become "equal to the greatest masters." He told a friend, Edmond Malone, that this book so delighted and inflamed his mind "that Raphael appeared to him superior to the most illustrious names of ancient or modern time."

Young Reynolds painted his first oil painting, now in the possession of Deble Boger, Esq., of Anthony, near Plymouth, when he was twelve years old. It was a portrait of Rev. Thomas Smart, a tutor in the family of Lord Edgcumbe. In church, while Smart was preaching, Joshua made a sketch on his thumb-nail of the minister. He enlarged this sketch in a boat-house, using part of the sail for his canvas.

Good Samuel Reynolds began to wonder whether a boy who could paint at twelve would make a successful apothecary, and, not being able to decide the question alone, he consulted Mr. Craunch. This gentleman, of small fortune, resided at Plympton, and was the father of pretty Betsy Craunch, a sweetheart of Peter Pindar (Dr. Wolcot). The lad himself said, "he would rather be an apothecary than an ordinary painter; but if he could be bound to an eminent master, he should choose the latter."

Mr. Craunch advised the study of art, and through his influence and that of his friend, a lawyer, Mr. Cutcliffe of Bideford, the lad was sent to Thomas Hudson, the principal portrait painter in England, living in Great Queen Street, Lincoln's Inn, London. He was the pupil of Richardson, married his daughter, and thus Reynolds was brought again under a kindred influence to that which had inspired him in the "Theory of Painting."

Hudson was to receive six hundred dollars for care of his pupil, half of which was loaned by a married sister till he should be able to repay her. The boy made drawings from ancient statuary and from Guercino, and was delighted with his work, writing home to his father, "While I am doing this I am the happiest creature alive."

One morning, while purchasing some pictures for Hudson at an auction room, he was overjoyed to see a great poet, Alexander Pope, enter the place, and bow to the crowd, who opened a passage for him. Among others, Pope shook hands with the ardent young artist. He described the poet as "about four feet six inches high; very hump-backed and deformed. He wore a black coat, and, according to the fashion of that time, had on a little sword. He had a large and very fine eye, and a long, handsome nose; his mouth had those peculiar marks which are always found in the mouths of crooked persons, and the muscles which run across the cheek were so strongly marked that they seemed like small cords."

Though bound to Hudson for four years, at the end of two years Joshua was dismissed, ostensibly for neglect to carry a picture at the time ordered, but in reality, it is believed, because the master was jealous that he had painted so admirably the portrait of an elderly serving-woman in the house. He returned to Devonshire, and settled at Plymouth, where he soon painted about thirty portraits of the magnates of the neighborhood, at fifteen dollars apiece.

He worked earnestly, saying, "Those who are determined to excel must go to their work whether willing or unwilling, morning, noon, and night, and they will find it to be no play, but, on the contrary, very hard labor."

Young Reynolds made a portrait in 1746 of Captain Hamilton, father of the Marquis of Abercorn, which was the first of his pictures which brought the artist into notice. He also painted Hamilton in a picture with Lord and Lady Eliot. The latter married Hamilton after her husband's death.

"This Captain Hamilton," we find in Prior's Life of Malone, "was a very uncommon character; very obstinate, very whimsical, very pious, a rigid disciplinarian, yet very kind to his men. He lost his life as he was proceeding from his ship to land at Plymouth. The wind and sea were extremely high; and his officers remonstrated against the imprudence of venturing in a boat where the danger seemed imminent. But he was impatient to see his wife, and would not be persuaded. In a few minutes after he left the ship, the boat was upset and turned keel upwards.

"The captain, being a good swimmer, trusted to his skill, and would not accept a place on the keel, in order to make room for others, and then clung to the edge of the boat. Unluckily, he had kept on his great-coat. At length, seeming exhausted, those on the keel exhorted him to take a place beside them, and he attempted to throw off the coat; but, finding his strength fail, told the men he must yield to his fate, and soon afterwards sank, while singing a psalm."

This year, young Reynolds, now twenty-three, painted his own portrait. Says Tom Taylor, in his "Life and Times of Sir Joshua Reynolds," begun by Charles Robert Leslie, the royal academician, and finished by Taylor, "It is masterly in handling, and powerful, almost Rembrandtesque, in chiaro-oscuro. The hair flows, without powder, in long ringlets over the shoulders. The white collar and ruffled front of the shirt are thrown open. A dark cloak is flung over the shoulders."

This year, 1746, Samuel Reynolds died, and the young painter took his two unmarried sisters to Plymouth to provide for them in his new home. Reynolds learned much at this time from William Gandy, whose father had been a successful pupil of Van Dyck. One of this painter's maxims, which Joshua never forgot, was that "a picture ought to have a richness in its texture, as if the colors had been composed of cream or cheese, and the reverse of a hard and husky or dry manner."

Three years later, an unlooked-for pleasure came to Reynolds. He had always longed to visit Rome for study, but his father was too poor to provide the means, and artists, as a rule, do not grow rich early in their career, if at all. The famous Admiral Keppel, then a commodore only twenty-four years old, appointed to a command in the Mediterranean, put into Plymouth for repairs to his ship. Here, at the house of Lord Edgcumbe, he met the young painter, and was so pleased with his courteous manner and frank kindly nature that he offered him passage on his vessel. The offer was gladly accepted, and they sailed for Lisbon, May 11, 1749. From here they went to Cadiz, Gibraltar, Tetuan, Algiers, the Island of Minorca, where Reynolds painted nearly all the officers of the garrison, then to Genoa, Leghorn, Florence, and, finally, Rome. "Now," he said, "I am at the height of my wishes, in the midst of the greatest works of art that the world has produced."

He remained at Rome two years, his married sisters, Mrs. Palmer and Mrs. Johnson, advancing the money for his expenses. He studied and copied many of the works of Raphael, Michael Angelo, Titian, Rubens, Rembrandt, and others, and filled several journals with his art notes. Two of these books are now carefully preserved in the British Museum, two in the Sloane Museum, and several in the Lenox Gallery in New York.

At first, Reynolds was disappointed in the works of Raphael, but, said he, "I did not for a moment conceive or suppose that the name of Raphael, and those admirable paintings in particular, owed their reputation to the ignorance and the prejudice of mankind; on the contrary, my not relishing them as I was conscious I ought to have done was one of the most humiliating things that ever happened to me. I found myself in the midst of works executed upon principles with which I was unacquainted.

"I felt my ignorance, and stood abashed. All the indigested

notions of painting which I had brought with me from England, where the art was at the lowest ebb,—it could not, indeed, be lower,—were to be totally done away with and eradicated from my mind. It was necessary, as it is expressed on a very solemn occasion, that I should become as a little child. Notwithstanding my disappointment, I proceeded to copy some of those excellent works. I viewed them again and again; I even affected to feel their merits, and to admire them more than I really did. In a short time a new taste and new perceptions began to dawn upon me, and I was convinced that I had originally formed a false opinion of the perfection of art, and that this great painter was entitled to the high rank which he holds in the estimation of the world....

"Having since that period frequently revolved the subject in my mind, I am now clearly of opinion that a relish for the higher excellences of the art is an acquired taste, which no man ever possessed without long cultivation and great labor and attention.... It is the florid style which strikes at once, and captivates the eye, for a time, without ever satisfying the judgment. Nor does painting in this respect differ from other arts. A just and poetical taste and the acquisition of a nice discriminative musical ear are equally the work of time."

In making the studies from Raphael in the Vatican, Reynolds caught so severe a cold as to produce deafness, from which he never recovered, and was obliged to use an ear-trumpet all his life. He could not help observe the superficiality of the average tourist. He said, "Some Englishmen, while I was in the Vatican, came there, and spent above six hours in writing down whatever the antiquary dictated to them. They scarcely ever looked at the paintings the whole time. Instead of examining the beauties of the works of fame, and why they were esteemed, they only inquire the subject of the picture and the name of the painter, the history of a statue and where it is found, and write that down."

Later, Reynolds journeyed to Bologna, Modena, Parma, and Venice, studying the methods of the Venetian painters. He says, "When I observed an extraordinary effect of light and shade in any picture, I took a leaf out of my pocketbook, and darkened every part of it in the same gradation of light and shade as the picture, leaving the white paper untouched to represent the light, and this without any attention to the subject, or to the drawing of the figures. A few trials of this kind will be sufficient to give their conduct in the management of their lights. After a few experiments, I found the paper blotted nearly alike. Their general practice appeared to be, to allow not above a quarter of the picture for the light, including in this portion both the principal and secondary lights; another quarter to be kept as dark as possible; and the remaining half kept in mezzotint or half-shadow. Rubens appears to have admitted rather more light than a quarter, and Rembrandt much less, scarcely an eighth: by this conduct, Rembrandt's light is extremely brilliant, but it costs too much; the rest of the picture is sacrificed to this one object."

Reynolds longed to be at home again. So great was his love for England that when, at Venice, he heard at the opera a ballad that had been popular in London, it brought tears to his eyes.

Reynolds settled in London on his return from the Continent, after spending three months in Devonshire. He took a suite of handsome apartments in St. Martin's Lane, his sister Frances, six years younger than himself, being his housekeeper. She failed to make her brother happy, through her peculiar temperament. She was, says Madame d'Arblay, "a woman of worth and understanding, but of a singular character; who, unfortunately for herself, made, throughout life, the great mistake of nourishing a singularity which was her bane, as if it had been her greatest blessing.... It was that of living in an habitual perplexity of mind and irresolution of conduct, which to herself was restlessly tormenting, and to all around her was teasingly wearisome.

"Whatever she suggested or planned one day was reversed the next; though resorted to on the third, as if merely to be again rejected on the fourth; and so on almost endlessly; for she rang not the changes on her opinions and designs, in order to bring them into harmony and practice, but wavering, to stir up new combinations and difficulties, till she found herself in the midst of such chaotic obstructions as could chime in with no given purpose, but must needs be left to ring their own peal, and to begin again just where they began at first."

Frances copied her brother's pictures, which copies, Reynolds said, "make other people laugh, and me cry." Dr. Samuel Johnson said she was "very near to purity itself;" and of her "Essay on Taste," "There are in these few pages or remarks such a depth of penetration, such nicety of observation, as Locke or Pascal might be proud of."

Reynolds now painted the portraits of Sir James Colebrooke, the Duchess of Hamilton, the Countess of Coventry, and the Dukes of Devonshire and Grafton. The two ladies were two beautiful Irish sisters. Horace Walpole tells us "how even the noble mob in the drawing-room clambered upon chairs and tables to look at them; how their doors were mobbed by crowds eager to see them get into their chairs, and places taken early at the theatres when they were expected; how seven hundred people sat up all night, in and about a Yorkshire inn, to see the Duchess of Hamilton get into her post-chaise in the morning; while a Worcester shoemaker made money by showing the shoe he was making for the Countess of Coventry."

The latter, the elder and lovelier, died seven years after her marriage, from consumption. The Duchess of Hamilton, Reynolds painted again five years later, and a third time in a red dress and hat, on horseback, the Duke standing near her.

"The evident desire which Reynolds had," writes Northcote, his pupil and biographer, "to render his pictures perfect to the utmost of his ability, and in each succeeding instance to surpass the former, occasioned his frequently making them inferior to what they had been in the course of the process; and when it was observed to him that probably he had never sent out to the world any one of his paintings in as perfect a state as it had been, he answered 'that he believed the remark was very just; but that, notwithstanding, he certainly gained ground by it on the whole, and improved himself by the experiment;' adding, 'if you are not bold enough to run the risk of losing, you can never hope to gain.'

"With the same wish of advancing himself in the art, I have heard him say that whenever a new sitter came to him for a portrait, he always began it with a full determination to make it the best picture he had ever painted; neither would he allow it to be an excuse for his failure to say 'the subject was a bad one for a picture;' there was always nature, he would observe, which, if well treated, was fully sufficient for the purpose."

The portrait of his friend Admiral Keppel, standing on a sandy beach, and back of him a tempestuous sea, did much to establish the reputation of Reynolds. He painted eight other pictures of this brave man, who entered the navy at ten and at eighteen had been round the world.

"Keppel was the first of many heroes painted by Reynolds," writes Leslie, "who was never excelled, even by Velasquez, in the expression of heroism. So anxious was he to do all possible justice to his gallant friend, and so difficult did he find it to please himself, that after several sittings he effaced all he had done, and began the picture again....

"From an early period Reynolds adopted what he strongly recommended in his Discourses, the practice of drawing with the hair pencil instead of the port-crayon; and this constant use of the brush gave him a command of the instrument, if ever equalled, certainly never exceeded, for there are marvels of delicacy and of finish in his execution, combined with a facility and a spirit unlike anything upon the canvases of any other painter. I am far from meaning that in the works of other great masters there are not many excellences which Reynolds did not possess; but what I would note is that, though he was all his life studying the works of other artists, he could not, and it was fortunate that he could not, escape from his own manner into theirs."

Reynolds once said to Northcote, "There is not a man on earth who has the least notion of coloring; we all of us have it equally to seek for and find out, as at present it is totally lost to the art.... I had not an opportunity of being early initiated in the principles of coloring; no man, indeed, could teach me. If I have never been settled with respect to coloring, let it at the same time be remembered that my unsteadiness in this respect proceeded from an inordinate desire to possess every kind of excellence that I saw in the works of others, without considering that there are in coloring, as in style, excellences which are incompatible with each other; however, this pursuit, or, indeed, any similar pursuit, prevents the artist from being tired of his art.... I tried every effect of color; and, leaving out every color in its turn, showed every color that I could do without it. As I alternately left out every color, I tried every new color, and often, it is well known, failed....

"I considered myself as playing a great game; and, instead of beginning to save money, I laid it out faster than I got it, in purchasing the best examples of art that could be produced, for I even borrowed money for this purpose. The possession of pictures by Titian, Vandyck, Rembrandt, etc., I considered as the best kind of wealth." He said, in order to obtain one of Titian's best works he "would be content to ruin himself."

Reynolds was probably never surpassed in the drawing of the face, but was not always correct in the human form, because of insufficient knowledge of anatomy.

During Reynolds's second year in London, he had one hundred and twenty sitters, dukes and duchesses, members of Parliament, and reigning beauties. That of Mrs. Bonfoy, daughter of the first Lord Eliot, is, says Leslie, "one of his most beautiful female portraits, and in perfect preservation. The lady is painted as a half-length, in a green dress, with one hand on her hip, and the head turned, with that inimitable grace of which Reynolds was master beyond all the painters who ever painted women."

Already Reynolds had become the friend of the great-hearted, great-minded Dr. Samuel Johnson, who came and went at all hours to the artist's home, and who, when about to be arrested for trivial debts, was again and again befriended by the artist's purse. In 1756, Reynolds painted for himself a half-length of Johnson, with a pen in his hand, sitting at a table. This picture is used in Boswell's Life.

For Johnson's "Idler" Reynolds wrote three papers, sitting up one whole night to complete them, and by so doing was made ill for a time.

He also painted a young lad, the son of Dr. Mudge, who was very anxious to visit his father on his sixteenth birthday, but was prevented through illness. "Never mind, I will send you to your father," said Reynolds, and he sent a speaking likeness, which was of course a gift. He seldom, however, made presents of his pictures, for he said they were usually not valued unless paid for.

About this time, Sir William Lowther, a young millionnaire, died, leaving twenty-five thousand dollars to each of thirteen companions. Each companion very properly commissioned Reynolds to paint for him the portrait of so considerate and generous a friend.

In 1758 and 1759, the artist was overwhelmed with work. In one year there were one hundred and fifty sitters, among them the Prince of Wales, afterwards George III.; Lady Mary Coke, afterwards believed to have been secretly married to the Duke of York, brother of George III.; and the fair and frail Kitty Fisher, very agreeable and vivacious, speaking French with great fluency, who died five years after her marriage, "a victim of cosmetics," it is said. Sir Joshua painted seven beautiful portraits of her. The most interesting represents her holding a dove in her lap, while its mate is about to descend to it from a sofa on which she is reclining. There are three of these, one being in the Lenox collection in New York.

Reynolds also painted the famous Garrick this year, and thirteen years later Garrick and his wife. Leslie writes: "Reynolds had to light the eyes with that meteoric sensibility, and to kindle the features with that fire of life which would deepen into the passion of Lear, sparkle in the vivacity of Mercutio, or tremble in the fatuousness of Abel Drugger. He had to paint the man who, of all men that ever lived, presents the most perfect type of the actor; quick in sympathy, vivid in observation, with a body and mind so plastic that they could take every mould, and give back the very form and pressure of every passion, fashion, action; delighted to give delight, and spurred to ever higher effort by the reflection of the effect produced on others, no matter whether his audience were the crowd of an applauding theatre, a table full of noblemen and wits, a nursery group of children, or a solitary black boy in an area; of inordinate vanity, at once the most courteous, genial, sore, and sensitive of men; full of kindliness, yet always quarrelling; scheming for applause even in the society of his most intimate friends; a clever writer, a wit and the friend of wits.

"Mrs. Garrick, though always the delight and charm of Garrick's house, was now no longer the lovely, light-limbed, laughing Eva Maria Violette, for love of whom Garrick, twenty-five years before, had dressed in woman's clothes that he might slip a letter into her chair, without compromising her, or offending her watchful protectress, Lady Burlington, and who had witched the world as a dancer, while she won friends among the titled and the great by her grace, good-humor, and modest sweetness of disposition. In Lord Normanton's gallery is a most fascinating sketch of her, which must have been painted in the first years of Sir Joshua's acquaintance with her. Slight as it is, those who have seen will not easily forget it. In the picture of her sitting with her husband, painted this year, she appears of matronly character, with a handsome, sensitive, kindly face; the dress is painted with singular force and freedom."

In 1759, Reynolds painted his first Venus, reclining in a wooded landscape, while Cupid looks in through the boughs. Mason, the poet, writes: "When he was painting his first Venus, I was frequently near his easel; and although before I came to town his picture was in some forwardness, and the attitude entirely decided, yet I happened to visit

165

him when he was finishing the head from a beautiful girl of sixteen, who, as he told me, was his man Ralph's daughter, and whose flaxen hair, in fine natural curls, flowed behind her neck very gracefully.

"But a second casual visit presented me with a very different object; he was then painting the body, and in his sitting chair a very squalid beggar-woman was placed, with a child, not above a year old, quite naked, upon her lap. As may be imagined, I could not help testifying my surprise at seeing him paint the carnation of the goddess of beauty from that of a little child, which seemed to have been nourished rather with gin than with milk, and saying that 'I wondered he had not taken some more healthy-looking model;' but he answered, with his usual naïveté, that, 'whatever I might think, the child's flesh assisted him in giving a certain morbidezza to his own coloring, which he thought he should hardly arrive at had he not such an object, when it was extreme (as it certainly was), before his eyes."

Among the many famous portraits of this year and the next was that of the Countess Waldegrave, Horace Walpole's beautiful niece Maria, afterwards Duchess of Gloucester. The earl was the most trusted friend of George II., and, for a short time, prime minister. Walpole mentions the countess being mobbed in the park one Sunday when in company with Lady Coventry, so that several sergeants of the guards marched before and behind them to keep off the admiring crowd. Also that of the beautiful Elizabeth Gunning, afterward Duchess of Argyle, and the sister of Admiral Keppel, afterwards Marchioness of Tavistock. "This is one of the painter's loveliest and best preserved female portraits. The dress is white, with a rose in the bosom, and the expression inimitably maidenly and gentle."

This year, Reynolds removed to a fine home in Leicester Square, where he remained as long as he lived, having a suburban home at Richmond Villa. His own painting-room was octagonal, "about twenty feet long and sixteen in breadth. The window which gave the light to the room was square, and not much larger than one-half the size of a common window in a private house; whilst the lower part of this window was nine feet four inches from the floor. The chair for his sitters was raised eighteen inches from the floor, and turned on casters. His palettes were those which are held by a handle, not those held on the thumb. The stocks of his pencils were long, measuring about nineteen inches. He painted in that part of the room nearest to the window, and never sat down when he worked."

He had now raised his prices to twenty-five, fifty, and one hundred guineas for the three classes of portraits,—head, half-length, and full-length, and his income from his work was thirty thousand dollars a year. He purchased, says Northcote, "a chariot on the panels of which were curiously painted the four seasons of the year in allegorical figures. The wheels were ornamented with carved foliage and gilding; the liveries also of his servants were laced with silver. But, having no spare time himself to make a display of this splendor, he insisted on it that his sister Frances should go out with it as much as possible, and let it be seen in the public streets to make a show, which she was much averse to, being a person of great shyness of disposition, as it always attracted the gaze of the populace, and made her quite ashamed to be seen in it. This anecdote, which I heard from this very sister's own mouth, serves to show that Sir Joshua Reynolds knew the use of quackery in the world. He knew that it would be inquired whose grand chariot this was, and that, when it was told, it would give a strong indication of his great success, and, by that means, tend to increase it."

The next year, Reynolds painted, among others, the Rev. Laurence Sterne, "at this moment the lion of the town, engaged fourteen deep to dinner, 'his head topsy-turvy with his success and fame,' consequent on the appearance of the first instalment of his 'Tristram Shandy.'" The picture is now in the gallery of the Marquis of Lansdowne, by whom it was purchased on the death of Lord Holland.

"Sterne's wig," writes Leslie, "was subject to odd chances from the humor that was uppermost in its wearer. When by mistake he had thrown a fair sheet of manuscript into the fire instead of the foul one, he tells us that he snatched off his wig, 'and threw it perpendicularly, with all imaginable violence, up to the top of the room.' While he was sitting to Reynolds, this same wig had contrived to get itself a little on one side; and the painter, with that readiness in taking advantage of accident, to which we owe so many of the delightful novelties in his works, painted it so, for he must have known that a mitre would not sit long bishop-fashion on the head before him, and it is surprising what a Shandean air this venial impropriety of the wig gives to its owner....

"In 1768, Sterne lay dying at the 'Silk bag shop in Old Bond Street,' without a friend to close his eyes. No one but a hired nurse was in the room, when a footman, sent from a dinner table where was gathered a gay and brilliant party—the Dukes of Roxburgh and Grafton, the Earls of March and Ossory, David Garrick and David Hume—to inquire how Dr. Sterne did, was bid to go upstairs by the woman of the shop. He found Sterne just a-dying. In ten minutes, 'Now it is come,' he said, put up his hand as if to stop a blow, and died in a minute.

"His laurels—such as they were—were still green. The town was ringing with the success of the 'Sentimental Journey,' just published.... Sterne's funeral was as friendless as his death-bed. Becket, his publisher, was the only one who followed the body to its undistinguished grave, in the parish burial-ground of Marylebone, near Tyburn gallows-stand.... His grave was marked down by the body-snatchers, the corpse dug up, and sold to the professor of anatomy at Cambridge. A student present at the dissection recognized under the scalpel the face of the brilliant wit and London lion of a few seasons before."

In 1761, the year of the marriage and coronation of George III., Reynolds painted three of the most beautiful of the ten bridesmaids,— Lady Elizabeth Keppel; Lady Caroline Russell, "in half-length, sitting on a garden-seat, in a blue ermine-embroidered robe over a close white-satin vest. She is lovely, with a frank, joyous, innocent expression, and has a pet Blenheim spaniel in her lap—a love-gift, I presume, from the Duke of Marlborough, whom she married next year;" and Lady Sarah Lenox, whom George III. had loved, and would have married had not his council prevented. She married, six years later, Sir Joshua's friend, Sir Charles Bunbury, was divorced, married General Napier, and became the mother of two illustrious sons, Sir William and Sir Charles. Four years later, Reynolds painted another exquisite picture of her "kneeling at a footstool before a flaming tripod, over which the triad of the Graces look down upon her as she makes a libation in their honor.... Lady Sarah was still in the full glow of that singular loveliness which, it was whispered, had four years ago won the heart of the king, and all but placed an English queen upon the throne. Though the coloring has lost much of its richness, the lakes having faded from Lady Sarah's robes, and left what was once warm rose-color a cold, faint purple, the picture takes a high place among the works of its class—the full-length allegorical."

Five years after this, Lord Tavistock, a young man of rare promise, who had married Lady Keppel, was killed by falling from his horse. His beautiful wife never recovered from this bereavement, and died in a few months at Lisbon, of a broken heart.

All these years were extremely busy ones for the distinguished artist. He disliked idle visitors, saying: "These persons do not consider that my time is worth, to me, five guineas an hour." He belonged to several literary and social clubs, and was a lifelong and devoted friend to such men as Edmund Burke, Johnson, and Goldsmith.

When he was ill, Johnson wrote him: "If the amusement of my company can exhilarate the languor of a slow recovery, I will not delay a day to come to you, for I know not how I can so effectually promote my own pleasure as by pleasing you, in whom, if I should lose you, I should lose almost the only man whom I call a friend."

Reynolds had now raised his prices to thirty guineas for a head, seventy for a half-length, and one hundred and fifty for a full-length, one half to be paid at the first sitting.

In 1766, when he was forty-three, a frequent visitor to the studio was Angelica Kauffman, the pretty Swiss artist, whom he usually enters in his notebooks as "Miss Angel," and whom it is believed he loved and wished to marry. She was, at this time, twenty-five years old, very attractive, and admired by everybody for her genius and loveliness.

Mrs. Ellet, in her "Women Artists," says: "At the age of nine, this child of genius was much noticed on account of her wonderful pastel pictures. When her father left Morbegno, in Lombardy, in 1752, to reside in Como, she found greater scope for her ingenious talent, and better instruction in that city; and, in addition to her practice with the brush and pencil, she devoted herself to studies in general literature and in music. Her proficiency in the latter was so rapid, and the talent evinced so decided, besides the possession of a voice unusually fine, that her friends, a few years afterward, urged that her life should be devoted to music. She was herself undecided for some time to which vocation she should consecrate her powers."

In the native city of her father, Schwarzenberg, Angelica painted in fresco the figures of the Twelve Apostles after copper engravings from Piazetta, an unusual work for a woman. After some years in Milan and Florence, Angelica went to Rome in 1763, where she painted the portrait of Winkelmann, then sixty years old, and other famous people, and was taken to London by the accomplished Lady Wentworth, wife of the British resident.

Here, says Mrs. Ellet, "she found open to her a career of brilliant success, productive of much pecuniary gain. Her talents and winning manners raised her up patrons and friends among the aristocracy. Persons attached to the court engaged her professional services, and the most renowned painter in England, Sir Joshua Reynolds, was of the circle of her friends.... She was numbered among the painters of the Royal Society, and received the rare honor, for a woman, of an appointment to a professorship in the Academy of Arts in London, being, meanwhile, universally acknowledged to occupy a brilliant position in the best circles of fashionable society."

Reynolds painted her portrait twice, and she painted his for his friend, Mr. Parker of Saltram. She was declared by some persons to be "a great coquette." Once she professed to be enamoured of Nathaniel Dance; to the next visitor she would disclose the great secret, "that she was dying for Sir Joshua Reynolds."

When at the height of her fame, either because she had refused a prominent lord, who sought to be revenged, or through the jealousy of another artist, a fearful deception was practised upon her.

"A low-born adventurer," says Mrs. Ellet, "who assumed the name of a gentleman of rank and character—that of his master, Count Frédéric de Horn—played a conspicuous part at that time in London society, and was skilful enough to deceive those with whom he associated. He approached our artist, who was then about twenty-six, and in the bloom of her existence. He paid his respects as one who rendered the deepest homage to her genius; then he passed into the character of an unassuming and sympathizing friend. Finally, he appealed to her romantic generosity, by representing himself as threatened with a terrible misfortune, from which she only could save him by accepting him as her husband. A sudden and secret marriage, he averred, was necessary.

"Poor Angelica, who had shunned love on the banks of Como and under the glowing skies of Italy, and since her coming to London had rejected many offers of the most advantageous alliance, that she might remain free to devote herself to her art, was caught in the fine-spun snare, and yielded to chivalrous pity for one she believed worthy of her heart's affection. The marriage was celebrated by a Catholic priest, without the formality of writings and without witnesses.

"Angelica had received commissions to paint several members of the royal family and eminent personages of the court, and her talents had procured her the favorable notice of the Queen of England. One day, while she was painting at Buckingham Palace, her Majesty entered into conversation with her, and Angelica communicated to her royal friend the fact of her marriage. The queen congratulated her, and sent an invitation to the Count de Horn to present himself at court. The impostor, however, dared not appear so openly, and he kept himself very close at home, for he well knew that it could not be long before the deception would be discovered.

"At length, the suspicions of Angelica's father, to whom her marriage had been made known, led him to inquiries, which were aided by friends of influence. About this time, some say, the real count returned, and was surprised at being frequently congratulated on his marriage. Then came the mortifying discovery that the pretended count was a low impostor. The queen informed Angelica, and assured her of her sympathy.

"The fellow had been induced to seek the poor girl's hand from motives of cupidity alone, desiring to possess himself of the property she had acquired by her labors. He now wished to compel her to a hasty flight from London. Believing herself irrevocably bound to him, Angelica resolved to submit to her fate; but her firmness and strength of nature enabled her to evade compliance with his requisition that she should leave England, till the truth was made known to her—that he who called himself her husband was already married to another woman, still living. This discovery made it dangerous for the impostor to remain in London, and he was compelled to fly alone, after submitting unwillingly to the necessity of restoring some three hundred pounds obtained from his victim, to which he had no right.

"The false marriage was, of course, immediately declared null and void. These unhappy circumstances in no way diminished the interest and respect manifested for the lady who, in plucking the rose of life, had been so severely wounded by its thorns; on the contrary, she was treated with more attention than ever, and received several unexceptionable offers of marriage. But all were declined; she chose to live only for her profession....

"After fifteen years' residence in England, when the physician who attended her suffering father advised return to Italy, and the invalid expressed his fear of dying and leaving her unprotected,

170

Angelica yielded to her parent's entreaties, and bestowed her hand upon the painter Antonio Zucchi."

He was then fifty-three, and she forty. He lived fourteen years after this, and the marriage seems to have been a happy one. Much of the time was spent in Rome, where Angelica became the friend of Goethe, Herder, and others. Goethe said of her: "The good Angelica has a most remarkable, and, for a woman, really unheard-of talent; one must see and value what she does, and not what she leaves undone. There is much to learn from her, particularly as to work, for what she effects is really marvellous.... The light and pleasing in form and color, in design and execution, distinguish the numerous works of our artist. No living painter excels her in dignity, or in the delicate taste with which she handles the pencil."

Her "Allegra" and "Penserosa," "Venus and Adonis," "The Death of Heloïse," "Sappho Inspired by Love," "Leonardo da Vinci dying in the arms of Francis I.," "The Return of Arminius," painted for Joseph II., and the "Vestal Virgin," are among her best known works. She died seven years after her husband, and, as at the funeral of Raphael, her latest pictures were borne after her bier. She was buried in St. Andrea della Fratte, and her bust was preserved in the Pantheon. Such is the sad history of the woman whom it is believed Reynolds loved, and wished to marry.

In 1768 the Royal Academy was founded, chiefly by the exertions of West, the painter, and Sir William Chambers. Reynolds was unanimously chosen its first president, and was immediately knighted by the king. He left a sitter to go to St. James's and receive the honor, and then returned to his sitter. When the president delivered his first discourse, probably on account of his deafness, he did not speak loud enough to be heard. A nobleman said to him, "Sir Joshua, you read your discourse in a tone so low that I scarce heard a word you said."

"That was to my advantage," said Sir Joshua, with a smile.

Reynolds suggested the addition of a few distinguished honorary members to the Academy: Dr. Johnson, as professor of Ancient Literature; Goldsmith, professor of Ancient History, and others. Goldsmith wrote his brother, says Allan Cunningham, in his Life of Reynolds: "I took it rather as a compliment to the institution than any benefit to myself. Honors to one in my situation are something like ruffles to a man who wants a shirt."

Goldsmith was very fond of Reynolds, and dedicated to him his "Deserted Village," in these words: "I can have no expectations, in an address of this kind, either to add to your reputation or to establish my own. You can gain nothing from my admiration, as I am ignorant of the art in which you are said to excel, and I may lose much by the severity of your judgment, as few have a juster taste in poetry than you. Setting interest, therefore, aside, to which I never paid much attention, I must be indulged at present in following my affections. The only dedication I ever made was to my brother, because I loved him better than most other men. He is since dead. Permit me to inscribe this poem to you."

At the first exhibition of the Academy, among the pictures which attracted the most notice were Sir Joshua's Miss Morris as Hope nursing Love,—the lady was the daughter of a governor of one of the West-India Islands, and, going upon the stage as Juliet, was so overpowered by timidity that she fainted and died soon afterwards,— the Duchess of Manchester and her son, as Diana disarming Cupid; and pretty Mrs. Crewe, the daughter of Fulke Greville, whom he had painted at sixteen as Psyche, and at nineteen as St. Genevieve reading in the midst of her flock.

Tom Taylor says: "The Mrs. Crewe should class as one of his loveliest pictures—most touching and pathetic in the expression given by the attitude rather than the face; for the eyes are cast down on the book, and the features are nearly hidden by the hand which supports the head. The landscape is beautiful in color, and powerfully relieves the figure, clothed in a simple white dress, the light of which is distributed through the picture by the sheep feeding or resting about their pretty shepherdess. Walpole notes the harmony and simplicity of the picture, and calls it, not unjustly, 'one of his best.'"

Each year, Reynolds's discourses were eagerly listened to at the Academy. "A great part of every man's life," he said, "must be spent in collecting materials for the exercise of genius. Invention is little but new combination. Nothing can come of nothing. Hence the necessity for acquaintance with the works of your predecessors. But of these, who are to be models—the guides?" The answer is, "Those great masters who have travelled with success the same road.... Try to imagine how a Michael Angelo or a Raphael would have conducted themselves, and work yourself into a belief that your picture is to be seen and observed by them. Even enter into a kind of competition with these great masters; paint a subject like theirs; a companion to any work you think a model. Test your own work with the model.... Let your port-crayon be never out of your hands. Draw till you draw as mechanically as you write. But, on every opportunity, paint your studies instead of drawing them. Painting comprises both drawing and coloring. The Venetians knew this, and have left few sketches on paper.... Have no dependence on your own genius; if you have great talents, industry will improve them; if you have but moderate abilities, industry will supply their deficiency. Nothing is denied to well-directed labor—nothing is to be obtained without it.... Without the love of fame you can never do anything excellent; but by an excessive and undistinguishing thirst after it you will come to have vulgar views; you will degrade your style, and your taste will be entirely corrupted.... I mention this because our exhibitions, while they produce such admirable effects by nourishing emulation and calling out genius, have also a mischievous tendency by seducing the painter to an ambition of pleasing indiscriminately the mixed multitude of people who resort to them."

To Barry, the artist, who was in Rome, he wrote: "Whoever is resolved to excel in painting, or indeed in any other art, must bring all his mind to bear upon that one object, from the moment he rises till he goes to bed. The effect of every object that meets the painter's eye may give a lesson, provided his mind is calm, unembarrassed with other objects, and open to instruction. This general attention, with other studies connected with the art, which must employ the artist in his closet, will be found sufficient to fill up life, if it were much longer than it is.... Whoever has great views, I would recommend to him, whilst at Rome, rather to live on bread and water than lose those advantages which he can never hope to enjoy a second time, and which he will find only in the Vatican.... The Capella Sistina is the production of the greatest genius that was ever employed in the arts.... If you neglect visiting the Vatican often, and particularly the Capella Sistina, you will neglect receiving that peculiar advantage which Rome can give above all other cities in the world. In other places you will find casts from the antique, and capital pictures of the great masters, but it is there only that you can form an idea of the dignity of the art, as it is there only that you can see the works of Michael Angelo and Raphael. If you should not relish them at first, which may probably be the case, as they have none of those qualities which are captivating at first sight, never cease looking till you feel something like inspiration come over you, till you think every other painter insipid in comparison, and to be admired only for petty excellences."

In 1770, Sir Joshua painted a picture called "The Babes in the Woods," which is now in the collection of Viscount Palmerston. Reynolds loved to find picturesque beggar children on the street, and would send them to his studio to be painted. Northcote says he would often hear the voice of a little waif, worn with sitting, say plaintively, "Sir,—sir,—I'm tired!"

"It happened once," says Leslie, "as it probably often did, that one of these little sitters fell asleep, and in so beautiful an attitude that Sir Joshua instantly put away the picture he was at work on, and took up a fresh canvas. After sketching the little model as it lay, a change took place in its position; he moved his canvas to make the change greater, and, to suit the purpose he had conceived, sketched the child again. The result was the picture of the 'Babes in the Wood.'"

This year, Sir Joshua brought the thirteen-year-old daughter, Theophila, of his widowed sister, Mrs. Palmer, to live with him in London, and three years later her elder sister, Mary, who afterward became the Marchioness of Thomond. He painted Theophila, called Offy, as "A Girl Reading," at which the young miss was offended, saying, "I think they might have put 'A Young Lady.'"

Sir Joshua offered to take to his home the sons of his other sister,

173

Mrs. Johnson—he had not forgotten how these two sisters had loaned him money when he was poor—but Mrs. Johnson declined his offer, fearing the temptations of London, and being greatly opposed to her brother's habit of painting on Sundays. One son went into the church and died young; another went to India, and Reynolds took great interest in his welfare. Later, two of Mrs. Johnson's daughters lived with Sir Joshua.

In 1773, he painted and exhibited "The Strawberry Girl," which represents Offy Palmer, creeping timidly along, and looking anxiously around with her great black eyes. Sir Joshua always maintained that this was one of the "half-dozen original things" which he said no man ever exceeded in his life's work. Later the picture was purchased by the Marquis of Hertford for ten thousand five hundred dollars.

F. S. Pulling, of Exeter College, Oxford, says, in his Life of Sir Joshua: "What a love Reynolds had for children, childless though he was himself! What a marvellous knowledge of their ways, and, even of their thoughts! With the peer's son or the beggar's child it was the same. The most fastidious critic finds it impossible to discover faults in these child portraits; the whole soul of the painter has gone into them, and he is as much at home with the gypsy child as with little Lord Morpeth. As Mr. Stephens well observes, 'Reynolds, of all artists, painted children best ... knew most of childhood, depicted its appearances in the truest and happiest spirit of comedy, entered into its changeful soul with the tenderest, heartiest sympathy, played with the playful, sighed with the sorrowful, and mastered all the craft of infancy.... His 'Child Angels' was not painted till 1786. It consists of simply five different representations of the same face, that of Frances Gordon. The perfect loveliness of this picture is beyond dispute.... These are human faces, it is true, but can you imagine any purer, more innocent, more gentle faces?... I, for one, am perfectly content to accept these faces as those of the most lovely beings God ever created."

A picture of a nymph with a young Bacchus, really the portrait of the beautiful young actress, Mrs. Hartley, "whose lovely face and lithe, tall, delicate figure had rapidly won for her the leading place at Covent Garden," is now in the possession of Mr. Bentley, who refused an offer of ten thousand dollars for it.

Sir Joshua was now elected mayor of Plympton, his native town, an honor which he greatly prized; and received the degree of D. C. L. from Oxford University. Oliver Goldsmith had died, and on the day of his death Sir Joshua did not touch a pencil, "a circumstance the most extraordinary for him," says Northcote, "who passed no day without a line." He acted as executor for his dead friend, and found, to his amazement, that his debts were ten thousand dollars.

Reynolds was as ever the centre of a charming circle. Miss Burney, the author of "Evelina," liked his countenance and manners; the former she pronounced "expressive, soft, and sensible; the latter, gentle, unassuming, and engaging." Hannah More, too, was greatly pleased with the distinguished painter.

"Foremost among the beauties of this brilliant time," says Leslie, "was Sir Joshua's pet in childhood, now the irresistible young queen of ton, Georgiana, Duchess of Devonshire. She effaced all her rivals, Walpole tells us, without being a beauty. 'Her youth, figure, glowing good-nature, sense, lively modesty, and modest familiarity make her a phenomenon.' The young duchess was now sitting to him in the full flush of her triumph as arbitress of fashion, the most brilliant of the gay throng who danced and played the nights away at the Ladies' Club, masqueraded at the Pantheon, and promenaded at Ranelagh. Marie Antoinette herself had scarcely a gayer, more devoted, and more obsequious court. It was this beautiful young duchess who set the fashion of the feather headdresses, now a mark for all the witlings of the time. Sir Joshua has painted her in her new-fashioned plumes, in the full-length now at Spencer House....

"Another beautiful sitter of this year was Eliza, the youthful wife of Richard Brinsley Sheridan. The young couple were now emerging from the first difficulties of their married life. Her exquisite and delicate loveliness, all the more fascinating for the tender sadness which seemed, as a contemporary describes it, to project over her the shadow of early death; her sweet voice, and the pathetic expression of her singing; the timid and touching grace of her air and deportment, had won universal admiration for Eliza Ann Linley. From the days when, a girl of nine, she stood with her little basket at the pump-room door, timidly offering the tickets for her father's benefit concerts, to those when in her teens she was the belle of the Bath assemblies, none could resist her beseeching grace. Lovers and wooers flocked about her; Richard Walter Long, the Wiltshire miser, laid his thousands at her feet....

"Nor had she resisted only the temptation of money; coronets, it was whispered, had been laid at her feet as well as purses. When she appeared at the Oxford oratorios, grave dons and young gentlemen commoners were alike subdued. In London, where she sang at Covent Garden in the Lent of 1773, the king himself was said to have been fascinated as much by her eyes and voice as by the music of his favorite Händel. From all this homage Miss Linley had withdrawn to share love in a cottage with Sheridan at East Burnham, after a runaway match in March, 1772, and after her husband had fought two duels in her cause with a Captain Matthews. When she began to sit to Sir Joshua, Richard Brinsley Sheridan was only known as a witty, vivacious, easy-tempered, and agreeable young man of three and twenty, with nothing but his wits to depend on; but, before the picture was finished, he was famous as the author of 'The Rivals.'"

Sir Joshua painted Mrs. Sheridan as St. Cecilia. "She had a way of gathering little children about her, and singing their childish songs, with 'such a playfulness of manner, and such a sweetness of look and voice,' says one, in describing her so engaged, 'as was quite enchanting.'... Mrs. Sheridan was gentleness personified, and sang without pressing; but her husband, proud of her as he was, would never allow her to sing in public after their marriage, and was even chary of permitting her to delight their friends with her sweet voice in private. She was the lovely model for the Virgin in Reynolds's 'Nativity,' for which the young Duke of Rutland paid him six thousand dollars, an unexampled price for an English picture at that time. It was burnt at Belvoir Castle. She died a few years later, living long enough to witness her husband's great success, and not long enough to see him overwhelmed with debts, partly the result of drink."

In 1780, Sir Joshua painted the ladies Maria, Laura, and Horatia Waldgrave, grand-nieces of Horace Walpole. "He never had more beautiful sitters," says Leslie; "and in none of his pictures has he done more justice to beauty. Their bright faces are made to tell with wonderful force, by the white dresses and powdered têtes worn by all three. They are sitting round a work-table. Lady Laura, in the centre, winds silk on a card from a skein held by Lady Horatia; while Lady Maria, on the right, bends over her tambouring frame. The action admits of a natural arrangement of the heads, in full-face, three-quarters, and profile; and it is impossible to conceive an easier, prettier way of grouping three graceful, high-bred young ladies." At this time, all three of these young ladies were in sorrow. The young Duke of Ancaster, to whom Horatia was betrothed, had just died suddenly, and two prominent lords to whom the other sisters were engaged had broken their promises. Lady Maria married, four years later, the Earl of Euston; Laura, her cousin, Lord Chewton; and Horatia, Lord Hugh Seymour.

Sir Joshua painted two years later the beautiful but unhappy Mrs. Musters, whose son John married Mary Chaworth, Byron's first love. "The fine full-length of her as Hebe, with the eagle, still hangs at Colwich Hall. Another full-length, with a spaniel at her feet, painted in 1777, the year of her marriage, is at Petworth. It is interesting to compare the two, and note the wear and tear of five years in the reign of a queen of fashion." The eagle was a pet of Sir Joshua, kept in a yard outside the studio.

In 1783, when Mrs. Siddons was the leading actress of the time, she sat to Reynolds. Taking her hand, he led her up to his platform with the words, "Ascend your undisputed throne: bestow on me some idea of the Tragic Muse." "On which," she said, "I walked up the steps, and instantly seated myself in the attitude in which the Tragic Muse now appears." He inscribed his name on the border of her drapery, saying, "I could not lose the honor this opportunity afforded me of going down to posterity on the hem of your garment." Sir Thomas Lawrence called this the finest portrait in the world of a woman, and Mrs. Jameson says, "It was painted for the universe and posterity." This picture was purchased, in 1822, by the first Marquis of Westminster, for nearly nine thousand dollars. Reynolds also painted Miss Kemble, her sister, "a very sweet and gentle woman."

This year, 1784, a friendship of thirty years was severed by the death of Dr. Johnson. On his death-bed, he made three requests of Sir Joshua: never to use his pencil on Sundays; to read the Bible whenever possible, and always on Sundays; and to forgive him a debt of thirty pounds, which he had borrowed of him, as he wished to leave the money to a poor family. Reynolds was present at the funeral, when his friend was laid beside Garrick, in the south transept of Westminster Abbey.

Reynolds said of his friend: "His pride had no meanness in it; there was nothing little or mean about him.

"Truth, whether in great or little matters, he6 held sacred. From the violation of truth, he said, in great things your character or your interest was affected, in lesser things your pleasure is equally destroyed. I remember, on his relating some incident, I added something to his relation, which I supposed might likewise have happened: 'It would have been a better story,' says he, 'if it had been so; but it was not.' Our friend, Dr. Goldsmith, was not so scrupulous; but he said he only indulged himself in white lies, light as feathers, which he threw up in the air, and, on whomever they fell, nobody was hurt. 'I wish,' says Dr. Johnson, 'you would take the trouble of moulting your feathers.'

"As in his writings not a line can be found which a saint would wish to blot, so in his life he would never suffer the least immorality or indecency of conversation, or anything contrary to virtue or piety, to proceed without a severe check, which no elevation of rank exempted them from.

"The Christian religion was with him such a certain and established truth that he considered it as a kind of profanation to hold any argument about its truth."

At sixty-three years of age, Reynolds was as busy as ever. Miss Palmer wrote to her cousin in Calcutta: "My uncle seems more bewitched than ever with his palette and pencils. He is painting from morning till night, and the truth is that every picture he does seems better than the former. He is just going to begin a picture for the Empress of6 Russia, who has sent to desire he will paint her an historical one. The subject is left to his own choice, and at present he is undetermined what to choose."

He chose "The Infant Hercules strangling the Serpents." Rogers says: "Reynolds, who was always thinking of his art, was one day walking with Dr. Lawrence, near Beaconsfield, when they met a fine rosy little peasant boy—a son of Burke's bailiff. Reynolds patted him on the head, and, after looking earnestly in his face, said: 'I must give

177

more color to my Infant Hercules.'" He took such great pains with this work that he used to say of the picture: "There are ten under it, some better, some worse." The Empress sent him as pay for this a gold box, with her cipher in diamonds, and seven thousand five hundred dollars.

In his "Gleaners," painted in 1788, the centre figure, with a sheaf of corn on her head, was the portrait of a beautiful girl, Miss Potts, who afterwards became the mother of Sir Edwin Landseer.

In 1789, he lost the sight of his left eye, through overwork, but he still preserved the sweet serenity of his nature, and was not depressed. He amused himself with his canary bird, which was so tame that it would sit upon his hand; but one morning it flew out of the window, and never returned.

On December 10, 1790, Reynolds gave his fifteenth and last Discourse to the Academy. In closing, he said to the crowded audience: "I reflect, not without vanity, that these Discourses6 bear testimony of my admiration of that truly divine man; and I should desire that the last words I should pronounce in this Academy and from this place might be the name of Michael Angelo."

As Reynolds descended from the chair, Edmund Burke stepped forward, and, taking his hand, addressed him in the words of Milton,—

> "The angel ended, and in Adam's ear
> So charming left his voice, that he awhile
> Thought him still speaking, still stood fixed to hear."

This year, he allowed Sheridan to buy the picture of his wife, "St. Cecilia," at half-price. Reynolds 'said it was "the best picture he ever painted," and added, in the letter to Sheridan: "However, there is now an end of the pursuit; the race is over, whether it is won or lost."

The next year, in May, 1791, Sir Joshua sat for his picture for the last time to the Swedish artist, Beda, at the request of the Royal Academy of Sweden. He had sent his picture to Florence, on being elected an honorary member of that famous Academy. In October of this year he became almost totally blind.

Burke wrote to his son Richard in January, 1792: "Our poor friend, Sir Joshua, declines daily. For some time past he has kept his bed.... At times he has pain; but for the most part is tolerably easy. Nothing can equal the tranquillity with which he views his end. He congratulates6 himself on it as a happy conclusion of a happy life. He spoke of you in a style that was affecting. I don't believe there are any persons he values more sincerely than you and your mother."

Reynolds died tranquilly between eight and nine on Thursday evening, February 23, 1792. He was buried in St. Paul's, on Saturday, March 3, ninety-one carriages following the body to the grave. There were ten pall-bearers, the Duke of Dorset, Duke of Leeds, Duke of Portland, Marquis Townshend, Marquis of Abercorn, Earl of Carlisle,

Earl of Inchiquin, Earl of Upper Ossory, Lord Viscount Palmerston, and Lord Eliot.

By will he left to his niece Offy, who had married, in 1781, a wealthy Cornish gentleman, Mr. Gwatkin, fifty thousand dollars; to his sister Frances the use, for life, of twelve thousand five hundred dollars; to Burke, ten thousand dollars, and cancelled a bond for the same amount of money borrowed; a thousand dollars to each of his executors; five thousand dollars to a servant who had lived with him more than thirty years; all the remainder of his property, about five hundred thousand dollars, to his niece, Miss Palmer. Such an amount of money earned by an artist, making his own way in life from poverty, was indeed wonderful. The number of his pictures is estimated at three thousand.

Burke wrote of him, the pages blurred with his tears: "Sir Joshua Reynolds was, on very many6 accounts, one of the most memorable men of his time. He was the first Englishman who added the praise of the elegant arts to the other glories of his country. In taste, in grace, in facility, in happy invention, and in the richness and harmony of coloring, he was equal to the great masters of the renowned ages. In portrait he went beyond them; for he communicated to that description of the art, in which English artists are the most engaged, a variety, a fancy, and a dignity derived from the higher branches, which even those who professed them in a superior manner did not always preserve when they delineated individual nature. His portraits remind the spectator of the invention of history and the amenity of landscape. He possessed the theory as perfectly as the practice of his art. To be such a painter, he was a profound and penetrating philosopher.

"In full affluence of foreign and domestic fame, admired by the expert in art and by the learned in science, courted by the great, caressed by sovereign powers, and celebrated by distinguished poets, his native humility, modesty, and candor never forsook him, even on surprise or provocation; nor was the least degree of arrogance or assumption visible to the most scrutinizing eye in any part of his conduct or discourse.

"His talents of every kind, powerful from nature, and not meanly cultivated by letters, his social virtues in all the relations and all the habitudes of life, rendered him the centre of a very6 great and unparalleled variety of agreeable societies, which will be dissipated by his death. He had too much merit not to excite some jealousy, too much innocence to provoke any enmity. The loss of no man of his time can be felt with more sincere, general, and unmixed sorrow."

Mrs. Jameson says: "The pictures of Reynolds are, to the eye, what delicious melodies are to the ear,—Italian music set to English words; for the color, with its luxurious, melting harmony, is Venetian, and the faces and the associations are English.... More and more we learn to sympathize with that which is his highest characteristic, and

179

which alone has enabled him to compete with the old masters of Italy; the amount of mind, of sensibility, he threw into every production of his pencil, the genial, living soul he infused into forms, giving to them a deathless vitality."

One secret of Reynolds's popularity, outside his genius, was the fact that he never spoke ill of the work of other painters. Northcote says he once asked Sir Joshua what he thought of two pictures by Madame Le Brun, who at that time was the most popular artist in France in portraiture.

"'They are very fine,' he answered.

"'How fine?' I said.

"'As fine as those of any painter.'

"'Do you mean living or dead?'

"'Either living or dead,' he answered briskly.

"'As fine as Van Dyke?'

"He answered tartly, 'Yes, and finer.'

"I said no more, perceiving he was displeased at my questioning him."

Leslie says of him: "He felt deeply and almost impatiently the gulf between the technical merits of his pictures and those of the great Venetians or Rembrandt, whom at different epochs he worshipped with equal reverence. I have no doubt his inferiority to these men in power, in mastery of materials, and in certainty of method was just as apparent to Sir Joshua as it is to any unbiassed judge who now compares his pictures with those of Titian, Rembrandt, or Velasquez....

"Estimating Reynolds at his best, he stands high among the great portrait painters of the world, and has achieved as distinct a place for himself in their ranks as Titian or Tintoret, Velasquez or Rembrandt."

SIR EDWIN LANDSEER

Sir Edwin Landseer, born in 1802, in London, on or about March 7, was the fifth child in a family of seven children. The father, John Landseer, a most skilful engraver, was the author of some books on the art of engraving and archæology. He once gave a course of lectures before the Royal Institution. The mother, whose maiden name was Miss Potts, was a gifted and beautiful woman, whose portrait was painted by Sir Joshua Reynolds.

The boy Edwin began to draw very early in life. Miss Meteyard quotes these words from John Landseer: "These two fields were Edwin's first studio. Many a time have I lifted him over this very stile. I then lived in Foley Street, and nearly all the way between Marylebone and Hampstead was open fields. It was a favorite walk with my boys; and one day when I had accompanied them, Edwin stopped by this stile to admire some sheep and cows which were quietly grazing. At his request I lifted him over, and, finding a scrap of paper and a pencil in my pocket, I made him sketch a cow. He was very young6 indeed then—not more than six or seven years old.

"After this we came on several occasions, and as he grew older this was one of his favorite spots for sketching. He would start off alone, or with John (Thomas?) or Charles, and remain till I fetched him in the afternoon. I would then criticise his work, and make him correct defects before we left the spot. Sometimes he would sketch in one field, sometimes in the other, but generally in the one beyond the old oak we see there, as it was more pleasant and sunny."

While still very young, the lad learned the process of etching from his father and elder brother Thomas, the latter one of the most eminent of engravers. At seven, he drew and etched the heads of a lion and a tiger, "in which," says Frederick G. Stephens, "the differing characters of the beasts are given with marvellous craft, that would honor a much older artist than the producer. The drawing of the tiger's whiskers—always difficult things to manage—is admirable in its rendering of foreshortened curves."

At thirteen he drew a magnificent St. Bernard dog. Edwin saw him in the streets of London, in charge of a man servant. He followed the dog to the residence of his owner, and obtained permission to make a sketch of him. The animal was six feet four inches long, and, at the middle of his back, stood two feet seven inches in height. These creatures are capable of carrying one 6hundredweight of provisions from a neighboring town to the monks at the Monastery of St. Bernard, eighteen miles.

Stephens says: "It is really one of the finest drawings of a dog that have ever been produced. We do not think that even the artist at any time surpassed its noble workmanship. The head, though expansive and domical in its shape, is small in proportion to that of a Newfoundland dog; the brow is broad and round; the eyes, according to the standard commonly assumed for large dogs, are far from being large, and are very steadfast in their look, without fierceness; the ears are pendulous, placed near to the head, and fleshy in substance." A live dog, admitted into the room with this picture, became greatly excited.

When Edwin was thirteen, in 1815, he exhibited some pictures at the Royal Academy; a mule, and a dog with a puppy. The following year he became a student at the Royal Academy. He was a bright, manly boy, with light, curly hair, gentle and graceful in manner, and diligent in his work. Fuseli, the keeper of the Academy, was much pleased with him, and, looking around the room upon the students, would say, "Where is my little dog boy?" This was in allusion to the picture of Edwin's favorite dog, Brutus, lying at full length of his chain, near a red earthenware dish. The picture, though very small, was sold in 1861 for seventy guineas.

In 1818, "Fighting Dogs Getting Wind" was exhibited at Spring Gardens, and caused a great sensation. The Examiner said, in a review of the works of the Society of Painters in Oil and Water-Colors, "Landseer's may be called the great style of animal painting, as far as it relates to the execution and color, and the natural, as far as it concerns their portraiture. Did we see only the dog's collar, we should know that it was produced by no common hand, so good is it, and palpably true. But the gasping and cavernous and redly stained mouths, the flaming eyes, the prostrate dog, and his antagonist standing exultingly over him; the inveterate rage that superior strength inflames but cannot subdue, with the broad and bright relief of the objects, give a wonder-producing vitality to the canvas."

Landseer also exhibited this year the "White Horse in a Stable." It disappeared from the studio, and twenty-four years later, in 1842, it was discovered in a hayloft, where it had been hidden by a dishonest servant. It was sent to Honorable H. Pierrepont, for whom it was painted, with a letter from Landseer, saying that he had not retouched the picture, "thinking it better when my early style was unmingled with that of my old age."

In 1819, "The Cat Disturbed" was exhibited, afterwards engraved with the title of "The Intruder." It represents a cat chased to the upper part of a stable by a dog, into whose place she had ventured. Dr. Waagen said, "This picture exhibits a power of coloring and a solidity of execution recalling such masters as Snyders and Fyt."

About this time a lion in the Exeter Change Menagerie died, and the young artist succeeded in getting the body and dissecting it, acting upon Haydon's advice, of years before, to "dissect animals, the only mode of acquiring a knowledge of their construction."

The result was the painting of two large pictures, six feet by eight, and six feet by seven feet six inches respectively: "A Lion Disturbed at his Repast," and "A Lion Enjoying his Repast," followed by a third, "A Prowling Lion."

In 1821, the chief pictures exhibited were "The Rat-Catchers," where four dogs are catching rats in an old barn; and "Pointers, To-ho," a hunting-scene, which sold in 1872 for over ten thousand dollars. The following year, Landseer received from the directors of the British Institution seven hundred and fifty dollars as a prize for "The Larder Invaded." Eighteen other pictures came from Landseer's studio this year.

The most famous of Sir Edwin's early works was "The Cat's-Paw," sold for five hundred dollars, and now owned by the Earl of Essex. Its present value is over fifteen thousand dollars.

"The scene," says Stephens, "is a laundry or ironing-room, probably in some great house, to which a monkey of most crafty and resolute disposition has access. The place is too neat and well maintained to be part of a poor man's house. The ironing-woman has left her work, the stove is in full combustion, and the hand of some one who appreciated the good things of life has deposited on its level top, together with a flatiron, half a dozen ripe, sound chestnuts. To the aromatic, appetizing odor of the fruit was probably due the entrance of the monkey, a muscular, healthy beast, who came dragging his chain and making his bell rattle. He smelt the fruit and coveted them; tried to steal them off the cooking-place with his own long, lean digits, and burnt his fingers.

"He looked about for a more effective means, and, heedless of the motherhood of a fine cat, who with her kittens was ensconced in a clothes-basket, where she blandly enjoyed the coverings and the heat, pounced upon puss, entangled as she was in the wrappings of her ease. Puss resisted at first with offended dignity and wrath at being thus treated before the faces of her offspring. She resisted as a cat only can, with lithe and strenuous limbs; the muscular, light, and vigorous frame of the creature quivered with the stress of her energy; she twisted, doubled her body, buckled herself, so to say, in convulsions of passion and fear, but still, surely, without a notion of the object of her captor.

"Yet he had by far the best of the struggle, for her tiger-like claws were enveloped in the covering which erst served her so comfortably; and, kicking, struggling, squalling, and squealing as strength departed from her, she flounced about the room, upset the coal-scuttle on the floor, and hurled her mistress's favorite flower-pot in hideous confusion on the 'ironing-blanket.' It was to no purpose, for the quadruped, with muffled claws, was no match for her four-handed foe. He dragged her towards the stove, and dreadful notions of a fate in its fiery bowels must have arisen in her heart as nearer and still more near the master of the situation brought his victim.

"Stern, resolute, with no more mercy than the cat had when some unhappy mouse felt her claws—claws now to be deftly yet painfully employed, Pug grasped her in three of his powerful hands, and, as reckless of struggles as of yells, squeals, and squalls, with the fourth stretched out her soft, sensitive, velvety forepaw—the very mouse-slayer itself—to the burning stove and its spoils. What cared he for the bared backs or the spiteful mewlings of her miserable offspring, little cats as they were? He made their mother a true 'cat's-paw.'"

Soon after the exhibition of this picture, Sir Walter Scott came to London and took the young painter to Abbotsford. The novelist greatly admired Landseer's work, saying, "His dogs are the most magnificent things I ever saw, leaping and bounding and grinning all over the canvas." After this, Landseer visited Scotland nearly every year, charmed by its scenery and enjoying the hospitality of the nobles.

In his thirty-second year, it seemed necessary that the painter should have a home removed from the soot and noisy traffic of London. A small house and garden, with a barn suitable for a studio, were purchased at No. 1 St. John's Wood, a suburban region, which derives its name from having been owned by the priors of the Hospital of the Knights of St. John of Jerusalem. A premium of a hundred pounds being demanded for the house, Landseer was about to break off negotiations, when a friend said: "If that is the only obstacle, I will remove it. Go to the lawyers, and tell them to make out the lease, and that as soon as it is ready for signatures, you will pay the sum required; and I will lend you the money, which you can repay when it suits you, without interest."

The painter returned the money loaned, in instalments of twenty pounds each. Here he lived for nearly fifty years, his sister, Mrs. Mackenzie, being his housekeeper. Here he received more famous people than any other English painter save Joshua Reynolds. Here, as he grew wealthy, he brought his dogs and other pets; here the father, John Landseer, to whom the son was ever devotedly attached, died.

A writer in Cornhill says: "There were few studios formerly more charming to visit than Landseer's. Besides the genial artist and his beautiful pictures, the habitués of his workshop (as he called it) belonged to the élite of London society, especially the men of wit and distinguished talents—none more often there than D'Orsay, with his good-humored face, his ready wit and delicate flattery. 'Landseer,' he would call out at his entrance, 'keep de dogs off me' (the painted ones). 'I want to come in, and some of dem will bite me—and dat fellow in de corner is growling furiously.'"

In 1826, when Landseer was twenty-four years old, "Chevy Chase" was painted, now at Woburn Abbey, the property of the Duke of Bedford. It is an illustration of the old ballad:—

"To drive the deer with hound and horne
Erle Percy took his way,

184

The chiefest harts in Chevy Chase
To kill and bear away."

This year, he was made an associate of the Royal Academy, an honor seldom given to so young a man. He was made a full member at thirty. His first important picture exhibited after this, in 1827, was "The Chief's Return from Deer-stalking." "It is," says Stephens, "one of the best of his compositions, the subject giving scope to all his powers in dealing with dogs, deer, and horses. Across the backs of a white and a black pony two magnificent antlered deer are bound. A young chief and his old companion, a mountaineer,—with traces of the wear and tear of a hard life on his cheeks and in his gaunt eyes,—step by the head of one of the horses. They go slowly and heedfully down the hill. Two dogs pace with them; one of these turns to a deer's skull which lies in the herbage."

"The Monkey who had seen the World" appeared at the same time as "The Chief's Return," and was engraved by Gibbon as "The Travelled Monkey." The monkey, who has returned from his travels and meets his friends, is dressed in a cocked hat and laced coat, with a wide cravat, breeches, buckled shoes, and a pendent eyeglass. The latter, especially, astonishes his friends. Thomas Baring gave fifteen hundred guineas for this painting, and bequeathed it to Lord Northbrook.

Another picture of this time, engraved by John Pye, was thus described in the Catalogue: "William Smith, being possessed of combativeness, and animated by a love of glory, enlisted in the 101st Regiment of Foot. At the Battle of Waterloo, on the 18th of July following, a cannon-ball carried off one of his legs; thus commenced and terminated William's military career. As he lay wounded on the field of battle, the dog here represented, blind with one eye, and having also a leg shattered apparently by a musket-ball, came and sat beside him, as 'twere for sympathy.

"The dog became William's prisoner, and, when a grateful country rewarded William's services by a pension and a wooden leg, he stumped about accompanied by the dog, his friend and companion. On the 15th of December, 1834, William died. His name never having been recorded in an extraordinary Gazette, this public monument, representing the dog at a moment when he was ill, and reclining against the mattress on which his master died, is erected to his memory by Edwin Landseer and John Pye."

In this year, 1827, there was also exhibited the well-known "Scene at Abbotsford," with the celebrated Maida, Sir Walter Scott's favorite dog, in the foreground. Six weeks after the picture was painted, the dog died. "High Life" and "Low Life," exhibited in 1831, noteworthy on account of their size, being eighteen inches by thirteen and a half, were bequeathed by Robert Vernon to the nation, and are now in the

National Gallery. "High Life" represents a gentle and slender stag-hound in a handsome home; "Low Life," a brawny bulldog, in a rude stone doorway.

Hamerton says: "Everything that can be said about Landseer's knowledge of animals, and especially of dogs, has already been said. There was never very much to say, for there was no variety of opinion and nothing to discuss. Critics may write volumes of controversy about Turner and Delacroix, but Landseer's merits were so obvious to every one that he stood in no need of critical explanations. The best commentators on Landseer, the best defenders of his genius, are the dogs themselves; and so long as there exist terriers, deer-hounds, bloodhounds, his fame will need little assistance from writers upon art."

In 1832, "Spaniels of King Charles's Breed" was exhibited; now in the National Gallery, as a gift from Mr. Vernon. Both these spaniels, pets of Mr. Vernon, came to a violent end. The white Blenheim spaniel fell from a table and was killed; the true "King Charles" fell through the railings of a staircase, and was picked up dead at the bottom. The picture was painted in two days, illustrating Landseer's wonderful rapidity of execution. Yet this power, as Stephens well says, "followed more than twenty years' hard study."

Stephens records an amazing instance of Landseer's power. "A large party was assembled one evening at the house of a gentleman in the upper ranks of London society; crowds of ladies and gentlemen of distinction were present, including Landseer, who was, as usual, a lion; a large group gathered about the sofa where he was lounging. The subject turned on dexterity and facility in feats of skill with the hand. No doubt, the talk was ingeniously led in this direction by some who knew that Sir Edwin could do wonders of dexterous draughtsmanship, and were not unwilling to see him draw, but they did not expect what followed.

"A lady, lolling back on a settee, and rather tired of the subject, as ladies are apt to become when conversation does not appeal to their feelings or their interests, exclaimed, after many instances of manual dexterity had been cited: 'Well, there's one thing nobody has ever done, and that is to draw two things at once.' She had signalized herself by quashing a subject of conversation, and was about to return to her most becoming attitude, when Landseer said: 'Oh, I can do that; lend me two pencils, and I will show you.'

"The pencils were got, a piece of paper was laid on the table, and Sir Edwin, a pencil in each hand, drew simultaneously, and without hesitation, with the one hand the profile of a stag's head, and all its antlers complete, and with the other hand the perfect profile of a horse's head. Both drawings were full of energy and spirit, and, although, as the occasion compelled, not finished, they were, together and individually, quite as good as the master was accustomed to produce with his right hand alone; the drawing by the left hand was not inferior to that by the right."

In 1834, "Suspense," a bloodhound watching at a closed door for his wounded master, "A Highland Shepherd Dog rescuing Sheep from a Snowdrift," and "A Scene of the Old Time at Bolton Abbey" were exhibited. For the last, Landseer was paid two thousand dollars. It is now owned by the Duke of Devonshire, and is valued at more than fifteen thousand dollars. Queen Victoria and Prince Albert made etchings from this and from several others of Landseer's works.

In 1835, "A Sleeping Bloodhound" (Countess) was exhibited. It was bequeathed by Mr. Jacob Bell to the National Gallery. "The hound was, one dark night (at Wandsworth), anxiously watching her master's return from London. She heard the wheels of his gig and his voice, but, in leaping from the balcony where she watched, she missed her footing, and fell all but dead at her master's feet. Mr. Bell (the owner of the dog) placed the hound in his gig and returned to London, called Sir Edwin Landseer from his bed, and had a sketch made then and there of the dying animal."

In 1837 came "The Highland Shepherd's Chief Mourner," representing the interior of a plain Highland home, the coffin of the shepherd in the centre, covered by his maud for a pall, his only mourner the dog who rests his head upon the coffin. A well-worn Bible is on a stool in front, with a pair of spectacles.

Ruskin calls this picture "one of the most perfect poems or pictures (I use the words as synonymous) which modern times have seen. Here the exquisite execution of the crisp and glossy hair of the dog, the bright, sharp touching of the green bough beside it, the clear painting of the wood of the coffin and the folds of the blanket, are language,—language clear and expressive in the highest degree. But the close pressure of the dog's breast against the wood; the convulsive clinging of the paws, which has dragged the blanket off the trestle; the total powerlessness of the head, laid close and motionless upon its folds; the fixed and tearful fall of the eye in its utter hopelessness; the rigidity of repose, which marks that there has been no motion nor change in the trance of agony since the last blow was struck upon the coffin-lid; the spectacles marking the place where the Bible was last closed, indicating how lonely has been the life, how unwatched the departure, of him who is now laid solitary in his sleep,—these are all thoughts; thoughts by which the picture is separated at once from hundreds of equal merit as far as the mere painting goes,—by which it ranks as a work of high merit, and stamps its author, not as the neat imitator of the texture of a skin or the fold of a drapery, but as a Man of Mind."

"The Portrait of the Marquis of Stafford and the Lady Evelyn Gower," in 1838, is considered Landseer's best portrait-picture. "A Distinguished Member of the Humane Society," exhibited in 1838, is the picture of a large Newfoundland dog named Paul Pry. "He lies in the broad sunlight, and the shadow of his enormous head is cast sideways on his flank as white as snow. He looks seaward with a watchful eye, and his quickness of attention is hinted at by the gentle lifting of his ears. The painting of the hide, here rigid and there soft; here shining with reflected light, there like down; the masses of the hair, as the dog's habitual motions caused them to grow; the foreshortening of his paws as they hang over the edge of the quay, and the fine sense of chiaro-oscuro displayed in the whole, induce us to rank it," says Stephens, "with the painter's masterpieces."

Landseer was now thirty-six years old, famous and honored, a welcome guest at the palaces of royalty. In 1835 he had painted Dash, the favorite spaniel of the Duchess of Kent, the pet of whom Leslie speaks in his autobiography: "The Queen Victoria, I am told, had studied her part very diligently, and she went through it extremely well. I don't know why, but the first sight of her in her robes brought tears into my eyes, and it had this effect upon many people; she looked almost like a child. She is very fond of dogs, and has one very favorite little spaniel, who is always on the lookout for her return when she has been from home. She had of course been separated from him on that day longer than usual, and when the state coach drove up to the steps of the palace, she heard him barking with joy in the hall, and exclaimed, 'There's Dash!' and was in a hurry to lay aside the sceptre and ball she carried in her hands, and take off the crown and robes, to go and wash little Dash."

In 1839 Landseer painted a picture of the Queen, which she gave to Prince Albert; the next year, the Queen and the Duke of Wellington reviewing a body of troops; in 1842, "The Queen and Children;" the Princess Royal with her pony and dog; the Queen and the Princess Royal; "Windsor Castle in the Present Time;" Islay, the Queen's pet terrier; Sharp, her favorite; Princess Alice in a cradle, with the dog Dandie Dinmont; Alice with the greyhound Eos, belonging to Prince Albert, and later "Her Majesty the Queen in the Highlands," "Prince Albert at Balmoral," which was engraved for the Queen's book, "Leaves from a Diary in the Highlands;" Princess Beatrice on horseback, the Queen at Osborne, and the Queen on a white horse.

Landseer was always a favorite with the royal family. In the last painful years of his life, when he suffered from overtaxed nerves, they were his devoted friends. He writes to his sister from Balmoral, June, 1867: "The Queen kindly commands me to get well here. She has to-day been twice to my room to show additions recently added to her already rich collection of photographs. Why, I know not, but since I have been in the Highlands I have for the first time felt wretchedly weak, without appetite. The easterly winds, and now again the unceasing cold rain, may possibly account for my condition, but I can't get out. Drawing tires me; however, I have done a little better to-day. The doctor residing in the castle has taken me in hand, and gives me leave to dine to-day with the Queen and the rest of the royal family.... Flogging would be mild compared to my sufferings. No sleep, fearful cramp at night, accompanied by a feeling of faintness and distressful feebleness."

When Landseer was in good health, he was the most genial of companions. He was the intimate friend of Dickens, Thackeray, Browning, and other noted men. Leslie tells the following incident at a dinner party at the house of Sir Francis Chantrey, the sculptor. "Edwin Landseer, the best of mimics, gave a capital specimen of Chantrey's manner, and at Chantrey's own table. Dining at his house with a large party, after the cloth was removed from the beautifully polished table,—Chantrey's furniture was all beautiful,—Landseer's attention was called by him to the reflections, in the table, of the company, furniture, lamps, etc. 'Come and sit in my place and study perspective,' said our host, and went himself to the fire. As soon as Landseer was seated in Chantrey's chair, he turned round, and, imitating his voice and manner, said to him: 'Come, young man, you think yourself ornamental; now make yourself useful, and ring the bell.' Chantrey did as he was desired; the butler appeared, and was perfectly bewildered at hearing his master's voice, from the head of the table, order some claret, while he saw him standing before the fire."

Some one urged Sydney Smith to sit to Landseer for his portrait. He is said to have replied in the words of the Syrian messenger to the prophet Elisha: "Is thy servant a dog, that he should do this great thing?"

At another time Landseer was talking to Sydney Smith about the drama, and said: "With your love of humor, it must be an act of great self-denial to abstain from going to the theatres." The witty clergyman replied, "The managers are very polite; they send me free admissions which I can't use, and, in return, I send them free admissions to St. Paul's."

Bewick, the artist, said: "Sir Edwin has a fine hand, a correct eye, refined perceptions, and can do almost anything but dance on the slack wire. He is a fine billiard-player, plays at chess, sings when with his intimate friends, and has considerable humor.

"Landseer is sensitive, delicate, with a fine hand for manipulation,—up to all the finesse of the art; has brushes of all peculiarities for all difficulties; turns his picture into all manner of situation and light; looks at it from between his legs,—and all with the strictly critical view of discovering hidden defects, falsities of drawing, or imperfections. See to what perfection he carries his perception of surface, hair, silk, wool, rock, grass, foliage, distance, fog, mist, smoke! how he paints the glazed or watery eye!"

A writer in the London Daily News says: "Sir Edwin's method of composition was remarkably like Scott's, except in the point of the early rising of the latter. Landseer went late to bed, and rose very late, coming down to breakfast at noon; but he had been composing perhaps for hours. Scott declared that the most fertile moments for resources, in invention especially, were those between sleeping and waking, or rather before opening the eyes from sleep, while the brain was wide awake. This, much prolonged, was Landseer's time for composing his pictures. His conception once complete, nothing could exceed the rapidity of his execution."

In 1840, at the country house of Mr. William Wells, Landseer had his first violent illness associated with severe depression, to which attacks he was subject all the rest of his life. He went abroad for a time, travelling in France, Switzerland, and Austria, but he was constantly longing for his studio, where, he said, "his works were starving for him."

"Coming events cast their shadows before them," sometimes called "The Challenge," a vigorous stag bellowing his defiance to hunters or other animals of his kind; "Shoeing," which has been engraved many times, the mare, Old Betty, belonging to his friend Mr. Jacob Bell; and "The Otter Speared," a huntsman surrounded by yelping dogs, while he uplifts a poor otter on his spear, were all exhibited in 1844, and won great praise.

From Sir Edwin's sporting-scenes many persons gained the impression that he was a keen sportsman, which was not the case. Ewen Cameron, an old forest keeper of Glencoe, who for more than twenty-four years accompanied Landseer with the sketch-book and gun, tells how the highland gillies were annoyed when a magnificent stag came bounding toward them, and Sir Edwin hastily thrust his gun into their hands, saying, "Here! take! take this!" while he pulled out his book and began to sketch. They murmured greatly in Gaelic, but, says Cameron, "Sir Edwin must have had some Gaelic in him, for he was that angry for the rest of the day, it made them very careful of speaking Gaelic in his hearing after."

The companion pictures "Peace" and "War," painted in 1846—the former a beautiful scene on a cliff overlooking Dover harbor, the latter a ruined cottage with a dying horse and dead rider near the door—were sold to Mr. Vernon for seventy-five hundred dollars. The publishers of the engravings from these pictures paid Landseer fifteen thousand dollars for them. "The Stag at Bay," belonging to the Marquis of Breadalbane, one of Landseer's strongest pictures, appeared the same year.

In 1848, "A Random Shot," one of the artist's most pathetic pictures, was painted. Stephens thus describes it: "It is a snow piece, the scene high on the mountain, whose most distant ridges rise above the mist. The snow lies smooth; and for miles, so far as the eye can penetrate the vapor, there is nothing but snow, which covers, but does not hide, the shapes of the hilltops. A few footprints show that a doe has come hither, attracted, doubtless, by her knowledge of a pool of unfrozen water which would assuage her thirst. Some careless shooter, firing into a herd of deer, had hit the doe, whose fawn was with her, and, mortally wounded, she came to die; the poor fawn had followed. There the victim fell; there the innocent one strove, long after the mothers form was cold, to obtain milk where an unfailing source had been. The mother has fallen on her side; the long limbs, that once went so swiftly, are useless, and the last breath of her nostrils has melted the snow, so that, stained with her blood, the water trickled downwards until it froze again."

Monkhouse says, in his "Landseer Studies": "He painted dogs and deer as no man ever painted them before; he inspired one with a humor and both with a poetry beyond all parallel in art; he added to this a feeling for the grandeur and sublimity of nature, which gave to his pictures a charm and a sentiment which all can feel; he never painted anything false or ignoble, vulgar or unmanly; he won as an artist purely the affection and admiration of a whole people as scarcely any man, not a poet, or a soldier, or a statesman, or a philosopher, has ever won them before....

"Landseer may be said to have mastered other animals, but the deer mastered him. He raised dogs almost to the scale of humanity, but deer raised him to a level of higher being. His love for the deer may not have been so deep, but it was more elevating, less self-regarding, and it ended at last in stimulating his imagination to produce pictures deeper in thought and more awful in sentiment than any attempted by an animal painter before."

A writer in Cornhill says: "Landseer's perceptions of character were remarkably acute. Not only did he know what was passing in the hearts of dogs, but he could read pretty closely into those of men and women also. The love of truth was an instinct with him; his common phrase about those he estimated highly was that 'they had the true ring.' This was most applicable to himself; there was no alloy in his metal; he was true to himself and to others. This was proved in many passages of his life, when nearly submerged by those disappointments and troubles which are more especially felt by sensitive organizations such as that which it was his fortune—or misfortune—to possess.

"It was a pity that Landseer, who might have done so much for the good of the animal kind, never wrote on the subject of their treatment. He had a strong feeling against the way some dogs are tied up, only allowed their freedom now and then. He used to say a man would fare better tied up than a dog, because the former can take his coat off, but a dog lives in his forever. He declared a tied-up dog, without daily exercise, goes mad, or dies, in three years.

"His wonderful power over dogs is well known. An illustrious lady asked him how it was that he gained his knowledge. 'By peeping into their hearts, ma'am,' was his answer. I remember once being wonderfully struck with the mesmeric attraction he possessed with them. A large party of his friends were with him at his house in St. John's Wood; his servant opened the door; three or four dogs rushed in, one a very fierce-looking mastiff. The ladies recoiled, but there was no fear; the creature bounded up to Landseer, treated him like an old friend, with most expansive demonstrations of delight. Some one remarking 'how fond the dog seemed of him,' he said, 'I never saw it before in my life.'

"Would that horse-trainers could have learned from him how horses could be broken in or trained more easily by kindness than by cruelty. Once when visiting him he came in from his meadow looking somewhat dishevelled and tired. 'What have you been doing?' we asked him. 'Only teaching some horses tricks for Astley's, and here is my whip,' he said, showing us a piece of sugar in his hand. He said that breaking in horses meant more often breaking their hearts, and robbing them of all their spirit...."

In 1850, the "Dialogue of Waterloo" was produced, with the Duke of Wellington and his daughter-in-law, the Marchioness Douro, on the battlefield. It is said that eighteen thousand dollars were paid for the copyright of this painting.

This year, Landseer was made a knight, at the age of forty-eight. The next year, 1851, he painted the well-known "Monarch of the Glen." "The Midsummer Night's Dream" of the same year, painted for the great engineer, Isambard K. Brunel, who ordered a series of Shakespearian subjects from different artists, at four hundred guineas each, was afterwards sold to Earl Brownlow for fourteen thousand dollars.

In 1857, in "Scene in Brae-mar—Highland Deer," we have, says Stephens, "the grandest stag which came from his hands. This was sold in 1868 for four thousand guineas." "The Maid and the Magpie," painted for Jacob Bell, and by him presented to the nation, appeared in 1858. The pretty girl is about to milk a cow, but turns to listen to her lover, when a magpie steals a silver spoon from one of the wooden shoes at her side. In connection with this picture, M. F. Sweetser tells this incident:

"Sir Edwin once painted a picture for Jacob Bell for one hundred guineas, which the latter soon afterwards sold for two thousand guineas. Placing the latter amount in Landseer's bank, Mr. Bell narrated the circumstance, suppressing both his own name and that of the purchaser, and adding that the seller would not keep the money, but wanted another picture painted for it. The master was so charmed with this generous act that he said, 'Well, he shall have a good one.' And afterwards, pressing Bell to tell him who his benefactor was, the latter exclaimed, in the words of Nathan, the Israelite: 'I am the man.' The picture which resulted was 'The Maid and the Magpie.'"

In 1860, "Flood in the Highlands," called by Stephens "probably the strongest of all his pictures," was painted. He was now fifty-eight. "I remember him," says Stephens, "during the painting of this picture, on the Tuesday before it was sent to the Academy,—putting a few touches on the canvas. He looked as if about to become old, although his age by no means justified the notion; it was not that he had lost activity or energy, or that his form had shrunk, for he moved as firmly and swiftly as ever,—indeed he was rather demonstrative, stepping on and off the platform in his studio with needless display,—and his form was stout and well filled.

"Nevertheless, without seeming to be overworked, he did not look robust, and he had a nervous way remarkable in so distinguished a man, one who was usually by no means unconscious of himself, and yet, to those he liked, full of kindness. The wide green shade which he wore above his eyes projected straight from his forehead, and cast a large shadow on his plump, somewhat livid features, and, in the shadow, one saw that his eyes had suffered. The gray 'Tweed' suit, and its sober trim, a little emphatically 'quiet,' marked the man; so did his stout, not fat nor robust, figure; rapid movements, and utterances that glistened with prompt remarks, sharp, concise, with quiet humor, but not seeking occasions for wit, and imbued throughout with a perfect frankness, distinguished the man."

In 1864, "Man proposes, God disposes," was painted, an Arctic incident suggested by the finding of the relics of Sir John Franklin. The purchaser of this picture, Sweetser says, paid Landseer twenty-five hundred pounds for it.

In 1865, "The Connoisseurs" was painted, and presented by Sir Edwin to the Prince of Wales. It represents two dogs looking over the shoulders of the artist, while he makes a drawing. Monkhouse says: "The man behind his work was seen through it,—sensitive, variously gifted, manly, genial, tender-hearted, simple, and unaffected, a lover of animals and children and humanity; and if any one wishes to see at a glance nearly all we have written, let him look at his own portrait, painted by himself, with a canine connoisseur on either side."

"Lady Godiva's Prayer," painted in 1866, was sold in 1874 for £3360, or nearly seventeen thousand dollars. This year, Sir Edwin first appeared as a sculptor, in a vigorous model of a "Stag at Bay." In 1867 his bronze Lions were placed at the base of the Nelson monument in Trafalgar Square, thus associating two great names. The government had commissioned him to execute this work eight years before, in 1859, but sickness and other matters had prevented. That this commission was a care to him, is shown by a letter to a friend: "I have got trouble enough; ten or twelve pictures about which I am tortured, and a large national monument to complete.... If I am bothered about anything and everything, no matter what, I know my head will not stand it much longer."

Again he writes: "My health (or rather condition) is a mystery beyond human intelligence. I sleep well seven hours, and awake tired and jaded, and do not rally till after luncheon. J. L. came down yesterday and did her best to cheer me.... I return to my own home in spite of a kind invitation from Mr. and Mrs. Gladstone to meet Princess Louise at breakfast."

"The Swannery invaded by Sea-Eagles" was one of Landseer's most notable later works. "The Sick Monkey," painted in 1870, was purchased by Thomas Baring for three thousand guineas, and bequeathed to Lord Northbrook, the Viceroy of India.

When Sir Charles Eastlake died, the presidency of the Royal Academy was urged upon Landseer, but he declined. He had become wealthy through his painting, his property amounting to about one million two hundred and fifty thousand dollars, which he left mostly to his brothers and sisters.

Sir Edwin's life was now drawing to its close. Miss Mackey says, in Cornhill, concerning his last long illness: "Was ever any one more tenderly nursed and cared for? Those who had loved him in his bright wealth of life now watched the long days one by one telling away its treasure. He was very weak in body latterly, but sometimes he used to go into the garden and walk round the paths, leaning on his sister's arm. One beautiful spring morning, he looked up and said: 'I shall never see the green leaves again;' but he did see them, Mrs. Mackenzie, his sister, said. He lived through another spring. He used to lie in his studio, where he would have liked to die. To the very end he did not give up his work; but he used to go on, painting a little at a time, faithful to his task.

"When he was almost at his worst, so some one told me, they gave him his easel and his canvas, and left him alone in the studio, in the hope that he might take up his work and forget his suffering. When they came back, they found that he had painted the picture of a little lamb lying beside a lion. This and 'The Font' were the last pictures ever painted by that faithful hand.

"'The Font' is an allegory of all creeds and all created things coming together into the light of truth. The Queen is the owner of 'The Font.' She wrote to her old friend and expressed her admiration for it, and asked to become the possessor. Her help and sympathy brightened the sadness of those last days for him. It is well known that he appealed to her once, when haunted by some painful apprehensions, and that her wise and judicious kindness came to the help of his nurses. She sent him back a message, bade him not be afraid, and to trust to those who were doing their best for him, and in whom she herself had every confidence....

"He wished to die in his studio, his dear studio, for which he used to long when he was away, and where he lay so long expecting the end; but it was in his own room that he slept away. His brother was with him. His old friend came into the room. He knew him and pressed his hand."

Landseer died on the morning of October 1, 1873, and was buried October 11, with distinguished honors, in St. Paul's Cathedral.

TURNER

"Turner was unquestionably, in his best time, the greatest master of water color who had ever lived. He may have been excelled since then in some special departments of the art, in some craft of execution, or in the knowledge of some particular thing in nature; but no one has ever deserved such generally high rank as Turner in the art of water-color painting. His superiority even goes so far that the art, in his hands, is like another art, a fresh discovery of his own.

"The color, in his most delicate work, hardly seems to be laid on the paper by any means known to us, but suggests the idea of a vaporous deposit, and besides the indescribable excellence of those parts of Turner's water-colors which do not look as if they were painted at all, there is excellence of another kind in those parts which exhibit dexterities of execution. Nor is the strange perfection of his painting in water color limited to landscape; his studies of still life, birds and their plumage, bits of interiors at Petworth, etc., are evidence enough that, had he chosen to paint objects rather than effects, he might have been as wonderful an object painter as William Hunt was, though in a different and more elevated manner." Thus writes Philip Gilbert Hamerton.

Turner was born April 23, 1775, in Maiden Lane, London, over a barber shop, in which his father, William Turner, lived and worked. The latter was an economical, good-natured, uneducated man, who taught his boy to be honest and saving.

The mother, Mary Turner, belonged to a family of Marshalls or Mallords near Nottingham, superior in position to the family of William Turner. She had an ungovernable temper, and is said to have led the barber "a sad life." Later, she became insane, and was sent to an asylum.

The boy William very early began to show his skill in drawing. In his first school at New Brentford, when he was ten years old, his birds, flowers, and trees on the walls of the room attracted attention, so that his schoolmates often did his work in mathematics for him while he made sketches. His father had intended him to be a barber, but, perceiving the lad's talent, encouraged him, hung his drawings in his shop windows, and sold them for a few pence or shillings each.

At twelve years of age, William was sent to "Mr. Palice, a floral drawing-master" in Soho; at thirteen, to a Mr. Coleman at Margate, where he loved and studied the sea; and at fourteen, to the Royal Academy. Meanwhile, he earned money by coloring prints, making backgrounds and skies for architects' plans, and copying pictures for Dr. Munro, who lived in one of the palaces on the Strand. This

195

physician owned many Rembrandts and Gainsboroughs, with sketches by Claude, Titian, Vandevelde, and others.

This house proved a valuable place for study to the barber's son, who considered himself fortunate to receive half a crown and a supper for each evening's work.

When pitied by some one in later life, because of the hard work of his boyhood, he said, "Well! And what could be better practice?"

In 1792, when he was seventeen, he received a commission from Mr. J. Walker, an engraver, to make drawings for his Copperplate Magazine, and soon after from Mr. Harrison for his Pocket Magazine. To make these sketches, the youth travelled through Wales, on a pony lent him by a friend, and on foot, with his baggage in his handkerchief tied to the end of a stick, through Nottingham, Cambridge, Lincoln, Peterborough, Windsor, Ely, the Isle of Wight, and elsewhere.

"The result of these tours," says W. Cosmo Monkhouse, "may be said to have been the perfection of his technical skill, the partial displacement of traditional notions of composition, and the storing of his memory with infinite effects of nature."

His first water color at the Royal Academy Exhibition was a picture of Lambeth Palace, when he was fifteen, and his first oil painting at the exhibition, according to Redgrave, the "Rising Squall, Hot Wells," when he was eighteen. Hamerton thinks "Moonlight," a study in Milbank, was his first exhibited work in oil. "The picture," he says, "shows not the least trace of genius, yet it has always been rather a favorite with me for its truth to nature in one thing. All the ordinary manufacturers of moonlights—and moonlights have been manufactured in deplorably large quantities for the market—represent the light of our satellite as a blue and cold light; whereas in nature, especially in the southern summer, it is often pleasantly rich and warm. Turner did not follow the usual receipt, but had the courage to make his moonlight warm, though he had not as yet the skill to express the ineffably mellow softness of the real warm moonlights in nature."

At twenty-one, Turner hired a house in Hand Court, and began to teach drawing in London and elsewhere at ten shillings a lesson. But he soon grew impatient of his fashionable pupils, and the teaching was abandoned.

At twenty-two, he journeyed into the counties of Yorkshire and Kent, and soon produced "Morning on the Coniston Fells," in 1798; "Cattle in Water; Buttermere Lake," 1798; and "Norham Castle on the Tweed." Twenty years afterward, as he was passing Norham Castle, with Cadell, an Edinburgh publisher, he took off his hat to the castle. Cadell expressed surprise. "Oh," said Turner, "I made a drawing or painting of Norham several years ago. It took; and from that day to this I have had as much to do as my hands could execute."

In Yorkshire, the rising young artist, natural and genial in manner, though small and somewhat plain in person, made many warm friends. He was often a guest at Farnley Hall, owned by Mr. Hawkesworth Fawkes, who afterward adorned his home with fifty thousand dollars' worth of Turner's pictures.

Mr. Fawkes's son speaks of "the fun, frolic, and shooting we enjoyed together, and which, whatever may be said by others of his temper and disposition, have proved to me that he was, in his hours of distraction from his professional labors, as kindly-hearted a man, and as capable of enjoyment and fun of all kinds, as any I ever knew."

Mrs. Wheeler, a friend in these early years, says: "Of all the light-hearted, merry creatures I ever knew, Turner was the most so; and the laughter and fun that abounded when he was an inmate of our cottage was inconceivable, particularly with the juvenile members of the family."

Somewhere between the ages of nineteen and twenty-three, a sorrow came which seemed completely to change Turner's nature. While at the Margate school, he had fallen in love with the sister of a schoolmate; the love had been reciprocated, and an engagement followed a few years later. During a long absence in his art work, their letters were intercepted by the young lady's stepmother, who finally prevailed upon her to become engaged to another. A week before the wedding, Turner arrived at Margate, and besought her to marry him; but his betrothed considered herself in honor bound to the new lover. The marriage proved a most unhappy one, and Turner remained a disappointed and solitary man through life.

His art now became his one absorbing thought; he worked early and late, often rising for work at four o'clock in the morning, saying sadly that there were "no holidays for him."

In 1799, when he was twenty-four, he was made an associate of the Royal Academy, and a full academician in 1802. Hamerton says: "His election is the more remarkable, that he had done nothing whatever to bring it about, except his fair hard work in his profession. He was absolutely incapable of social courtiership in any of its disguises. He gave no dinners, he paid no calls, he did nothing to make the academicians believe that he would be a credit to their order in any social sense. Even after his election, he would not go to thank his electors, in obedience to the established usage. 'If they had not been satisfied with my pictures,' he said to Stothard, 'they would not have elected me. Why, then, should I thank them? Why thank a man for performing a simple duty?' His views on the subject were clearly wrong, for the rules of good manners very frequently require us to thank people for performing simple duties, and the academicians were not under any obligation to elect the young painter so soon; but how completely Turner's conduct in this matter proves that he can only have been elected on his merits!...

"His elevation to the full membership was of immense value to him in his career, and he knew this so well that he remained deeply attached to the Academy all his life. He was associate or member of it for a full half-century, and during fifty years was only three times absent from its exhibitions."

This year, 1802, he removed to 64 Harley Street, taking his plain old father home to live with him. He took his first tour on the Continent, this year, making studies of Mont Blanc, the Swiss lakes and mountain passes. The exhibitions of 1803 to 1806 contained, among other pictures, "The Vintage at Macon," the celebrated "Calais Pier" in a gale; "The Source of the Arveiron," "Narcissus and Echo," "Edinburgh from Calton Hill;" his famous "Shipwreck," now in the National Gallery; and the magnificent "Goddess of Discord choosing the Apple of Contention in the Garden of Hesperides," also in the National Gallery.

In 1807, Turner began, at the suggestion of his friend, Mr. W. F. Wells, the Liber Studiorum, issued in dark blue covers, each containing five plates, the whole series of one hundred plates to be divided into historical, landscape, pastoral, mountainous, marine, and architectural. The work was intended as a rival to Claude Lorraine's Liber Veritatis.

After seventy plates had been published, the project came to an end in 1816, because of disagreement with engravers, and lack of patronage. The principal pictures were "Æsacus and Hesperia," "Jason," "Procris and Cephalus," the "Fifth and Tenth Plagues of Egypt," "Christ and the Woman of Samaria," "Rizpah," "Raglan Castle," the "River Wye," "Solway Moss," "Inverary," the "Yorkshire Coast," "Mer de Glace," the "Lake of Thun," "St. Gothard Pass," the "Alps from Grenoble," "Dunstanborough Castle," and others.

"So hopeless and worthless did the enterprise seem, at one time," says M. F. Sweetser, "that Charles Turner, the engraver, used the proofs and trials of effect as kindling paper. Many years later, Colnaghi, the great print-dealer, caused him to hunt up the remaining proofs in his possession, and gave him fifteen hundred pounds for them. 'Good God!' cried the old engraver, 'I have been burning bank-notes all my life.'... In later days three thousand pounds had been paid for a single copy of the Liber."

"The most obvious intention of the work," says Monkhouse, "was to show Turner's own power, and there never was, and perhaps never will be again, such an exhibition of genius in the same direction. No rhetoric can say for it as much as it says for itself in those ninety plates, twenty of which were never published. If he did not exhaust art or nature, he may be fairly said to have exhausted all that was then known of landscape art, and to have gone further than any one else in the interpretation of nature....

"Amongst his more obvious claims to the first place among landscape artists are his power of rendering atmospherical effects, and the structure and growth of things. He not only knew how a tree looked, but he showed how it grew. Others may have drawn foliage

198

with more habitual fidelity, but none ever drew trunks and branches with such knowledge of their inner life.... Others have drawn the appearance of clouds, but Turner knew how they formed. Others have drawn rocks, but he could give their structure, consistency, and quality of surface, with a few deft lines and a wash; others could hide things in a mist, but he could reveal things through mist. Others could make something like a rainbow, but he, almost alone, and without color, could show it standing out, a bow of light arrested by vapor in mid-air, not flat upon a mountain, or printed on a cloud.... If we seek the books from which his imagination took fire, we have the Bible and Ovid; the first of small, the latter of great and almost solitary power. Jason, daring the huge glittering serpent; Syrinx, fleeing from Pan; Cephalus and Procris; Æsacus and Hesperia; Glaucus and Scylla; Narcissus and Echo. If we want to know the artists he most admired and imitated, or the places to which he had been, we shall find easily nearly all the former, and sufficient of the latter to show the wide range of his travel. In a word, one who has carefully studied the Liber has indeed little to learn of the range and power of Turner's art and mind, except his color and his fatalism."

In 1808, Turner was appointed professor of perspective in the Royal Academy, which position he held for thirty years, though he rarely gave lectures to students, owing to his confused manner and obscurity in the use of language. Ruskin says: "The zealous care with which Turner endeavored to do his duty is proved by a large existing series of drawings, exquisitely tinted, and often completely colored, all by his own hand, of the most difficult perspective subjects; illustrating not only directions of line, but effects of light, with a care and completion which would put the work of any ordinary teacher to utter shame. In teaching generally, he would neither waste time nor spare it; he would look over a student's drawing at the Academy, point to a defective part, make a scratch on the paper at the side, say nothing. If the student saw what was wanted, and did it, Turner was delighted; but if the student could not follow, Turner left him."

Turner this year moved to the Upper Mall, Hammersmith, where his garden extended to the Thames. In this he had a summer-house, where some of his best work was done. He still retained the Harley-Street house, and lived in it much the life of a recluse. Mr. Thornbury tells the following incident:—

"Two ladies called upon Turner while he lived in Harley Street. On sending in their names, after having ascertained that he was at home, they were politely requested to walk in, and were shown into a large sitting-room without a fire. This was in the depth of winter; and lying about in various places were several cats without tails. In a short time our talented friend made his appearance, asking the ladies if they felt cold. The youngest replied in the negative; her companion, more curious, wished she had stated otherwise, as she hoped they might have been shown into his sanctum or studio. After a little conversation he offered them wine and biscuits, which they partook of for the novelty, such an event being almost unprecedented in his house. One of the ladies bestowing some notice upon the cats, he was induced to remark that he had seven, and that they came from the Isle of Man."

Turner was fond of his pet cats, and would let no harm come to them. After he had moved, in 1812, to 47 Queen-Anne Street, one of his favorite pictures, "Bligh Shore" was used as a covering for a window. A cat desiring to enter the window scratched the picture severely, and was about to be punished for the offence, by Mrs. Danby, the housekeeper, when Turner said, "Never mind," and saved the cat from the whipping.

At his house in Twickenham, which he bought and rebuilt in 1813 or 1814, calling it Solus Lodge on account of his desire to be alone, and afterwards Sandycomb Lodge, the boys named him "Blackbirdy," because he protected the blackbirds in the adjacent trees, not allowing their nests to be robbed. Turner sold this place after having owned it about twelve years, because his aged father, whom he always called "Dad," was always working in the garden and catching cold.

The eccentric artist must have been at this time quite rich, as well as famous. He had painted "The Sun rising in Mist," in 1807; the well-known "Wreck of the Minotaur," in 1810; "Apollo killing the Python," in 1811; "Hannibal and his Army crossing the Alps in a Snowstorm," in 1812; and "Crossing the Brook," and "Dido building Carthage," in 1815. "The first ('Crossing the Brook')," says Monkhouse, "is the purest and most beautiful of all his oil pictures of the loveliness of English scenery, the most simple in its motive, the most tranquil in its sentiment, the perfect expression of his enjoyment of the exquisite scenery in the neighborhood of Plymouth. The latter ('Dido building Carthage'), with all its faults, was the finest of the kind he ever painted, and his greatest effect in the way of color before his visit to Italy."

It is said that "Crossing the Brook" was painted for a gentleman who ordered it with the promise of paying twenty-five hundred dollars for it, but was disappointed in it when finished, and refused to take it. Turner was afterwards offered eight thousand dollars for it, but would not sell it.

In 1815, the artist, now forty years old, was again disappointed in love. He wrote to one of his best friends, Rev. H. Scott Trimmer, vicar of Heston, concerning his sister, Miss Trimmer: "If she would but waive her bashfulness, or, in other words, make an offer instead of expecting one, the same (Sandycomb Lodge) might change occupiers." But Miss Trimmer had, at this time, another suitor, whom she married, and Turner never again attempted to win a wife.

In 1817, "The Decline of the Carthaginian Empire" was exhibited, a companion piece to the Building of Carthage. Years later, Sir Robert Peel, Lord Hardinge, and others, offered twenty-five thousand dollars to Turner for the two pictures, intending to present them to the National Gallery. "It's a noble offer," said the painter, "but I have willed them." He had already made his will, privately, giving these and other pictures to the nation.

The artist is said to have once remarked to his friend Chantrey, the sculptor: "Will you promise to see me rolled up in the 'Carthage' at my burial?"

"Yes," was the reply; "and I promise you also that, as soon as you are buried, I will see that you are taken up and unrolled."

In 1819, Turner made his first visit to Italy, after which his works became remarkable for their color. In 1823, says Monkhouse, "he astonished the world with the first of those magnificent dreams of landscape loveliness with which his name will always be specially associated: 'The Bay of Baiæ, with Apollo and the Sibyl.'"

The "Rivers of England" was published in 1826, with sixteen engravings after Turner's designs. Monkhouse says: "For perfect balance of power, for the mirroring of nature as it appears to ninety-nine out of every hundred, for fidelity of color to both sky and earth, and form (especially of trees), for carefulness and accuracy of drawing, for work that neither startles you by its eccentricity nor puzzles you as to its meaning, which satisfies without cloying, and leaves no doubt as to the truth of its illusion, there is none to compare with these drawings of his of England after his first visit to Italy."

During this year, 1826, among other pictures, Turner exhibited his "Cologne—the Arrival of a Packet-boat—Evening." "There were," says Hamerton, "such unity and serenity in the work, and such a glow of light and color, that it seemed like a window opened upon the land of the ideal, where the harmonies of things are more perfect than they have ever been in the common world." The picture was hung between two of Sir Thomas Lawrence's portraits, the golden color of the "Cologne" dulling their effect. Turner at once covered his picture with lampblack, thereby spoiling it for the public view. When reproached by the critics, he said: "Poor Lawrence was so unhappy. It will all wash off after the Exhibition." "Was there ever," says Hamerton, "a more exquisitely beautiful instance of self-sacrifice?" The "Cologne" was sold, in 1854, to Mr. John Naylor, for two thousand guineas.

Turner made designs for twenty illustrations in Rogers's poem of "Italy," for which, it is asserted, he would accept but five guineas each, as the execution of the work pleased him so well; thirteen illustrations for "The Provincial Antiquities of Scotland," for which Sir Walter Scott wrote the letter-press; and twenty-six pictures for Finden's "Illustrations of the Bible." Turner generally received from twenty to one hundred guineas for each drawing used, which was returned to him that he might sell it, if he so desired.

In 1827 the first part of his largest series of prints was published:

"England and Wales." The work was discontinued twelve years later, because it was not a pecuniary success.

Bohn offered twenty-eight hundred pounds for the copper plates and stock, but Turner himself bid them in, at the auction, for three thousand pounds, saying to Bohn: "So, sir, you were going to buy my 'England and Wales' to sell cheap, I suppose—make umbrella prints of them, eh? But I have taken care of that."

He disliked steel engravings, or any plan to cheapen or popularize art. He once told Sir Thomas Lawrence that he "didn't choose to be a basket engraver." Being asked what he meant, he replied: "When I got off the coach t'other day at Hastings, a woman came up with a basketful of your 'Mrs. Peel,' and wanted to sell me one for a sixpence."

The painter's hard-working life, with little comfort save what fame brings to a man who eagerly seeks it, received its greatest shock in the death of the aged father, in 1830. Turner said, "The loss was like that of an only child." His friends the Trimmers said, "He never appeared the same man after his father's death."

The plain barber had lived with his son for thirty years, and had seen him gain wealth and renown. He could do little save to encourage with his affection and be proud and grateful for the painter's success. And this was enough. He was buried in St. Paul's, Covent Garden, the artist writing this inscription for his monument:—

IN THE VAULT
BENEATH AND NEAR THIS PLACE
ARE DEPOSITED THE REMAINS OF
WILLIAM TURNER,
MANY YEARS AN INHABITANT OF THIS PARISH,
WHO DIED
SEPTEMBER 21ST, 1830.
TO HIS MEMORY AND OF HIS WIFE,
MARY ANN,
THEIR SON J. M. W. TURNER, R. A.,
HAS PLACED THIS TABLET,
AUGUST, 1832.

In 1832, Turner exhibited his memorable "Childe Harold's Pilgrimage; Italy," in which he seemed to combine the mountains, the trees, the cities, and the skies he had loved in that beautiful country. From 1833 to 1835 he produced his exquisite series, "The Rivers of France." Ruskin says: "Of all foreign countries, Turner has most entirely entered into the spirit of France; partly because here he found more fellowship of scene with his own England; partly because an amount of thought which will miss of Italy or Switzerland will fathom France; partly because there is in the French foliage and forms of ground much that is especially congenial with his own peculiar choice of form.... He still remains the only, but in himself the sufficient, painter of French landscape."

In 1833 Turner exhibited the first of his eleven remarkable Venetian pictures, one of the finest being, "The Sun of Venice going to Sea." "The characteristics which they have in common," says Hamerton, "are splendor of color and carelessness of form; the color being, in most instances, really founded upon the true Venetian color, but worked up to the utmost brilliance which the palette would allow, the forms simply sketched, exactly on the principles of the artist's own free sketching in water colors.... It is believed, and with probability, that he blocked out the picture almost entirely in pure white, with only some very pale tinting, just to mark the position of the objects, and that this white preparation was thick and loaded from the beginning. On this he afterwards painted thinly in oil or water-color, or both, so that the brilliance of the white shone through the color, and gave it that very luminous quality which it possesses. This is simply a return to the early Flemish practice of painting thinly on a light ground, with the difference, however, that Turner made a fresh ground of his own between the canvas and his bright colors, and that the modelling of the impasto with the brush was done in this thick white. The result was to unite the brilliance of water-color to the varied and rich surface of massive oil-painting."

These pictures called forth much adverse criticism, but they soon had a Herculean defender in the "Oxford Undergraduate" of 1836, the Ruskin of "Modern Painters." In 1839, Turner exhibited "The fighting Téméraire tugged to her last berth to be broken up, 1838." Thornbury tells how the subject was suggested to Turner.

"In 1838, Turner was with Stanfield and a party of brother artists on one of those holiday excursions, in which he so delighted, probably to end with whitebait and champagne at Greenwich. It was at these times that Turner talked and joked his best, snatching, now and then, a moment to print on his quick brain some tone of sky, some gleam of water, some sprinkling light of oar, some glancing sunshine cross-barring a sail. Suddenly there moved down upon the artist's boat the grand old vessel that had been taken prisoner at the Nile and that led the van at Trafalgar. She loomed pale and ghostly, and was being towed to her last moorings at Deptford by a little fiery, puny steam-tug.

"'There's a fine subject, Turner,' said Stanfield," and the suggestion was gladly acted upon.

Hamerton says: "The picture is, both in sentiment and execution, one of the finest of the later works. The sky and water are both magnificent, and the shipping, though not treated with severe positive truth, is made to harmonize well with the rest, and not stuck upon the canvas, as often happens in the works of bad marine painters. The sun sets in red, and the red, by the artist's craft, is made at the same time both decided in hue and luminous, always a great technical difficulty. Golden sunsets are easy in comparison, as every painter knows. This picture has more than once been associated by critics with the magnificent 'Ulysses deriding Polyphemus,' which was painted ten years earlier. Both are splendid in sky and water, and both are florid in color. Mr. Ruskin's opinion is that the period of Turner's central power, 'entirely developed and entirely unabated, begins with the Ulysses, and closes with the Téméraire.'

"This decade had been a time of immense industry for Turner. In that space he had made more than four hundred drawings for the engraver, had exhibited more than fifty pictures in the Royal Academy, and had executed, besides, some thousands of sketches, and probably many private commissions which cannot easily be ascertained."

One reason of his aversion to society was his desire to save time for this great amount of work. The Téméraire, though sought by several persons, the artist refused to sell at any price, and bequeathed it to the nation.

From 1840 to 1845, Turner painted a few pictures of great power. The "Slave Ship, slavers throwing overboard the dead and dying, typhoon coming on," was exhibited in 1840. It became the property of Mr. Ruskin, who sold it, and it is now in the Boston Museum of Fine Arts. It represents a sunset on the Atlantic after a storm. It is gorgeous in color, and is regarded by many as the grandest sea which Turner ever painted. The "Snowstorm," in 1842, was harshly criticised, and called "soapsuds and whitewash." The picture represents a steamer off a harbor in a storm, making signals.

Ruskin says: "Turner was passing the evening at my father's house, on the day this criticism came out; and after dinner, sitting in his armchair, I heard him muttering low to himself at intervals, 'Soapsuds and whitewash!' again, and again, and again. At last I went to him, asking 'why he minded what they said.' Then he burst out: 'Soapsuds and whitewash! what would they have? I wonder what they think the sea's like? I wish they'd been in it!'"

Turner had been in the storm, and knew that he had painted truthfully. One night, when the Ariel left Harwich, he "got the sailors to lash him to the mast, to observe the storm," and remained there four hours, not expecting to survive it.

"Peace—Burial at Sea," now in the National Gallery, was exhibited also in 1842. It was painted to commemorate the funeral of Sir David Wilkie, the Scottish artist, which had taken place in June, 1841, off Gibraltar, some distance from shore. Whilst the picture was on the easel, Stanfield entered Turner's studio and said, "You're painting the sails very black," to which the artist made answer, "If I could find anything blacker than black, I'd use it."

The deaths of Chantrey, in 1841, and of Callcott, in 1844, deeply affected Turner. "In the death-chamber of the former," says George

Jones, "he wrung my hands, tears streaming from his eyes, and then rushed from the house without uttering a word." When William Frederick Wells, the artist, died a few years previously, Turner went to the house, sobbing like a child, and saying to the daughter, "O Clara, Clara! these are iron tears. I have lost the best friend I ever had in my life."

In 1843, he took his last journey to the Continent, making many sketches about Lake Lucerne, which was very dear to him. From 1847 to 1849, he paid several visits to the photographic artist Mayall, calling himself a master in chancery, as he did not wish to be recognized. He was deeply interested in the progress of photography. When Mayall was in pecuniary trouble in consequence of a lawsuit about patent rights, Turner, unasked, brought him fifteen hundred dollars, telling him to repay it sometime if he could. He gladly accepted the loan and paid it. After nearly two years, Turner found that his personality had become known, and could never be induced to visit the place again.

In 1850, he sent his last pictures to the Academy: "Æneas relating his Story to Dido," "Mercury sent to admonish Æneas," "The Departure of the Trojan Fleet," and "The Visit to the Tomb."

He was now seventy-five years old. In 1851, he exhibited no pictures, and ceased to attend the Academy meetings, which had always given him so much pleasure. David Roberts, the artist, wrote him, and begged to be allowed to see him. Two weeks later, Turner called at the studio. "I tried to cheer him up," says Roberts, "but he laid his hand upon his heart and replied, 'No, no; there is something here which is all wrong.' As he stood by the table in my painting-room, I could not help looking attentively at him, peering in his face, for the small eye (blue) was brilliant as that of a child, and unlike the glazed and 'lack-lustre eye' of age. This was my last look."

For several months, the aged artist was absent from his home in Queen-Anne Street. Finally, Hannah Danby, who had been his housekeeper for fifty years, and was said to have been his mistress, found a letter in the pocket of an old coat, which led her to believe he was in Chelsea. She and a relative sought him, and found him, December 18, 1851, very ill, in a small plain cottage on the banks of the Thames, owned by Sophia Caroline Booth. He was called "Admiral Booth" by her neighbors, who thought him an admiral in reduced circumstances. He died the day after his friends found him. An hour before his death, he was wheeled to the window to look out upon the Thames, and bathe in the sunshine which he so dearly loved.

"So died," says Monkhouse, "the great solitary genius, Turner, the first of all men to endeavor to paint the full power of the sun, the greatest imagination that ever sought expression in landscape, the greatest pictorial interpreter of the elemental forces of nature that ever lived.... Sunlight was his discovery; he had found its presence in shadow; he had studied its complicated reflections before he commenced to work in color. From monochrome he had adopted the low scale of the old masters, but into it he carried his light; the brown clouds, and shadows and mists, had the sun behind them, as it were, in veiled splendor. Then it came out and flooded his drawings and his canvases with a glory unseen before in art. But he must go on, refine upon this; having eclipsed all others, he must now eclipse himself. His gold must turn to yellow, and yellow almost into white, before his genius could be satisfied with its efforts to express pure sunlight."

Turner was buried in St. Paul's Cathedral, between the tombs of Sir Joshua Reynolds and James Barry, the service being read by Dean Milman. By his will, he left all his pictures and drawings to the nation, to be preserved in a "Turner Gallery," specifying that "The Sun Rising in Mist" and "Dido building Carthage" should be hung between the two pictures painted by Claude, the "Seaport" and "Mill." During his life he is said to have refused two offers of five hundred thousand dollars for the pictures in his Queen-Anne Street house. He left one hundred thousand dollars to the Royal Academy, five thousand dollars for a monument to himself in St. Paul's, a few small bequests for relatives, money for a medal to be given for the best landscape exhibited at the Academy every two or three years, and the remainder of a large fortune for the maintenance of "poor and decayed male artists being born in England and of English parents only, and lawful issue;" the latter gift to be known as "Turner's Gift."

The will was contested by relatives, and, after four years of litigation, the testator's intention to provide for aged artists was disregarded, and the property given to the "nearest of kin." Such instances are teaching our great men to carry out their benevolent wishes in their lifetime. Though Turner had great faults,—it is stated that he drank to excess in later years,—he had great virtues. Though parsimonious with himself, he was generous to others. Ruskin tells these incidents:

"There was a painter of the name of Bird, and when Bird first sent a picture to the Academy for exhibition, Turner was on the hanging committee. Bird's picture had great merit; but no place for it could be found. Turner pleaded hard for it. No, the thing was impossible. Turner sat down and looked at Bird's picture a long time; then insisted that a place must be found for it. He was still met by the assertion of impracticability. He said no more, but took down one of his own pictures, sent it to the Academy, and hung Bird's in its place.... At the death of a poor drawing-master, Mr. Wells, whom Turner had long known, he was deeply affected, and lent money to the widow until a large sum had accumulated. She was both honest and grateful, and, after a long period, was happy enough to be able to return to her benefactor the whole sum she had received from him. She waited on him with it; but Turner kept his hands in his pocket. 'Keep it,' he said, 'and send your children to school and to church.' He said this in bitterness; he had himself been sent to neither."

Once, after sending an importunate beggar from his house, he relented, ran after her, and gave her a five-pound note.

Says Thornbury: "An early patron of Turner, when he was a mere industrious barber's son, working at three-shilling drawings in his murky bedroom, had seen some of them in a window in the Haymarket, and had bought them. From that time he had gone on buying and being kind to the rising artist, and Turner could not forget it. Years after, he heard that his old benefactor had become involved, and that his steward had received directions to cut down some valued trees. Instantly Turner's generous impulses were roused; his usual parsimony (all directed to one great object) was cast behind him. He at once wrote to the steward, concealing his name, and sent him the full amount; many, many thousands—as much as twenty thousand pounds, I believe.

"The gentleman never knew who was his benefactor; but, in time, his affairs rallied, and he was enabled to pay the whole sum back. Years again rolled on, and now the son of Turner's benefactor became involved. Again the birds of the air brought the news to the guardian angel of the family; again he sent the necessary thousands anonymously; again the son stopped the leak, righted himself, and returned the whole sum with thanks."

Ruskin says: "He had a heart as intensely kind and as nobly true as God ever gave to one of his creatures.... Having known Turner for ten years, and that during the period of his life when the highest qualities of his mind were in many respects diminished, and when he was suffering most from the evil speaking of the world, I never heard him say one depreciating word of living man or man's work. I never saw him look an unkind or blameful look. I never saw him let pass, without some sorrowful remonstrance or endeavor at mitigation, a blameful word spoken by another. Of no man but Turner whom I have ever known could I say this; and of this kindness and truth came, I repeat, all his highest power; and all his failure and error, deep and strange, came of his faithlessness." Probably Mr. Ruskin means lack of religious faith, as Mr. Thornbury says Turner feared that he would be annihilated.

Turner was a most pains-taking worker. "Every quarter of an inch of Turner's drawings," says Ruskin, "will bear magnifying; and much of the finer work in them can hardly be traced, except by the keenest sight, until it is magnified. In his painting of 'Ivy Bridge,' the veins are drawn on the wing of a butterfly not three lines in diameter; and I have one of his smaller drawings of 'Scarborough' in my own possession, in which the muscle shells on the beach are rounded, and some shown as shut, some as open, though none are as large as the letters of this type: and yet this is the man who was thought to belong to the 'dashing' school, literally because most people had not patience or delicacy of sight enough to trace his endless details."

He loved poetry, and sometimes attempted to write it. He was seldom true to nature in his work. Hamerton says: "With an immense and unwearied industry, Turner accumulated thousands and thousands of memoranda to increase his knowledge of what interested him, especially in the mountains, rivers, and cities of the Continent, and the coasts of his native island. Amidst all this wealth of gathered treasure, his imagination reigned and revelled with a poet's freedom. With a knowledge of landscape vaster than any mortal ever possessed before him, his whole existence was a succession of dreams. Even the hardest realities of the external world itself, granite and glacier, could not awaken him; but he would sit down before them and sketch another dream, there, in the very presence of the reality itself. Notwithstanding all the knowledge and all the observation which they prove, the interest of Turner's twenty thousand sketches is neither topographic nor scientific, but entirely psychological. It is the soul of Turner that fascinates the student, and not the material earth."

With little education from the schools, without distinguished ancestry, in the midst of many, disappointments and much censure, Turner came to great renown. He had talent, but he had also untiring industry and unlimited perseverance.

www.ingramcontent.com/pod-product-compliance
Lightning Source LLC
Chambersburg PA
CBHW011522240626
47154CB00009B/2930